New England
WATERFALLS

New England
WATERFALLS

A GUIDE TO MORE THAN 200 CASCADES AND WATERFALLS

Greg Parsons
&
Kate B. Watson

THE COUNTRYMAN PRESS
WOODSTOCK, VERMONT

If you believe any information found in this guide to be incorrect, please let
the authors and publisher know so that corrections may be made in futre
editions. The authors also welcome your comments and suggestions. Address all
correspondence to:

Editor
New England Waterfalls
The Countryman Press
PO Box 748
Woodstock, VT 05091

Outdoor activities are by their very nature potentially hazardous. The publishers
and authors have done their best to ensure the accuracy of all the information
in *New England Waterfalls,* however, they can accept no responsiblity for any
loss, injury or inconvenience sustained by any traveler as a result of information
or advice contained in this guide. Every effort was made to respect private
property. Users of *New England Waterfalls* are expected to respect notices of
private property. Future editions of this guide will reflect any changes in land
ownership. If you believe any property-related information to be incorrect,
please let us know.

Library of Congress Cataloging-in-Publication Data
Parsons, Greg, 1982–
     New England waterfalls : a guide to more than 200 waterfalls and cascades
/ Greg Parsons and Kate B. Watson.—1st ed.
        p. cm.
     ISBN 0-88150-545-5
     1. Hiking—New England—Guidebooks. 2. Waterfalls—New England—
Guidebooks. 3. New England—Guidebooks. I. Watson, Kate B., 1982– II. Title.
GV199.42.N38P37 2003
917.404'44—dc21   2003043833
Book design by Deborah Fillion
Page composition by PerfecType, Nashville, TN
Cover and interior photographs by Greg Parsons and Kate B. Watson with the
exception of Lye Brook Falls, on page 255, by Jon Binder
Illustration on page xix by Dan Maleck

Published by The Countryman Press
P.O. Box 748, Woodstock, VT 05091

Distributed by W.W. Norton & Company, Inc.
500 Fifth Avenue, New York NY 10110

Printed in the United States of America
10 9 8 7 6 5 4 3 2

Contents

Acknowledgments

New England Waterfalls: A Guide to More Than 200 Cascades and Waterfalls could never have come into being without the help of many wonderful people who shared their time and expertise with us. Each person below, in his or her own way, helped develop this guidebook into something much more special than what the two of us could have done alone.

There were five individuals who sparked our initial inspiration; Jon Binder, Peter Chapin, David Ellis, Robert Glaubitz, and Dean Goss. Their enthusiasm and love for New England waterfalls really created a passion within us to write this book for readers like you. Jon Binder, the creator of the web site Jon's Waterfalls of the Eastern United States, deserves extra thanks for sharing his artistic expertise and for contributing the photograph of Lye Brook Falls.

Two professors at Babson College deserve a tremendous amount of recognition for donating their valuable time and words of wisdom. Kerry Rourke, with her ideas on how to submit a book proposal, and our mentor, Martin Tropp, a professor with extraordinary passion for teaching, have both made our time at Babson College and the process of constructing this book a great learning experience.

Special thanks are also due to all those who joined us in discovering the whereabouts of these treasures. These individuals are Brett Lafortune, Sylvia Mello, Jason Mostacci, Garrett Parsons, Brian Petroccione, Heather Sargent, Brad Sullivan, and Jessica Taylor.

Major thanks also go to Editorial Director Kermit Hummel and the rest of the staff at The Countryman Press. Our literary agent, Madeline Morel, who guided us along each step of the way, and Daniel Maleck, creator of the "types of waterfalls" image in this guide. Both deserve our warmest gratitude.

Finally, both of us would like to thank our parents and the rest of our family and friends for their patience, excitement, and encouragement throughout this project.

Introduction

Our passion for New England waterfalls developed years before we met at Babson College. Our parents instilled a sense of respect and admiration for nature in us at a very young age. Greg was initially dragged kicking and screaming on daylong journeys through New England by his family. Travels during high school finally opened his mind to the wonders and attractions of the natural world. Meanwhile, Kate loved what New England had to offer from the beginning, and she pleaded to be taken on new trips continuously.

Soon after meeting at college, we began to take day trips all over New England, visiting a variety of places and, most importantly, a number of waterfalls. Day trips turned out to become regular activities for us. It was not long before we realized that many of New England's waterfalls were known only to local residents. As we racked up miles and miles of hiking, we wondered why so many of these wonderful places could not be found in existing guidebooks.

And so the idea for *New England Waterfalls* was born. Our main focus, we decided, was to share all these great places with our readers in a way that minimized the amount of hassle a day trip can bring. We wrote directions based on easily identifiable reference points, described trails in an easy-to-follow format, and snapped pictures that represent the actual beauty of these places. We also added nine classifications to each waterfall trip, including an overall rating—intended to give you a sense of comparison—and also information pertaining to the trail, such as the difficulty and altitude gain.

There you have it. *New England Waterfalls* is our contribution to the natural splendors of this region. We hope you enjoy our book.

THE SIX STATES

As you will begin to observe while sampling the waterfalls in this region, each New England state has its own peculiarities. A wide variety of experiences can be had as you move from state to state. As you will see below, the waterfalls of each state offer the enthusiast great variety in hiking terrain, geological structure, biological environments, and water characteristics.

CONNECTICUT

Connecticut's lack of mountainous topography tends to result in more seasonal falls. To ensure a flowing waterfall, it is best to plan your visit before the dry spells of summer.

Approximately half the Connecticut waterfalls described in this guide are under the protection of the state park system or other nonprofit organizations such as The Nature Conservancy. As a result, these waterfalls are often located in parks that also have picnic facilities. Many of these sites are furnished with picnic tables, fire pits, bathrooms, and ample parking. The enforcement of state park rules and regulations has kept most areas clean and prevented the sites from becoming local party zones.

MAINE

Large sections of Maine remain relatively undeveloped. Vast expanses of wilderness can be found throughout the state, but primarily in the northern half. These wildernesses harbor remote waterfalls yet to be publicly documented or even discovered. The best chance for discovering your own private New England waterfall has to be in the state of Maine. Wildlife sightings are also more common in this state because of the lack of development.

Expect long backcountry roads when reaching some of the trailheads for the waterfalls of Maine described in this guide. Low-clearance vehicles may not be able to access the formal trailhead parking areas. *Make sure to see individual descriptions for more information.* Some waterfalls do not even have a trailhead; more than a dozen popular waterfalls in Maine are accessible only by canoe. These waterfalls were omitted from this guide, but we still recommend visiting them if you enjoy lengthy canoe, kayaking, or whitewater rafting trips.

Maine may be the northernmost state of New England, but its swimming holes still manage to warm to refreshing temperatures with the sun's rays in summer. These swimming spots are very popular, both with local residents and among visitors from other states.

Some waterfalls require you to pay entrance fees. Public reserved lands, such as the KI Jo-Mary Multiple Use Forest, require a modest entrance fee. Baxter State Park, the home of Mount Katahdin and dozens of scenic waterfalls, also requires a fee for out-of-state residents.

MASSACHUSETTS

Waterfalls are few and far between in Massachusetts, making it difficult to visit more than a few in a day. The Berkshire region, where the bulk of waterfalls in this state can be found, is the only place where you can visit multiple waterfalls in a day.

Very few waterfalls in this state have swimming holes. Similar to Connecticut, most waterfalls are either located within the state park system or managed by organizations. The Trustees of Reservation, a nonprofit group dedicated to "preserving the Massachusetts landscape," has made a great effort to preserve several waterfall sites.

NEW HAMPSHIRE

It is no surprise that the majority of waterfalls in New Hampshire are found in or near the White Mountain National Forest. The high peaks of the White Mountains create hundreds of permanent and seasonal waterfalls. Within the last decade the White Mountain National Forest adopted a per-car fee for many of the trailhead parking lots. This fee, $3 in 2002, is used for maintenance of trails and roads, as well as related expenses. Other waterfalls in this region have become commercialized and are more costly to visit.

This guide's longest, most challenging hikes with the greatest elevation gains are found in New Hampshire. Unlike other states, many trips to waterfalls in New Hampshire can be extended by continuing farther on the trail to mountain summits, remote ponds and lakes, wilderness areas, and some of the finest scenic vistas in New England.

New Hampshire also offers backpacking opportunities, some of the coldest waterfall swimming holes, colorful foliage, and some of the tallest waterfalls in New England.

RHODE ISLAND

Rhode Island is not gifted with waterfalls like the other states. Our research indicates that Rhode Island only has one waterfall worthy of your attention. Perhaps there is still a waterfall or two to be discovered, which may end up in future editions of this guide.

VERMONT

Avid hikers may be left unsatisfied with the waterfall trips in Vermont; the majority of falls are roadside attractions or require hikes of less than 0.5 mile. The waterfalls in this state are most likely to please swimmers and those who are unable to hike long distances.

Many of Vermont's waterfalls have been partially altered or ruined altogether by dams created through hydroelectric projects and power stations. As a result, locals are actively protective of the waterfalls left in their natural state. The Vermont River Conservancy is one organization fighting to purchase and protect the lands that waterfalls lie on.

Vermont is home to the finest swimming holes known among New England waterfalls. Warm, refreshing, and clean, the swimming holes naturally attract a slew of visitors during summer months. The translucent emerald-green color, so familiar in tropical waters, creates lovely pools. Always carry a bathing suit and towel; you will surely need them.

DISCOVERIES ALONG THE WAY

- **Size does not matter.**
  There are no mathematical formulas to determine beauty based on height. Some of the most attractive and highly rated waterfalls in this guide are less than 30 feet in total drop.
- **Waterfall swimming holes are generally cold.**
  Swimming with waterfalls may well be the most enjoyable outdoor activity there is. Always remember, however, that rushing mountain waters never really get a chance to warm up to comfortable temperatures. Expect chilly to cold pools in almost all cases, with many of Vermont's swimming holes being the exception.
- **Many waterfalls in New England are world class in beauty and style.**
  New England offers some of the most picturesque falls in the world. If a photographic collection of the world's most scenic waterfalls were ever produced, some falls from New England would certainly be included.
- **Waterfalls are always endangered.**
  Plans for hydroelectric plants are occasionally proposed for sites at waterfalls. You will also find litter and even graffiti at some waterfalls in New England. Please do your part to ensure that waterfalls remain forever in their natural state.
- **No two waterfalls are exactly alike.**
  New England is such diverse waterfall territory that each one found is sure to be a new experience. You will be hard-pressed to find two

trails or falls that are comparable. Each new waterfall has its own geology, plant life, and style.

- **There are more waterfalls to be found and publicly documented.**
  Our original research indicated that approximately 300 waterfalls existed in New England. We now have information on more than 500 waterfalls, and there are many more rumored waterfalls that are still yet to be documented. Upstate Maine is sure to have dozens of uncrowded, unspoiled gems hiding in its multiple-use forests.

- **Waterfalls have a personality.**
  One visit to each waterfall is not enough. If you have visited a particular waterfall only once, you have not really grasped its personality. To see its true character you must visit in different seasons, and during different conditions. Check out the falls during dry and wet weather, when they're covered in snow, and during fall foliage. These ever-changing conditions create an unpredictable waterfall experience for each visit.

- **Animals use trails, too.**
  Do not forget that we are merely visitors to wildlife habitats. Large animals such as black bears, white-tailed deer, and bull moose are not commonly seen on the trail, but in rare instances you may spot one. If you respect that you are visiting their home, they will likely scamper away and avoid close contact.

SEASONALITY

Seasonality is an issue of great importance to the falls of New England. It refers to the fluctuations in the volume of water sources of waterfalls. In an ideal world each waterfall would always look the same, never losing any of its attractiveness or appeal. This just is not the case, though; seasonality is a factor to be considered before embarking on any trip described in this guide.

Our advice is simple: To reduce the likelihood of visiting a dried-up waterfall, visit it before the middle of June. Spring runoff from the previous winter can last throughout most of spring and, at times, even into summer. Unless a record-breaking drought has occurred, every waterfall in this guidebook will be flowing; we intentionally did not include other waterfalls we found to be too highly seasonal. Beyond the middle of June, however, each waterfall's character begins to change.

Here are some general guidelines that have proven themselves true in our travels.

- Mountain brooks are likely to dry up faster than lowland rivers.
- The waterfalls of northern New England survive for longer in summer than do the falls of the south.
- Falls at the base of a mountain are likely to remain longer than falls located halfway up a trail leading to the summit.
- Snowy winters mean longer waterfall seasons during the warmer months.
- If you are hiking along a stream to a waterfall, and there is little water flowing, you run the risk of uncovering a dried-up falls.
- When there is little volume flowing but the water source is abnormally wide, the falls are still likely to be quite powerful. We have been pleasantly surprised several times.
- You can expect a normally seasonal waterfall to be roaring with power for up to one week after a day of heavy rain. You are guaranteed a great show if you visit within three days of a storm.

Seasonality is not always a terrible thing; differences in water flow create new sparkling personalities and characteristic changes. Here are the benefits of seasonality:

- A trip to a dried-up falls can still be rewarding, especially if you have previously visited the waterfall when it was flowing with thundering power. You could witness the power of natural change.
- A swimming pool at the base of a falls may be too dangerous for swimming in May because of dangerous currents, but quite safe in July.
- Seasonality can also change major characteristics of a waterfall; for example, a 20-foot-wide mix of cascades during spring runoff can transform into an elusive 4-foot-wide plunge in July.

WATERFALL PHOTOGRAPHY

Mastering the art of photographing falling water requires using the right equipment along with creative techniques. Although it may seem like an art best reserved for the professionals, photographing waterfalls can actually be quite simple to learn, and improvement can be immediate and striking. After shooting hundreds of rolls of slide film in just about every waterfall condition, we have come up with some straightforward guidelines for beginner and advanced photographers alike.

CAMERA AND LENSES

A camera with manual shutter-speed adjustment is essential for above-average pictures. Although digital cameras save substantial money in film costs, single-lens-reflex (SLR) cameras are recommended by most professional photographers for capturing water in motion. Medium-format and large-format cameras have taken most of the highest-quality pictures of falling water we have seen, but are not practical for many shutterbugs. This is attributable to the added costs of these cameras, both for the camera itself and for developing costs. The added weight and size of the larger-format cameras makes backpacking more of a challenge. Point-and-shoot cameras are inexpensive, reliable pieces of equipment, but do not allow much manual control. SLR-type cameras allow you the flexibility of changing shutter speed, aperture, and lenses. For all these reasons, we suggest carrying an SLR-type camera on all waterfall expeditions.

You may want to carry several different lenses to cover every shooting situation. Many waterfalls are located in gorges and narrow ravines; requires wide-angle lenses, such as a 20mm lens, to encapsulate the entire falls into your picture. On the other hand, a telephoto zoom lens, such as a 100–300mm lens, may be needed to capture waterfalls located below a bridge or far beyond the practical limits of a trail. If carrying multiple lenses seems impractical or unjustifiable to you, a zoom lens such as a 28–90mm model—which begin at around $100—will suffice for the majority of waterfall situations.

SHUTTER SPEED AND TRIPODS

One of the best tips we can offer a waterfall photographer is always to carry a tripod. A tripod is essential for maintaining long shutter speeds (to eliminate camera shake, which can blur your picture). Also, tripods come in quite handy when you want to photograph yourself with these natural treasures and no one is around to snap the picture.

Long shutter speeds are essential to create the soft "angelhair" or "silky" look so common to waterfall photographs. Generally, speeds of 1/15 second or longer will blur the water to create this artistic effect. Long shutter speeds are also essential if you are photographing in gorges or basins, where, even on the sunniest days, the area around the falls receives little light.

Long shutter speeds are not always the top choice for falls, though. With the traditional block-type waterfall, we suggest using shorter shutter speeds, such as 1/60 second, because longer shutter speeds on such falls often create a portrait of pure white water that lacks detail. You will find that long shutter speeds work much better for thin plunges or other weak-powered waterfalls. Most of the shots in this book were taken at shutter speeds between 1 second and 1/10 of a second on ISO 50 film. The trick with shutter speed is not to be afraid to experiment.

SMALL APERTURE

Equally as important as shutter speed is proper exposure; aperture is often neglected in waterfall photography instructions. A small aperture is needed if you want to capture an entire waterfall landscape, including the wildflowers, trees, rocks, and any people around the falling water. We suggest experimenting with apertures between f/8 and f/22. Apertures of f/16 and f/19, for example, should capture everything in focus, from a boulder 6 feet in front of you to the trees on the side of a waterfall. Many photographers focus on the shutter speed alone; do not forget to take aperture into account when composing pictures. If you are using a high-speed film, you may be tempted to bring the aperture down to f/5.6 to reach a shutter speed of 1/10 second. With an aperture of f/5.6, you are running the risk of having certain areas of the picture come out blurry.

SLOW-SPEED FILM

To create the soft, angelhair water effect while keeping the foreground and background of the frame focused and sharp, slow-speed film is essential. Our personal favorites are those listed at ISO 100 or below, such as the slide films Fuji Velvia 50 and Kodak Kodachrome 64. Slow-speed film requires more light for proper exposure, which means you can use the longer shutter speeds that you will need to achieve most of your desired effects. For enlarging your pictures, slow-speed films are also ideal, because they are typically very sharp. This translates into bigger enlargements as compared to "faster" film, such as ISO 200 or ISO 400.

On sunny days, however, even the slowest films may not be able to get the long shutter speed you desire. For this, a polarizer or neutral density filter can be very useful in bringing the exposure to your desired level. These two types of filters require more light for an exposure. Polarizers usually require you to compensate with one and a half to two stops of extra light. For example, if you are set up with an aperture of f/13 and a shutter speed of 1/30 second, a polarizer will allow you to increase the shutter speed to 1/10 second or 1/8 second.

BRACKETING

Bracketing is a waterfall photographer's best friend. The meters inside your camera are affected by gleaming water and the dark walls of the gorges where many falls are found. To combat this problem, manually adjust the aperture or shutter speed around the suggested exposure from your camera's meter. We suggest taking exposures up to two stops in each direction to maximize your chance for a perfectly exposed picture. Although film and developing costs will increase, bracketing is often necessary in photographing falls. Very often, the correct exposure can be a full two stops away from the suggested exposure from your camera's meter.

An alternative to bracketing is using cheap "gray cards" or partial metering to find a suggested exposure. With partial metering, compare your camera's suggested exposures of different parts of the scene, such as the falling water, the underlying rock, trees, or even the sky.

FOREGROUND AND COMPOSITION

By making minor changes in the composition of your picture, you can turn an average shot into a professional one. Just try incorporating some natural features positioned around the waterfall into the photograph. Boulders in a streambed, hikers climbing the rock wall of a waterfall, or wildflowers along the trail are three suggestions that can add quality to your photos.

Finding foreground objects becomes necessary with waterfalls that have abnormally large pools at their base. Take the time to observe the entire landscape around the falls, searching for anything else that can help fill your camera's frame. This will enhance the quality of your pictures.

WEATHER AND WATERFALL PHOTOGRAPHY

Mother Nature is very difficult to predict, but some facts are certain. The melting snow of early spring powers most waterfalls in New England well into June. After June, however, an understanding of the relationships among weather, waterfalls, and photography takes on great importance.

You can expect the waterfalls throughout all of New England to be at their highest volume of the year in spring. You are not likely to find the thin veils of water you may see during summer. In spring months you can expect to photograph chaotic crashes of whitewater at most falls. Some waterfalls are yet to be swallowed up by overhanging tree coverage, which will begin to occur as summer rolls around.

During summer, the greens of the trees and mosses surrounding the falls will add color to your pictures. Unfortunately, at many falls water flow is greatly reduced or even eliminated; photographs can look empty. Yet for some cataracts, this is the best time to compose a picture. Photos of waterfalls such as Bridal Veil Falls of New Hampshire and March Cataract Falls of Massachusetts radiate romantic feelings, as they capture thin veils of cascading water.

A true waterfall photographer will also return during foliage and the winter season for new shots. If you want a typical postcard shot, capture the falls of northern New England during peak foliage. Two of the best waterfalls to shoot during this season are Arethusa Falls and Silver Cascade. Both of these are located in the White Mountain National Forest, and just about every color of foliage is represented within yards of the falling water.

Peak times for New England vary by state, with foliage usually near or at peak during the first two weeks of October for the northern states. The southern states often peak during the second and third weeks of the month.

Winter is the most difficult to photograph. The vibrant colors of spring and autumn are long gone, and your camera's meter is often fooled by the reflecting white of the snow. You will find that many waterfalls are closed for the season simply because they are too dangerous to visit. If the falls are reachable, be sure to bracket your exposures over a greater range to ensure that at least one photograph can make the scrapbook.

For any season, always carry a trash bag or two in your backpack in case the weather turns bad. Cameras are easily damaged by water, and the combined protection of a backpack and a trash bag may save your equipment from the weather.

HOW TO USE THIS GUIDE

This guidebook is centered on making your waterfall experiences as easy and enjoyable as possible. To know what you can expect with each trip, we have added simple classifications to each basic waterfall description and list them to provide a quick and easy summary of what the trip entails. Each of these classifications is clarified below.

RATING

Each waterfall is rated on a scale of one to five stars. A rating of one star identifies a waterfall lacking in many categories. These waterfalls are not impressive, nor are they photogenic or scenic. A rating of five stars, on the other hand, is for those special waterfalls that really deserve praise because

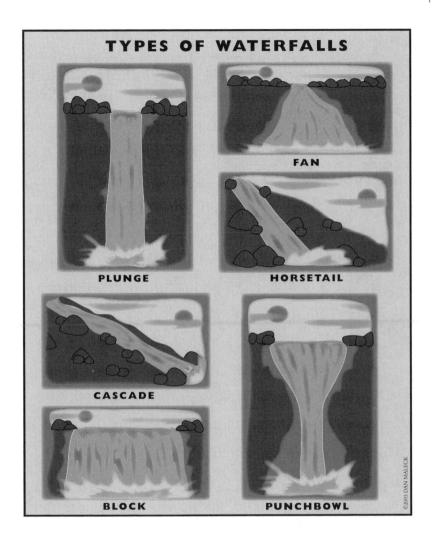

TYPES OF WATERFALLS

PLUNGE

FAN

HORSETAIL

CASCADE

BLOCK

PUNCHBOWL

they offer so much. If a particular waterfall has a rating of five stars, you can expect an outstandingly scenic attraction and, in most cases, one that is incredibly photogenic.

Every waterfall in this guide deserves your time and attention. If a trip has earned a rating of two, it does not mean that the waterfall should be excluded from your plans. It only suggests that you may want to supplement this particular waterfall with others in the area. For the dedicated enthusiast, every waterfall is a new special place.

TYPE

After visiting the waterfalls of New England, we have concluded that there are six distinguishable types. Everyone has a favorite style of waterfall, whether it is the classic block or the completely vertical drop of a plunge.

Block—a cascade, wider than it is tall, that usually covers the entire distance across a stream. Blocks are often referred to as being "classic" or "horseshoe" falls.

Cascade—a series of small drops, too many to count, that fall at a low angle of descent. Just about every type of waterfall usually has cascades shortly upstream or downstream from it.

Fan—a steep-angled cascade that fans out from a narrow width at the top to a larger base at the bottom. Most fans are also horsetails in that they maintain contact with rock during their descent.

Horsetail—a nearly vertical drop characterized by waters maintaining constant or almost constant contact with the underlying rock that they are flowing over.

Plunge—a waterfall in which water drops at an entirely vertical angle. Water flows over some broad ledge, usually an overhanging one, and does not make contact with underlying rock.

Punchbowl—characterized by water being contracted to a very narrow width and shot down into a plunge. Punchbowls are seldom found in this region.

HEIGHT

One of the first pieces of information people want to know about a waterfall is how tall it is. There is a tendency for people to believe that there is a direct correlation between height and beauty. We have found that this is just not so. Some of our favorite waterfalls are less than 20 feet in total drop, and one is a mere 6-foot drop.

In determining the height of the falls, we either separated the major drops—if they were distinguishable—or lumped the entire formation into one total drop. Some heights have been accurately measured, and a few have been reasonably estimated. In all cases the height reflects the elevation drop.

TRAIL LENGTH

All trail lengths listed are one-way, representing the distance from trailhead to the waterfall, unless otherwise noted. Some trails are loops, and they reflect the total hiking mileage covered on the trip. Before undertaking a hike, or deciding to skip a particular falls, consider other trail factors, such as altitude gain and trail difficulty. A 3-mile round trip with no altitude gain is much easier on your body than a 2-mile round trip with a 1,000-foot elevation change.

WATER SOURCE

The fourth characteristic is the water source of the waterfall. This tells you which brook, stream, creek, or river is feeding the formation. Several of the waterfalls described in this guide have water sources that are either unknown or too seasonal to be worthy of an official name.

ALTITUDE GAIN/LOSS

For the majority of waterfalls described in this guide, the altitude gain or loss on the trail was the prevalent factor in determining trail difficulty. For every 1,000 feet of elevation gain, average-paced hikers can expect to add about half an hour to their one-way trail time.

The trails that gain significant elevation in a short amount of distance can be hazardously slippery and muddy during the wet season. Unless you are prepared for the worst, avoid hiking trails that feature 500 or more feet of elevation gain over less than 2 miles of length in early spring. Examples include Beaver Brook Cascades of New Hampshire and Race Brook Falls of Massachusetts—both are sure to supply too many dangers to allow a pleasant overall experience.

TRAIL DIFFICULTY

The trails described in this guide are categorizied into one of five levels of difficulty: easy, easy side of moderate, moderate, moderate side of difficult, and difficult. To come up with a rating, we took into consideration trail distance, altitude gain, trail dangers such as the scale of muddy and slippery travel, and any challenges present that must be overcome, like crossing a river. All of the ratings are conservative, based on family-friendly hiking. Travelers with years of hiking experience can downgrade the hiking difficulty by one step.

Easy—generally flat, stable-foot terrain, with no challenging trail difficulties. These trails are perfect for families and safe for all.

Easy side of moderate—hikes involving a fair amount of navigating over rocks and roots on the trail. There also may be some elevation gain, mud in springtime, or sections of slippery travel after periods of rain, but nothing too difficult.

Moderate—trails offering a significant altitude gain, with steep and slippery stretches of terrain. Moderate hikes are still appropriate for families and children, as long as you take them in summer or fall. Water and snacks should be carried, because these hikes are usually longer and more time consuming than trails with lower ratings of difficulty.

Moderate side of difficult—only a handful of New England's waterfall trails approach a difficult rating; we purposely chose waterfalls in this guide that were challenging but not extraordinarily so. If you are hiking trails with a moderate side of difficult rating, you should be fully prepared with water, food, and other supplies, and you can expect demanding altitude gains. You may be required to cross a knee-deep river or scramble down a steep gorge wall. We suggest traveling in groups for trips with this rating.

Difficult—any trail marked difficult is reserved for the truly experienced. If you are not in great physical shape, skip these hikes—there are scores of other waterfalls with less potential for disaster. If you choose a difficult hike, bring at least 3 liters of water, food, a compass, and a few friends in case of emergency.

HIKING TIME

The approximate hiking time is based on a commonly followed hiking formula: A mile can be covered in half an hour, and for every 500 feet of elevation gain, an additional half hour is added. Extras, such as the time required to cross a river, scale a rock wall, or scramble down a riverbank, also add to the amount of approximate hiking time. As you might expect, our estimations can differ from the actual time it will take you to reach a waterfall. Our approximations are based on the average person's pace of travel: about 2 miles per hour. Experienced hikers may be able to cut down a travel time by nearly half; conversely, a family with children might need nearly double the amount of time.

Take note that approximate hiking time is for one-way travel. If you are wondering what the entire trip might take you, double the hiking time given and allow some time for exploration and enjoyment at the waterfall. For loop trails, the hiking time reflects the entire trip.

DELORME MAP

The idea behind including the coordinates of waterfalls in DeLorme's State Atlases and Gazetteers is to make it easier for you to map out your day; this in turn can allow you to visit more than just one waterfall per day. Be aware that only about half of the waterfalls that we describe are actually marked on DeLorme maps.

I. Connecticut

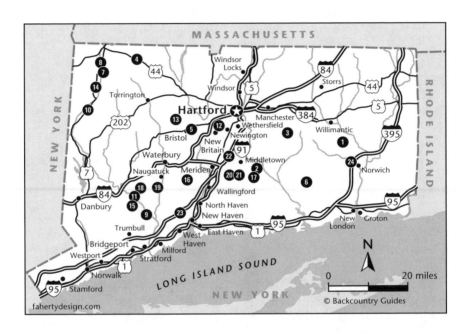

fahertydesign.com

BAILEY'S RAVINE
Franklin, New London County

Type: Plunges and slides

Height: Tallest plunge is 12 feet

Trail Length: 0.2 mile

Water Source: Bailey Brook

Altitude Gain/Loss: +20 feet

Difficulty: Easy

Hiking Time: 5 minutes

DeLorme Map: Page 38, A-1

Rating: ★★★½

DESCRIPTION Ayer's Gap, or Bailey's Ravine, as it is more commonly called, is a quiet little place just off CT 207. The main attraction, a 12-foot plunge, is followed by several smaller drops and waterslides. The falls here may not be anything spectacular, but the hemlock-surrounded ravine is pretty and rather secluded. The Nature Conservancy manages the 80 acres of Ayer's Gap Preserve and requires that visitors come between sunrise and sunset.

TRAIL INFORMATION The parking area is not actually the trailhead.

Bailey's Ravine

To reach the ravine, you must walk down CT 207 for a few hundred feet and take a left onto Ayer Road. Walk down Ayer Road for about 0.1 mile; the trailhead will be marked on your left. A well-used trail runs to the top of the falls. Lesser-used trails navigate around the ravine and the rest of the nature preserve.

DIRECTIONS From Lebanon, take CT 207 east. Continue traveling on CT 207 east for 1.5 miles past its junction with CT 32 and take a left into a parking pullout marked with a sign for BAILEY'S RAVINE. *To get to Lebanon,* take CT 2 south from Hartford to exit 18. Continue on CT 16 east to a right onto CT 207 east.

OTHER WATERFALLS NEARBY Yantic Falls.

2

BEAR HILL FALLS
Middletown, Middlesex County

Type: Plunges and cascades
Height: 30-foot total drop
Trail Length: 0.6 mile
Water Source: Unknown
Altitude Gain/Loss: Up 50 feet, down 30 feet

Difficulty: Easy side of moderate
Hiking Time: 20 minutes
DeLorme Map: Page 35, H-23
Rating: ★★½

DESCRIPTION Many waterfalls in the state of Connecticut are protected under the state park system or by nonprofit organizations. These waterfalls are well known, heavily visited, and widely publicized. While everyone is sure to enjoy these classics, some people seek waterfalls that are farther off the beaten path.

Not many cataracts in this state can offer the chance for privacy and isolation found at Bear Hill Falls. The falls are not impressive like nearby Wadsworth Big Falls or Westfield Falls, but unlike those falls, Bear Hill Falls remains undiscovered by nearly all but local residents. The trailhead is barely noticed on Aircraft Road, and the path to the falls is hardly tread upon. Bear Hill Falls may go days, even weeks, without a single visitor. This is where it gains its attraction: You have a good chance of being its sole viewer on a given day.

SPECIAL NOTE *Bear Hill Falls* is not an official name, but the term is often applied to this waterfall. David A. Ellis, proprietor of Ctwaterfalls.com, a web site dedicated to the natural splendor of Connecticut waterfalls, is believed to have first coined this waterfall's name.

TRAIL INFORMATION The trail to the falls begins across the street from the green MATTABASSET TRAIL sign. You will see a sign stating that the area is private property, but do not despair: The utility company that owns the area permits hiking. This sign, as you will see with a more careful look, prohibits only motorized vehicles from the trails.

As you travel the trail, you will find a fork, with the Mattabasset Trail veering right and the Bear Hill South Loop Trail leading to your left. Take the right fork and continue along the blue-square-blazed Mattabasset Trail to the falls. The trail is not well used, and deer are often seen as you hike to the waterfall.

DIRECTIONS From Middletown, take CT 9 south to exit 10. Follow signs to Aircraft Road. Travel on Aircraft Road for about 0.8 mile and you will see a small green sign on the right side of the road for the MATTABASSET TRAIL. Parking is limited to the embankment on the opposite side of the road.

OTHER WATERFALLS NEARBY Seven Falls, Wadsworth Big Falls, Wadsworth Little Falls, Westfield Falls.

3

BLACKLEDGE FALLS

Glastonbury, Hartford County

Type: Plunges
Height: 22–25 feet each
Trail Length: 0.5 mile
Water Source: Blackledge River
Altitude Gain/Loss: None

Difficulty: Easy
Hiking Time: 20 minutes
DeLorme Map: Page 45, J-18
Rating: ★★★★

DESCRIPTION Blackledge Falls is a set of two or three neighboring plunges, depending on the water volume of the Blackledge River. The plunges are similar in appearance, each being between 22 and 25 feet in height. If you bring along your water shoes or sandals, you can stand di-

Blackledge Falls

rectly underneath the middle waterfall and become instantly refreshed. The middle plunge is also a completely vertical drop, due to the overhanging ledge that the Blackledge River flows over.

Several trees prevent this waterfall from being one of the most photogenic in the state, but do not let that prevent you from enjoying the somewhat tropical appearance of Blackledge Falls. Be sure to check this one out in spring or after a rainstorm; during periods of dry weather, the rushing plunges can turn into small, unimpressive trickles of water. If not for being highly seasonal, Blackledge would certainly have made our Top 40 Waterfalls in New England list.

TRAIL INFORMATION Cross over the yellow gate to begin the trail. After 0.1 mile of hiking, you will begin to notice an abundance of side trails on all sides of you. Keep straight, following blue and white trail markers all the way to the falls. Expect an easy 20-minute walk to reach this waterfall.

DIRECTIONS From Hartford, take CT 2 south to exit 8. Turn onto CT 94 east. Continue on this road for 4.0 miles past its junction with CT 83. A sign for BLACKLEDGE FALLS is on your left, and a parking area is just down a dirt road on your right. The trail begins behind the sign for the falls.

OTHER WATERFALLS NEARBY Mill Pond Falls.

4

BUTTERMILK FALLS (NORFOLK)
Norfolk, Litchfield County

Type: Fan, cascades, and slides
Height: 20-foot total drop
Trail Length: Roadside
Water Source: Blackberry Creek
Altitude Gain/Loss: None

Difficulty: Easy
Hiking Time: Not applicable
DeLorme Map: Page 50, D-9
Rating: ★★★½

DESCRIPTION Hidden under a bridge and a few yards off a state highway, Buttermilk Falls lies peacefully between the backyards of two Norfolk residents. Surrounding the waterfall is a charming garden on the right and a quaint yellow house on the left.

This is one the best examples around of a fan-type waterfall. The waters of Blackberry Creek slide down smooth rocks, creating an almost perfect triangle shape. Below the fan are small cascades and warm little pools.

This Buttermilk Falls should not be confused with Buttermilk Falls of Plymouth, Connecticut, which is considerably larger in scale. Also, Buttermilk Falls of Plymouth is part of a nature preserve, offering you the opportunity to picnic and survey the area. Buttermilk Falls of Norfolk, on the other hand, lies on private property and can only be viewed from roadside. Yet it is still worth the quick stop if you happen to be in town or passing through.

TRAIL INFORMATION Follow the road back down to the bridge, where the falls begin their descent. The only views to be had are from the road or the sidewalk, as the river and waterfall are on private property.

DIRECTIONS From Canaan, take US 44 east into Norfolk. Immediately after US 44 east joins with CT 272, take the first right turn onto a road marked by a sign for GREENWOODS RD WEST/WEST SIDE GOLF CLUBS. The waterfall is just up the street, below the first bridge. *To get to Canaan, take US 7 north from Danbury.*

OTHER WATERFALLS NEARBY Campbell Falls, Great Falls of the Housatonic, Dean's Ravine Falls.

5

BUTTERMILK FALLS (PLYMOUTH)

Plymouth, Buttermilk Falls Nature Preserve, Litchfield County

Type: Horsetails, cascades, and slides
Height: 55-foot total drop
Trail Length: 0.2 mile to base of falls
Water Source: Hancock Brook
Altitude Gain/Loss: –30 feet

Difficulty: Easy side of moderate
Hiking Time: 5 minutes
DeLorme Map: Page 33, A-21
Rating: ★★★★

DESCRIPTION More than half a dozen waterfalls in New England are named Buttermilk Falls. Vermont's Buttermilk Falls is perhaps the most favored of the bunch, being one of the state's top swimming holes in terms of size and popularity. Other favorites include Buttermilk Falls of Norfolk, Connecticut, and Buttermilk Falls of Plymouth, Connecticut, which is the highlight of this chapter.

Plymouth's Buttermilk Falls is recommended for reasons other than swimming—most important among them is its elusive quality. From the top of the waterfall, where the trail first brings you, you are unable to get a full grasp of the height and beauty of the 55-foot waterfall. By scrambling to the bottom of the falls, however, you can really see the personality of Buttermilk Falls. The shaded horsetails, enclosed above almost entirely by hemlock trees, cut their way down to pools at your feet. There are plenty of flat trail sections adjacent to the brook that serve well for picnicking, picture taking, or gazing up at the falls. Small wildflowers and ferns around the rock-strewn river add to the beauty.

Buttermilk Falls (Plymouth)

TRAIL INFORMATION This short, blue-rectangle-marked trail can be as easy as you want to make it. From the parking lot to the top of the falls the trail is flat, and travel is quick. You will first reach a view from the top of the falls. Even though the well-worn trail ends here, the best views are to be had by descending to the base of the falls. A steep path has been created over the years for just this reason.

DIRECTIONS From New Britain, take CT 72 west to US 6. Take a left onto US 6, follow it for 1.7 miles, and take a left onto Scott Road. Follow Scott Road for 0.4 mile and turn left onto Washington Road. After 1.0 mile on Washington Road, turn right onto South Eagle Street and continue 1.7 miles to its end. Take a left onto South Main Street, then an immediate right onto Lane Hill Road. After a steep incline you will see a parking pull-off on the right and a sign for the NATURE PRESERVE.

OTHER WATERFALLS NEARBY Negro Hill Brook Falls, Mill Pond Falls, Spruce Brook Falls.

6

CHAPMAN FALLS

East Haddam, Devils Hopyard State Park,
Middlesex County

Type: Blocks	**Difficulty:** Easy
Height: 60-foot total drop	**Hiking Time:** 5 minutes
Trail Length: 0.1 mile	**DeLorme Map:** Page 37, J&K-13
Water Source: Eight Mile River	**Rating:** ★★★★★
Altitude Gain/Loss: –50 feet	

DESCRIPTION (HIGHLY RECOMMENDED) Chapman Falls is just as famous for a fascinating legend involving Satan as it is a popular state park day-trip destination. Posted on a billboard at the site is a Puritan belief that Satan once walked along the Eight Mile River and became infuriated as his tail became wet. To express his anger, he scampered up to the falls and stomped his hooves on each section, leaving scars in the boulders of the natural feature over which the falls descend. This is where Chapman Falls derives its alternative name, Devil's Hopyard.

In addition to the interesting legend, the falls are quite scenic. The Eight

Mile River drops about 60 feet in three bold segments. The waterfall is one of the most powerful in the state, and it is usually very crowded. This state park also calls for a picnic, so be sure to spend a combined few hours at the falls and at the picnic area.

During extremely dry weather, the falls may lose their "block" formation and become weak-flowing horsetails. Do not let this stop you from visiting, however: The entire area is still quite interesting, scenically speaking, and when fishing below the falls the odds are in your favor for catching trout!

TRAIL INFORMATION The falls are located just across the street from the parking lot. An obvious trail, lined with wooden fencing, guides you down a few steps to the base of the falls.

DIRECTIONS From Middletown, take CT 9 south to exit 7. Take CT 82 east into Haddam. Continue traveling on CT 82 east for 100 feet past its junction with CT 151 north and take a left onto Mount Pleasant Road. Follow Mount Pleasant Road for 5.8 miles and take a right onto Hopyard Road. Follow Hopyard Road for 0.8 mile and take a left onto an unmarked road; immediately after this, take another left into a large parking lot. There are several signs directing you to DEVIL'S HOPYARD STATE PARK, beginning on CT 82 and guiding you the rest of the way.

OTHER WATERFALLS NEARBY Bear Hill Falls, Seven Falls, Yantic Falls.

7

DEAN'S RAVINE FALLS
Canaan, Litchfield County

Type: Horsetails, cascades, and slides
Height: 50 feet
Trail Length: 0.4 mile
Water Source: Reed Brook
Altitude Gain/Loss: −100 feet

Difficulty: Easy side of moderate
Hiking Time: 15 minutes
DeLorme Map: Page 49, H-24
Rating: ★★★★½

DESCRIPTION (HIGHLY RECOMMENDED) This sister of New Hampshire's Ripley Falls resides in the small town of Canaan, Connecti-

Dean's Ravine Falls

cut. Dean's Ravine Falls is a steep drop of Reed Brook. Similar in shape, location, and personality, both cascades fall at approximately the same vertical angle, about 65 degrees. Other similarities include their widths, heavy exposure to the sun, and trail features. The only major difference is that Dean's Ravine is about half the drop of Ripley Falls. Both are equally stunning in beauty, even though Dean's Ravine is significantly shorter.

TRAIL INFORMATION Starting from the parking lot, this easy trail begins by traveling downstream with the brook. Soon the trail zigzags its way through steep terrain down to brook level. Instead of following the trail, many have skipped the switchbacks and trampled down the eroded "shortcut" trails. Please stay on the main trail to prevent further damage to the area. After about 0.4 mile you will reach the falls. If the trailside views are not sufficient, the fallen trees downstream can be used to cross the brook. This will put you directly below the waterfall, allowing for a completely different perspective.

DIRECTIONS From West Cornwall, take US 7 north. Take a left onto Lime Rock Station Road just after you pass the CANAAN TOWN LINE sign. Travel for about a mile on Lime Rock Station Road and take a left onto Music Mountain Road. Continue for 0.8 mile; the parking lot will be on your left. The trail begins to the left of the parking lot. *To get to West Cornwall,* take US 7 north from Danbury.

OTHER WATERFALLS NEARBY Great Falls of the Housatonic, Pine Swamp Brook Falls, Buttermilk Falls (Norfolk), Kent Falls.

8

GREAT FALLS OF THE HOUSATONIC
Canaan, Litchfield County

Type: Block and cascades
Height: 50 feet
Trail Length: 0.1 mile
Water Source: Housatonic River
Altitude Gain/Loss: –30 feet

Difficulty: Easy
Hiking Time: Not applicable
DeLorme Map: Page 49, F-23
Rating: ★★★★

DESCRIPTION During planned water releases in spring, the dam-controlled Great Falls of the Housatonic puts on a spectacular show for sightseers. This water flow is unsurpassed in power by any other waterfall in the region. When the water is flowing (and in summer months it generally is not), whitewater kayakers take to the strong currents below the falls. From the upper viewpoint near the top of the falls, it is always interesting to watch them paddle the powerful currents of rapids there.

The volume of water flowing over this 50-foot feature is impressive. If you are unable to make it to Niagara Falls this summer, this waterfall is about as close as you can get in New England.

TRAIL INFORMATION The trail follows a short, worn path to an upper viewpoint of the falls. For better views, you can also hack your way down to river level. When we visited, a deer appeared to make this area his home and was very protective of his space!

DIRECTIONS From the junction of US 7 and CT 126 in the section of Canaan known as Falls Village, take CT 126 north. Proceed for 0.3 mile, fork left, and follow a short road marked for FALLS VILLAGE. At the end of the road, take a right at a sign for the RIVER AND FALLS. Take the next left and drive over a bridge. Continue 0.4 mile beyond the bridge and take a right onto Falls Mountain Road. After 0.4 mile, there will be a small parking area on your right. *To get to Falls Village,* take US 7 north from Danbury or US 7 south from Canaan.

OTHER WATERFALLS NEARBY Dean's Ravine Falls, Pine Swamp Brook Falls, Buttermilk Falls (Norfolk), Kent Falls, Campbell Falls.

9

INDIAN WELL FALLS
Shelton, Indian Well State Park, Fairfield County

Type: Horsetail
Height: 15 feet
Trail Length: 0.2 mile
Water Source: Unknown
Altitude Gain/Loss: None

Difficulty: Easy
Hiking Time: 5 minutes
DeLorme Map: Page 24, G-2
Rating: ★★★★

Indian Well Falls

DESCRIPTION Indian Well Falls is a slender, 15-foot-tall horsetail that dumps into a circular pool nearly surrounded by steep rock walls. Managing to remain photogenic despite heavy tree cover, the falls welcome your artistic talent with several natural seats created by fallen trees.

The name *Indian Well* originates from the well-shaped circular gorge that the water flows over and into. Indian Well State Park closes at sunset, and make sure to leave your bathing suit at home—no swimming is allowed in the brook or at the falls, although (as you will notice) the temptation does exist.

TRAIL INFORMATION The trail begins across the street from the parking lot. There is a RULES AND REGULATIONS sign with an arrow pointing toward the falls trail. Wide and flat, this pathway takes you to the base of the falls with minimal effort. Climbing the steep walls around the falls is a different story. It can be quite difficult to access a bird's-eye view of this waterfall; you are better off enjoying it from below.

DIRECTIONS From Bridgeport, take CT 8 north to exit 14 in Shelton. Follow CT 110 north for 2.2 miles and take a right onto the road that leads into Indian Well State Park. After 0.4 mile on this road, pull into the parking area on your right.

OTHER WATERFALLS NEARBY Prydden Brook Falls, Wintergreen Falls, Kettletown Brook Falls, Southford Falls, Spruce Brook Falls.

10

KENT FALLS

Kent, Kent Falls State Park, Litchfield County

Type: Plunges and cascades

Height: Approximately 250-foot total drop

Trail Length: 0.3 mile to top of falls

Water Source: Kent Falls Brook

Altitude Gain/Loss: +250 feet

Difficulty: Easy side of moderate

Hiking Time: 10 minutes

DeLorme Map: Page 40, E-8&9

Rating: ★★★★★

DESCRIPTION (HIGHLY RECOMMENDED) Grab the peanut butter and jelly sandwiches and head over to Kent Falls State Park, one of Connecticut's most popular state parks and one of New England's top places for a picnic. Here you will find 250 feet of cascades and plunges and one of the finest, best-maintained parks in New England.

A trip to Kent Falls is one way to view just about every different classification of waterfall. There are plunges, horsetails, punchbowls, blocks, and fans. Many of the falls are also very photogenic, especially in the afternoon when the sun makes the water glitter.

The trail to the top of the falls is steep but manageable. Although we feel that the view when you first see this waterfall is alone worth a trip, make sure to climb the trail to see the rest of the variety this spot has to offer. Schedule a few hours when you visit Kent Falls. In addition to the falls you will find a small covered bridge, large grassy fields, and plenty of picnic tables and fire pits at this often crowded site.

TRAIL INFORMATION You can see the beginning of the falls from the large parking area. Cross through the covered bridge and head toward the cascades. The rest of Kent Falls lies up the Kent Falls Trail, which is a short but steep climb that begins to the right of the lowest falls.

DIRECTIONS From Sharon, take US 7 south. Continue traveling on US 7 south for 0.4 mile past the KENT TOWN LINE sign and pull into the

Kent Falls

parking lot for Kent Falls State Park on your left. If you are traveling north on US 7 from New Milford, continue on US 7 north for 5.1 miles past its junction with CT 341 in Kent. Both directions of US 7 have signs directing you to the state park.

OTHER WATERFALLS NEARBY Pine Swamp Brook Falls, Dean's Ravine Falls, Great Falls of the Housatonic.

11

KETTLETOWN BROOK FALLS
Southbury, Kettletown State Park, New Haven County

Type: Cascades

Height: 5 feet

Trail Length: 0.2 mile

Water Source: Kettletown Brook

Altitude Gain/Loss: None

Difficulty: Easy

Hiking Time: 5 minutes

DeLorme Map: Page 23, B-21

Rating: ★★

DESCRIPTION Kettletown State Park is a pleasant park that borders the section of the Housatonic River formally acknowledged as Lake Zoar. In addition to camping facilities, a beach, freshwater fishing, and a network of trails, the state park offers a short walk to a small waterfall. To our knowledge, these falls do not have a proper name. Due to their size, only 5 feet, they may never receive enough attention to warrant a name. Yet size is not all that matters. The falls do have a tempting swimming pool below them, and because they are only a few minutes' walk from the beach, we felt this natural feature had to be included in our guide.

TRAIL INFORMATION The falls are located 0.2 mile north of the beach, reached by hiking along the trail that parallels Kettletown Brook.

DIRECTIONS From the junction of US 6, CT 67, and I-84 in Southbury, take CT 67 south and, soon after, turn right onto CT 487 south (Kettletown Road). Follow CT 487 south for 3.4 miles to a right turn onto George's Hill Road. After 0.7 mile on George's Hill Road, turn right into Kettletown State Park and follow signs to the BEACH. The trail begins to the left end of the beach.

OTHER WATERFALLS NEARBY Prydden Brook Falls, Southford Falls, Indian Well Falls, Spruce Brook Falls.

12

MILL POND FALLS

Newington, Hartford County

Type: Fan

Height: 14 feet

Trail Length: Roadside

Water Source: Mill Pond

Altitude Gain/Loss: None

Difficulty: Easy

Hiking Time: Not applicable

DeLorme Map: Page 44, J-2

Rating: ★★★

DESCRIPTION Mill Pond Falls is formed from the outlet waters of Mill Pond, a flower-lined body of water with a paved route around its perimeter. The waterfall and pond have been made into a tiny little park by the town of Newington.

The waterfall is surrounded by an iron fence, which detracts from the beauty of both the wildflowers and the landscaped gardens. A red wooden walking bridge is set just above the waterfall. The bridge, railing, and flow-

Mill Pond Falls

ers can add significant character to a photograph or painting of the waterfall.

We do not suggest making a day of this waterfall, as it is quite small and rather unimpressive. Still, if you are in the area or looking for a new picnic area, Mill Pond Falls is sure to please you.

TRAIL INFORMATION The falls are clearly visible from the parking area.

DIRECTIONS From Hartford, take I-84 west to exit 39A and follow CT 9 south into Newington. Take exit 29 off CT 9 and, at the end of the off-ramp, turn left and follow the road signs toward CT 175, heading right after 0.1 mile onto CT 175. After traveling on CT 175 for 0.4 mile, you must take a left to continue on the highway. Take this left and continue on CT 175 east 1.2 miles farther. Next you must take a right onto CT 175 south. After 0.2 mile, take a left onto Garfield Street. The parking area is 0.1 mile ahead on your right, marked by a sign for MILL POND FALLS.

OTHER WATERFALLS NEARBY Westfield Falls, Buttermilk Falls (Plymouth).

13

NEGRO HILL BROOK FALLS

Burlington, Session Woods Wildlife Management Area, Hartford County

Type: Plunges
Height: 20 feet each
Trail Length: 2.9-mile loop
Water Source: Negro Hill Brook
Altitude Gain/Loss: Up 40 feet, down 40 feet

Difficulty: Easy
Hiking Time: 90-minute loop
DeLorme Map: Page 42, H-12
Rating: ★★★

DESCRIPTION The Sessions Woods Wildlife Management Area is a 455-acre preserve in Burlington that introduces visitors to wildlife management through self-guiding trails, various education programs, and an informative visitors center. The attractions of the management area include a beaver marsh, observation tower, and a set of three waterfall plunges on Negro

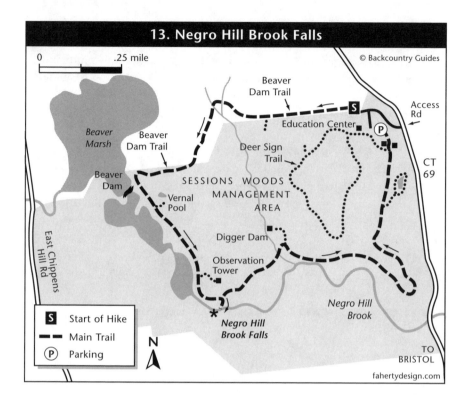

13. Negro Hill Brook Falls

0   .25 mile

© Backcountry Guides

Beaver Dam Trail

S

Access Rd

Beaver Marsh

Beaver Dam Trail

Education Center

P

Deer Sign Trail

CT 69

Beaver Dam

SESSIONS WOODS MANAGEMENT AREA

Vernal Pool

Digger Dam

East Chippens Hill Rd

Observation Tower

Negro Hill Brook

S Start of Hike

Negro Hill Brook Falls

- - - Main Trail

P Parking

N

TO BRISTOL

faherty design.com

Hill Brook. Each plunge is short in total drop, very narrow, and partially hidden between plates of rock.

Other published sources state that this waterfall is rather unimpressive. Negro Hill Brook Falls may not be tall, powerful, or particularly scenic, but it is still impressive to us. As a bonus, the trail to the waterfall has many "stops" where information is provided on the diverse biology of the park. You will also find several beaver dams and a boardwalk trail that leads out toward a beaver pond.

TRAIL INFORMATION The falls are accessed by following the Beaver Dam Trail. If you are facing the visitors center, head right toward the dirt road on your right, where the trail begins. When you reach the trailhead, essential trail maps can be found. These detail the trail network of the park and provide information on all its attractions and objectives.

The Beaver Dam Trail follows a dirt road for just under 3.0 miles. After about 1.4 miles of hiking, a WATERFALL sign will direct you onto a spur trail on your right. The falls are a short distance down that trail. When you return, continue the loop of the Beaver Dam Trail back to the visitors center and parking lot. Dogs are welcome on the trails as long as they remain leashed at all times.

DIRECTIONS From the junction of US 6 and CT 69 in Bristol, take CT 69 north for 3.7 miles; the entrance for the Session Woods Wildlife Management Area will be on your left. Follow the park road to the large parking lot in front of the visitors center. *To get to Bristol,* take I-84 west from Hartford to exit 38. Take US 6 west.

OTHER WATERFALLS NEARBY Buttermilk Falls (Plymouth), Mill Pond Falls.

Negro Hill Brook Falls

14

PINE SWAMP BROOK FALLS

Sharon, Litchfield County

Type: Cascades

Height: 30-foot total drop

Trail Length: Less than 0.1 mile

Water Source: Pine Swamp Brook

Altitude Gain/Loss: None

Difficulty: Easy

Hiking Time: Not applicable

DeLorme Map: Page 49, K&L-23

Rating: ★★★

DESCRIPTION This well-shaded waterfall, viewable only from US 7 in Sharon, consists of two sections of small cascades tumbling down through chasm walls. The waters of Pine Swamp Brook pass beneath you, flow underneath the state highway, and then dump into Housatonic River. It takes a true waterfall enthusiast to really appreciate this roadside attraction.

Although far from extraordinary, Pine Swamp Brook Falls is conveniently located on the route between Dean's Ravine and Kent Falls. For this reason, take a break off the highway and check out these small falls. Do not be one of the hundreds of people per day who must drive by this waterfall oblivious to the fact that a natural beauty lies directly beside them.

TRAIL INFORMATION From the parking area, walk back up the road heading north for a few yards; the falls will be visible on your left. There is a sign on the road for PINE SWAMP BROOK.

DIRECTIONS From Canaan, take US 7 south. Continue traveling on US 7 south for 4.0 miles past the SHARON TOWN LINE sign. The parking area will be on your right just after a sharp curve in the road. If you are traveling north on US 7, the parking area is on your left, 2.0 miles north of the Housatonic Meadows Campground in Sharon. *To get to Canaan,* take US 7 north from Danbury.

OTHER WATERFALLS NEARBY Dean's Ravine Falls, Great Falls of the Housatonic, Kent Falls.

15

PRYDDEN BROOK FALLS

Newtown, Paugussett State Forest, Fairfield County

Type: Plunges and cascades

Height: 25-foot plunge and 40 feet of cascades

Trail Length: 1.5 miles

Water Source: Prydden Brook

Altitude Gain/Loss: None (see notes)

Difficulty: Easy side of moderate

Hiking Time: 45 minutes

DeLorme Map: Page 23, B-21

Rating: ★★★★

DESCRIPTION The hike to Prydden Brook Falls is one of our favorites. For the majority of the trail, you walk along the west side of the Housatonic River. As you walk, you pass dozens of private river beaches. The climax of the trip is, of course, the waterfall itself.

This waterfall begins and ends as a plunge, with many sections of cascades between. The main attraction is a 25-foot horsetail, which is surrounded by a heavy growth of moss and plenty of tempting rocks for climbing. The entire feature receives little exposure to the sun, but on a clear day the sun sneaks its way through the trees onto the waterfall and illuminates the water and the vibrant greens of the moss.

Offering plenty of intimate explorations and a healthy 3.0-mile round-trip hike, Prydden Brook Falls is not to be missed. During fall months be sure to wear colorful clothing, as hunting is permitted in the state forest.

TRAIL INFORMATION The Zoar Trail begins to the east end of the parking lot behind an information board with the rules and regulations of the state forest. Well traveled and marked by sky-blue rectangles, the trail parallels the Housatonic River for the entire way to the waterfall, sometimes as close as 5 feet to the river, and up to a few hundred feet west of it. After 1.4 miles you will reach Prydden Brook; take a right spur trail down the falls. The trail is obvious, and the falls are viewable a few hundred feet before you get there, so you should not experience any difficulties reaching them. Although the altitude gain is modest, there are several hills to ascend and descend.

DIRECTIONS From the junction of CT 111 and CT 34 in the village of Stevenson, take CT 34 west for 0.2 mile. Take a right onto Great

Quarter Road and follow it for 1.1 miles to a fork. Take the left fork, and continue on Great Quarter Road for an additional 0.2 mile to its end, where a circular parking area can be found. *To get to Stevenson,* take CT 25 north from Bridgeport to CT 111 north.

OTHER WATERFALLS NEARBY Kettletown Brook Falls, Indian Well Falls, Southford Falls.

16

ROARING BROOK FALLS

Cheshire, New Haven County

Type: Horsetail and cascades

Height: 80-foot total drop

Trail Length: 0.5 mile

Water Source: Roaring Brook

Altitude Gain/Loss: +225 feet

Difficulty: Moderate

Hiking Time: 20 minutes

DeLorme Map: Page 34, J&K-1

Rating: ★★★★

DESCRIPTION One of the tallest waterfalls in the state, Roaring Brook Falls is a 60-foot horsetail with several feet of cascades below the main drop. Similar to Race Brook Falls of Massachusetts, the waterfall is surrounded by a variety of green plant life, causing it to play peek-a-boo with you from all viewing angles. Someone eventually determined the best view and placed a small wooden seat between two trees just off the trail. Instead of trying to view or photograph the entire falls, we suggest accepting the best seat in the house.

TRAIL INFORMATION The trail begins as a continuation of Roaring Brook Road. Follow this dirt road for about five minutes and you will approach a sign letting you know that the road just became private. Take a left here onto a new trail. From here to the falls, an orange-blazed trail will guide you across progressively steeper ground. About 0.3 mile into the woods, you will reach the falls. You can choose to either enjoy the views already attained or continue to the top of falls. We do not recommend continuing, because the trail becomes hazardously steep and the views are no more spectacular. Getting to the base of the falls is completely out of the question, due to the danger of sliding down the ravine into the cascading brook; we therefore ask that you stay on the trail.

DIRECTIONS From Waterbury, take exit 23 off I-84. Take CT 69 south until you reach its junction with CT 42. Take a left onto CT 42 east and follow it for 2.6 miles. Take a left onto Mountain Road, continue for 0.3 mile, then take a left onto Roaring Brook Road. Travel along this road for 0.5 mile and park at a small pull-off on your right before a metal gate, which is the trailhead for the falls.

OTHER WATERFALLS NEARBY Spruce Brook Falls, Wintergreen Falls, Westfield Falls.

17

SEVEN FALLS

Haddam & Middletown, Middlesex County

Type: Cascades
Height: Tallest cascade is 5 feet
Trail Length: 0.1 mile
Water Source: Bible Rock Brook
Altitude Gain/Loss: None

Difficulty: Easy
Hiking Time: Not applicable
DeLorme Map: Page 35, I-23
Rating: ★★ ½

DESCRIPTION With so many other noteworthy falls in the area, Seven Falls springs to life as a comfortable pit stop to enjoy a barbecue, sandwich, or some other picnic-suitable meal. Although the term *Seven Falls* suggests seven waterfalls, the actual number of cascades varies depending on the source. We can pick out only three sizable cascades, rather than seven.

Most waterfalls in this guide are large in either size or power, stunningly beautiful, or a combination of the three. To be honest, none of these characteristics is applicable to Seven Falls. All you can expect to find is several small cascades, and perhaps a few places to splash and explore. Do not make a special trip to this one unless you are in the mood for a picnic. We find this place to be a pleasant break from other travels in the area.

TRAIL INFORMATION All of the small cascades of Seven Falls are visible from the picnic area in front of the parking area.

DIRECTIONS From Middletown, take CT 9 south to exit 10. Follow Aircraft Road for 0.1 mile, and take a right onto CT 154 south. Follow

CT 154 south for 0.8 mile and take a left into the parking lot for the falls.

OTHER WATERFALLS NEARBY Bear Hill Falls, Wadsworth Big Falls, Wadsworth Little Falls, Westfield Falls, Chapman Falls.

18

SOUTHFORD FALLS

Southbury, Southford Falls State Park,
New Haven County

Type: Cascades and a small plunge	**Difficulty:** Easy
Height: 60-foot total drop	**Hiking Time:** 10 minutes
Trail Length: 0.3-mile loop	**DeLorme Map:** Page 32, L-12
Water Source: Eight-Mile Brook	**Rating:** ★★
Altitude Gain/Loss: None	

DESCRIPTION Your first impression of Southford Falls is that it is artificial. The remains of a mill are evident in the stonework around the top of the falls. Upon closer inspection, you realize that much of the waterfall is actually natural. Although not fully natural, Southford Falls seems to please the picnickers visiting the park and those fishing for trout in Papermill Pond, the water body above the waterfall.

There is nothing scenic or anything out of the ordinary here—just another chain of small waterfalls surrounded by an area best suited for a family picnic.

TRAIL INFORMATION The falls are located on the opposite end of the pond from the parking lot. A short 0.3-mile loop trail leads along the riverbank, through a covered bridge, and back up the other side of the falls. A great place for a short relaxing stroll.

DIRECTIONS From Waterbury, take I-84 west to exit 16, then follow CT 188 south for 0.5 mile past its junction with CT 67. The parking lot for the Southford Falls State Park will be on your left.

OTHER WATERFALLS NEARBY Kettletown Brook Falls, Spruce Brook Falls, Prydden Brook Falls, Indian Well Falls.

19

SPRUCE BROOK FALLS

Beacon Falls, Naugatuck State Forest,
New Haven County

Type: Plunges and cascades

Height: Largest plunge is 15 feet

Trail Length: 0.3 mile

Water Source: Spruce Brook

Altitude Gain/Loss: +50 feet

Difficulty: Easy side of moderate

Hiking Time: 10 minutes

DeLorme Map: Page 33, L-17&18

Rating: ★ ★ ★ ★

DESCRIPTION Spruce Brook Falls is one of two waterfalls described in this guide that allow visitors to wander behind a waterfall. It is much easier to get behind the falling waters of Bartlett Falls in Vermont, but in the southern half of New England, Spruce Brook Falls is the only waterfall you will find that you can manage to see the reverse of. The only way this is possible is by climbing down the embankment and wading through the river, then tucking yourself behind the falling water.

At the base of the main falls, the rushing water is forced into rocks, causing white foam to swirl around and look like a bubble bath. There are rust-colored pools; the one at the base of the falls appears to be about 6 feet deep. Cascades drop above and below the star waterfall, and farther downstream is a petite-sized waterslide, even a pool with a swirling eddy. Farther up the trail, beyond the main falls and cascades above, lies another noteworthy waterfall—a segmented cascade over an egg-shaped boulder that sits in the center of the brook.

The entire section of Spruce Brook we are describing lies in a ravine that supports an unusually large variety of plant life. This adds much color to the area. It could be said that this particular environment is one of the prettiest ravines in all of New England.

TRAIL INFORMATION The trail begins on the opposite side of the brook from the parking lot. The best way to reach it is by walking back up the road. Take a right onto the trail just after crossing the small bridge you drove in on. As you continue up the trail and begin passing the first cascades, expect steeper and more slippery terrain. *Footing can become quite difficult, so be careful.*

DIRECTIONS From Waterbury, take CT 8 south to exit 24. Take a right at the end of the off-ramp; after 0.1 mile, take another right and drive over a bridge. Immediately beyond the bridge, take a right onto Lopus Road; after 0.1 mile, take a right onto Cold Spring Road. Travel on Cold Spring Road for 1.1 mile and you will reach a fork. Take the right branch and continue for 0.25 mile farther to the parking area on your left. Be aware that Cold Spring turns into a rather rough road, and that exit 24 is only on the southbound side of CT 8.

OTHER WATERFALLS NEARBY Southford Falls, Roaring Brook Falls, Kettletown Brook Falls, Indian Well Falls, Prydden Brook Falls.

20

WADSWORTH BIG FALLS

Middlefield, Wadsworth Falls State Park,
Middlesex County

Type: Block	**Difficulty:** Easy
Height: 20 feet	**Hiking Time:** Not applicable
Trail Length: 0.1 mile	**DeLorme Map:** Page 35, H-16
Water Source: Coginchaug River	**Rating:** ★★★ ½
Altitude Gain/Loss: –25 feet	

DESCRIPTION One of the highest-volume waterfalls in New England, Wadsworth Big Falls is located on the western border of Wadsworth Falls State Park. It is a stereotypical "block"-type waterfall, wider than it is tall. Lacking much originality, beauty, or differentiation in any way, Wadsworth Big Falls earns its "highly recommended" award simply because you do not expect to find such a commanding waterfall in the heart of Connecticut. The currents of the river following the falls are just as impressive.

Do not expect peace and quiet at this particular waterfall. The parking lot can fill up even on chilly, rainy days in springtime. Its popularity can only be explained by its stunning volume and scale, especially considering how confined the area is. If seclusion and privacy are what you want, try nearby Wadsworth Little Falls—less than a mile away and accessed via a trail that starts at the same parking lot.

TRAIL INFORMATION From the parking lot, walk straight across a

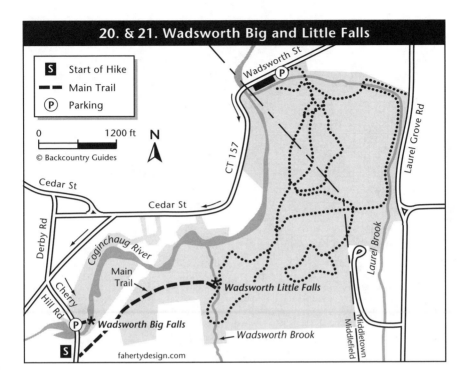

20. & 21. Wadsworth Big and Little Falls

S Start of Hike
━ ━ Main Trail
P Parking

0 ——————— 1200 ft
© Backcountry Guides

N

Wadsworth St

CT 157

Laurel Grove Rd

Cedar St

Cedar St

Derby Rd

Coginchaug River

Main Trail

Cherry Hill Rd

P ✳ Wadsworth Big Falls

S

faherty design.com

✳ Wadsworth Little Falls

Laurel Brook

Middletown Middlefield

← Wadsworth Brook

field and down the steps to the falls. There is also a cement overlook, surrounded by safety fences, at the top of the falls for a bird's-eye view of the falls.

DIRECTIONS In Middletown, take exit 16 off CT 9. Take CT 66 west to its junction with CT 157 south. Take a left onto CT 157 south and follow it for 1.6 miles; a sign for WADSWORTH FALLS STATE PARK will appear on your left. Although there is a large parking lot here, and trails can be seen leading into the woods, the parking lot for the falls is not here. Continue on CT 157 for 1.1 miles more, then take a left onto Cherry Hill Road. After 0.2 mile, turn left into a paved parking lot.

OTHER WATERFALLS NEARBY Wadsworth Little Falls, Westfield Falls, Bear Hill Falls, Seven Falls.

21

WADSWORTH LITTLE FALLS

*Middlefield, Wadsworth Falls State Park,
Middlesex County*

Type: Small plunges

Height: 40 feet

Trail Length: 0.5 mile

Water Source: Wadsworth Brook

Altitude Gain/Loss: –40 feet

Difficulty: Easy side of moderate

Hiking Time: 20 minutes

DeLorme Map: Page 35, H-16

Rating: ★★★½

DESCRIPTION To our surprise, Wadsworth Little Falls turned out to be two times taller than its neighbor, Wadsworth Big Falls. Wadsworth Little Falls probably earned its name from being much less powerful and seasonal than the Big Falls. When we visited in spring after two previous days of heavy rain, Little Falls was still rather weak.

For structure, this waterfall is composed of about two dozen step plunges, none taller than 3 feet. Although weak, Wadsworth Little Falls is a fine example of a staircase waterfall, and is a nice supplement to the power and popularity of the Big Falls.

TRAIL INFORMATION (See map on previous page) From the parking lot facing the field, take a right and continue walking along Cherry Hill Road. Cross the railroad tracks; the trailhead will soon be found on your left. The trail you are now on is the "Main Trail," an easily traveled pathway that navigates through the center of the park. Hike this red-or-ange-blazed trail for 0.4 mile, when you approach a junction. There will be a bench and a sign for LITTLE FALLS TRAIL, pointing left. Take this left, and follow the trail down to the falls. The last 100 feet are somewhat steep and often muddy—this part may not be best for children.

DIRECTIONS In Middletown, take exit 16 off CT 9. Take CT 66 west until you reach its junction with CT 157 south. Take a left onto CT 157 south and follow it for 1.6 miles; a sign for WADSWORTH FALLS STATE PARK will appear on your left. Although there is a large parking lot here, and trails can be seen leading into the woods, the parking lot for the falls is not here. Continue on CT 157 for 1.1 miles more, then take a left onto Cherry Hill Road. After 0.2 mile, take a left into a paved parking lot.

Wadsworth Little Falls

OTHER WATERFALLS NEARBY Wadsworth Big Falls, Westfield Falls, Bear Hill Falls, Seven Falls.

22

WESTFIELD FALLS
Middletown, Middlesex County

Type: Horsetail and plunge
Height: 18-foot plunge and 15-foot horsetail
Trail Length: Less than 0.1 mile
Water Source: Fall Brook
Altitude Gain/Loss: –30 feet

Difficulty: Easy
Hiking Time: 5 minutes
DeLorme Map: Page 35, E-15
Rating: ★★★½

DESCRIPTION Westfield Falls is a pair of drops about 30 feet apart from each other. On the left side of the structure is an 18-foot-tall plunge; to the right lies a 15-foot horsetail. The brook, which is separated by a rocky island before the falls, rejoins about 80 feet downstream. There is also a long slide a few feet downstream from the falls worth noting.

Westfield Falls is a beautiful waterfall. Due to its residential location, however, the surrounding area has fallen victim to vandalism, litter, and an interstate highway. Hopefully this waterfall will be cleaned up in the near future. If so, it will earn a much higher recommendation in any future editions of this guidebook.

TRAIL INFORMATION Step over the cinder blocks and walk along the dirt road in front of the parking lot for a few feet. To see the top of the falls first, continue straight down the dirt road. To get to the bottom of the falls—which we recommend—take a left onto a trail that heads into the woods. After 100 feet or so, take the right trail at the fork that appears. You will shortly be able to see and hear the waterfall.

DIRECTIONS From Middletown, take CT 66 west toward Middlefield. Take a right onto CT 217 north, continue for 2.4 miles, and take a left onto Miner Street. Follow Miner Street for 0.7 mile and leave your vehicle at the small parking area on your right. This area is outlined with cement blocks. You can also reach the falls by taking exit 21 off I-91, and following CT 372 east to a right turn onto CT 217 south.

Westfield Falls

OTHER WATERFALLS NEARBY Wadsworth Big Falls, Wadsworth Little Falls, Bear Hill Falls, Seven Falls, Mill Pond Falls.

23

WINTERGREEN FALLS

Hamden, New Haven County

Type: Cascades
Height: 15 feet
Trail Length: Less than 0.1 mile
Water Source: West Brook
Altitude Gain/Loss: None

Difficulty: Easy
Hiking Time: Not applicable
DeLorme Map: Page 24, G-12
Rating: ★★★

DESCRIPTION Thin sheaths of water slide and cascade over traprock at Wintergreen Falls, a near-roadside attraction located at the entrance to the

Wintergreen Falls

West Rock Nature Center in New Haven. Beyond the falls, the waters of West Brook travel through a deep red gorge. This tranquil little place is a distant 20 miles from the nearest waterfall, so you may opt to skip this trip. The majority of visitors to this waterfall seem to be the local children exploring their neighborhood.

TRAIL INFORMATION Wintergreen Falls is only feet from the parking area, reached by taking one of several short paths down to the brook. A primitive path leads around down a steep bank to the base of the falls. This is often very slippery and quite muddy, so it is best to enjoy the falls from either the top or side.

DIRECTIONS In New Haven, take exit 60 off CT 15. Travel on CT 10 south for 1.6 miles. Take a wide right turn onto Woodin Street just before a gas station. Follow Woodin Street for 1.7 miles and take a left onto Wintergreen Avenue. Follow Wintergreen for 0.6 mile; the parking area will be on your left after crossing underneath a bridge.

OTHER WATERFALLS NEARBY Indian Well Falls, Spruce Brook Falls, Negro Hill Brook Falls.

24

YANTIC FALLS

Norwich, New London County

Type: Plunge and cascades
Height: 40-foot plunge
Trail Length: Roadside
Water Source: Yantic River
Altitude Gain/Loss: None

Difficulty: Easy
Hiking Time: Not applicable
DeLorme Map: Page 38, G-4
Rating: ★★★★

DESCRIPTION As the legend goes, Yantic Falls was a favorite camping spot and battleground for the Mohegan Indians in the 1640s. Uncas, sachem of the Mohegans, led his people in a battle here against the Narragansetts, a major rival tribe. Legend states that during the fight, a group of Narragansetts chose to leap into the chasm of the Yantic River instead of surrendering. All of the warriors met their death in the turbulent cascades of Yantic Falls.

Today Yantic Falls is part dam and part natural. The main plunge is 35 to 40 feet in height, and the volume of water is one of the most power-ful in the state. The river continues through one of Connecticut's most impressive gorges before ending its descent and relaxing in calmer waters. Above the falls, a walking bridge and a railroad bridge have been con-structed, but they do not detract from the scenery.

TRAIL INFORMATION From the parking area, walk back up Yantic Street and take a left at the sign for the YANTIC FALLS AND INDIAN LEAP.

DIRECTIONS From Colchester, take CT 2 east toward Norwich. Take exit 29 for Norwichtown. At the end of the off-ramp, take a right, and you will be on the New London Turnpike, heading south. After 1.3 miles on the turnpike, take a left onto Newton Street. Just after this left turn, you will be faced with a fork. Veer right and follow Newton Street to its end. At the end of Newton Street, take a left onto Asylum Street, con-tinue 0.7 mile, and take a right onto Sherman Street. Follow Sherman, making sure to remain with the street as it takes a sharp right turn. At the end of Sherman, take a right onto Yantic Street. The parking lot is 0.1 mile up the road, on your right just past a set of black fencing.

OTHER WATERFALLS NEARBY Bailey's Ravine, Chapman Falls.

II. Maine

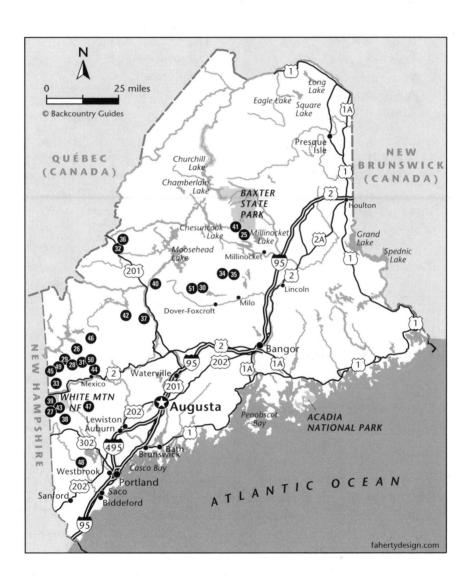

25

ABOL FALLS

Township 2, Range 10, Piscataquis County

Type: Cascades and rapids

Height: 5-foot total drop

Trail Length: Roadside

Water Source: West Branch
Penobscot River

Altitude Gain/Loss: None

Difficulty: Easy

Hiking Time: Not applicable

DeLorme Map: Page 50, E-5

Rating: ★★½

DESCRIPTION In early spring, when the West Branch of the Penobscot River is in its flood stage, Abol Falls is a wide, massively powerful cascade. As the spring months pass, the volume of water released by Ripogenus Dam upstream begins to diminish. Abol Falls becomes more of a small set of rapids, either Class II or III whitewater.

No matter what the season, though, you should visit for the unmatched vista of Mount Katahdin. The clear view of the mountain from the falls is difficult to beat. From the riverbank just southwest of the waterfall, you could compose a prizewinning photograph or painting of Abol Falls on the scenic West Branch of the Penobscot River, with Mount Katahdin highlighting the backdrop.

TRAIL INFORMATION Several truly primitive paths lead down to the river. Perhaps two or three visitors each year make their way down to the riverbank. There are also limited views from the dirt road.

DIRECTIONS From Bangor, take I-95 north to exit 56. Take a left onto ME 157, traveling west toward Millinocket. Just past ME 157's end in the town of Millinocket, turn right onto Katahdin Avenue. Follow signs toward Baxter State Park. As you approach Millinocket Lake on your right, you will need to switch over to the road running parallel and left of the road you are on. There are several paved lanes to do this, so be on the lookout when you approach Millinocket Lake and Spencer Cove. The road you switched to is called the Golden Road. Travel north on the Golden Road as it eventually crosses the West Branch of the Penobscot River over Abol Bridge. Continue for 100 feet or so beyond the bridge, take a left onto an unmarked dirt road, and drive for 0.7 mile; the falls can be seen off at a distance from the left side of the road.

OTHER WATERFALLS NEARBY Nesowadnehunk Falls, Gulf Hagas, Hay Brook Falls.

26

ANGEL FALLS
Township D, Franklin County

Type: Plunge
Height: 90 feet
Trail Length: 0.8 mile
Water Source: Mountain Brook
Altitude Gain/Loss: Down 50 feet, up 150 feet

Difficulty: Easy side of moderate (see notes)
Hiking Time: 30 minutes
DeLorme Map: Page 18, B-4
Rating: ★★★★

DESCRIPTION (HIGHLY RECOMMENDED) For years there has been a dispute over which waterfall—Angel Falls or Moxie Falls—is Maine's tallest single drop. Some accounts will say that Angel Falls, at 90 feet, is a foot taller than Moxie. Other sources have stated that they are both 90 feet tall. Regardless of which is the taller, however, each offers a wild remote treasure not commonly found in this region.

With surrounding cliff walls of up to 115 feet, Angel Falls is remarkably scenic. The 25-foot gap positioned on the top of the cliff wall can be explained by two theories, the first being erosion. Through the years it appears as if the water sliced its way through the cliff walls, causing the sediments to flow downstream. The other theory suggests that the perfectly sized and shaped boulder at the base of the waterfall used to sit in the gap above. Perhaps it was knocked out during the Ice Age or even by a great storm. We cannot say which theory is correct, but the gap on the cliff wall through which the water flows certainly distinguishes Angel Falls from all others in the region.

TRAIL INFORMATION For the first 0.2 mile of the hike to the falls, the trail follows an old dirt road that stems from Bemis Road. It is currently distinguishable from other roads only by a sign prohibiting kindling fires in the area. Follow this dirt road as it descends past a gravel pit on your left and a large dirt lot on your right. You should soon see two obvious trails. Take the left, red-blazed trail.

About 0.5 mile from the parking pull-offs, cross Berden Stream; on our visits, this required only minimal effort, though we have heard of people having difficulties crossing this stream during periods of high water. After crossing the stream, continue 0.3 mile farther, following the red markers as the trail skips back and forth across the brook before reaching the base of the falls.

DIRECTIONS From the junction of US 2 and ME 17 in Mexico, take ME 17 north and continue for 11.9 miles past the road that leads you to ME 120 (Frye Crossover Road). Take a left onto Houghton Road, which is 1.5 miles south of the TOWNSHIP E TOWN LINE sign. Follow Houghton Road for 0.25 mile and take a right onto Bemis Road. Follow Bemis Road for 3.4 miles and look for several parking pull-offs on your left. *To get to Mexico,* take ME 17 north from Augusta or US 2 east from Bethel.

OTHER WATERFALLS NEARBY Smalls Falls, Swift River Falls, Ellis Falls, The Cataracts, Dunn Falls.

27

BICKFORD SLIDES

Stow, White Mountain National Forest, Oxford County

Type: Cascades and slides
Height: Varies (see notes)
Trail Length: To lower slide, 0.7 mile; to upper slide, 1.1 mile
Water Source: Bickford Brook
Altitude Gain/Loss: To lower slide, +300 feet; to upper slide, +500 feet

Difficulty: Moderate
Hiking Time: 35 minutes to upper slide
DeLorme Map: Page 10, C-1
Rating: ★★★

DESCRIPTION Hidden in a deep ravine between Blueberry Mountain and Sugarloaf Mountain, Bickford Brook travels downstream toward its confluence with the Cold River. Along the way, hundreds of feet of cascades and slides adorn the brook, most accessible by a few popular hiking trails.

The first slides of the trail, appropriately named Lower Slides, are reached just after your first contact with the brook. These slides are about 50 feet in height and composed of cascades, slides, and delightful water chutes. Forget about exploring the Lower Slides; the sheer flume walls are very dangerous.

A 40-foot-tall, medium-angled slide with a dark, moderately attractive pool encompasses the Upper Bickford Slides. Set in a heavily shaded glen, the Upper Slides have very low water throughout most of the year. Although the area is remote and access can be confusing, the pool, with its

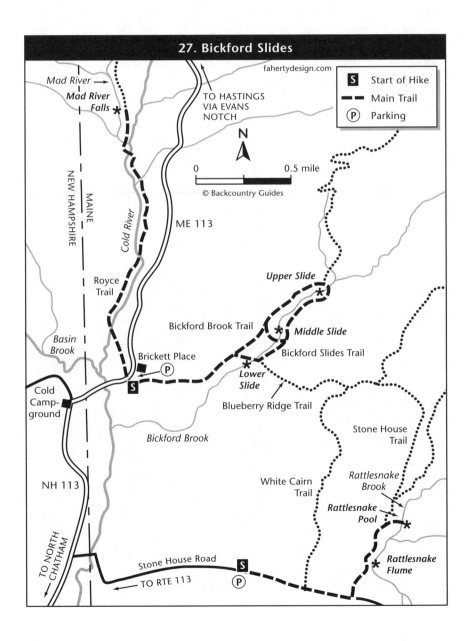

27. Bickford Slides

fahertydesign.com

Mad River
Mad River Falls
TO HASTINGS VIA EVANS NOTCH

S Start of Hike
- - - Main Trail
P Parking

N

0   0.5 mile
© Backcountry Guides

NEW HAMPSHIRE
MAINE

Cold River

ME 113

Royce Trail

Upper Slide

Bickford Brook Trail

Middle Slide

Basin Brook

Brickett Place
P

Bickford Slides Trail

Lower Slide

S

Cold Campground

Blueberry Ridge Trail

Bickford Brook

Stone House Trail

Rattlesnake Brook

White Cairn Trail

Rattlesnake Pool

NH 113

Rattlesnake Flume

TO NORTH CHATHAM

Stone House Road
S
P
← TO RTE 113

depths up to 5 feet, receives moderate use. We saw a troop of about a dozen towel-holding children being led by their guide to the swimming hole when we visited midweek toward the end of June.

TRAIL INFORMATION The trail to Bickford Slides begins at the parking lot behind the trail information boards. For the first 0.2 mile, it is a moderately steep climb. After climbing for about 10 minutes, you will reach a flat stretch; continue right to stay on the trail.

For the next 0.4 mile the trail gains altitude very slowly as you approach a fork. The left fork is for the Bickford Brook Trail; the right, which you will be taking, is the Blueberry Ridge Trail. Follow the ridge trail for 0.1 mile as it meanders down to the brook. At the waterside a white sign will appear pointing toward the Lower Slides and the trail that leads to the Upper Slides.

The Lower Slides are approximately 100 feet downstream, accessible by a worn path that parallels the brook. Take note that there are limited views of the slides from the trail, and scrambling off-trail is not recommended, as a fall from the river walls would be deadly. To reach the Upper Slides, continue back to where you first reached the brook. Two different trails continue on the other side. On your right is the Blueberry Ridge Trail; on your left, the trail to the upper falls. Both are yellow blazed, so be sure

Upper Bickford Slides

to take the left trail. Follow parallel to the brook for about 0.4 mile and you will reach a head-on view of the Upper Slides. If you are comfortable, scramble down to the base of the slides, where you will find one of the more popular swimming holes of the White Mountains.

DIRECTIONS From the junction of ME 113 and US 302 in Fryeburg, take ME 113 north, continuing past Chatham and 0.5 mile beyond the posted WHITE MOUNTAIN NATIONAL FOREST BOUNDARY sign. Take a right into the Brickett Place, where the parking lot can be found. *To get to Fryeburg,* take US 302 east from Conway.

OTHER WATERFALLS NEARBY Rattlesnake Flume and Pool, Mad River Falls, Hermit Falls (New Hampshire).

28

THE CATARACTS
Andover West Surplus, Oxford County

Type: Horsetails and cascades
Height: Approximately 60-foot total drop
Trail Length: 0.5 mile
Water Source: Frye Brook
Altitude Gain/Loss: +150 feet

Difficulty: Moderate
Hiking Time: 20 minutes
DeLorme Map: Page 18, D-2
Rating: ★★★

DESCRIPTION On our summer visits, The Cataracts consisted of many plunges dropping an estimated 60 feet. We have heard accounts, and seen some convincing pictures, that in the wet season this is a behemoth of raging cascades. When we visited, we only saw some lonely cascades and plunges. On a positive note, with the cascades gone we were able to explore the small caves near the waterfall between precipitous gorge walls.

During the summer, The Cataracts were also a scrambler's delight, with opportunities for hours of exploration. The many swimming holes are also refreshingly pleasing here. Perhaps your visit will reveal the personality of The Cataracts we have heard about.

TRAIL INFORMATION The Frye Brook Trail begins across the street from the parking area and travels up Cataracts Road, so steep and rough that it is hard to imagine how any motor vehicle could have once traveled along it. After a few minutes, fork right at a red HIKER sign directing you toward the falls with an arrow. Continue along the yellow-blazed trail; about 0.7 mile from the parking lot you will begin climbing at a more intense rate, with the gorge appearing on your right behind wooden fencing. The views are limited from the top, so backtrack a little, scout the easiest path down to the brook, and hike upstream to the falls. Be careful as you hike upstream, because many rocks are covered in moss and others are just weathered and very slippery. To reach the tallest drop, you must pass through a narrow cave and hike upstream. Continue along the brook for as long as you feel safe: The trail gets increasingly challenging as you begin to explore the cascades.

DIRECTIONS From the junction of ME 5 and ME 120 in the center of Andover, head west on Newton Street (identified on some maps as East B Hill Road). Follow Newton Street for 5.4 miles and look for a pull-off on your right across the street from a sign for CATARACT ROAD. *To get to Andover,* take ME 120 west from Rumford.

OTHER WATERFALLS NEARBY Dunn Falls, Ellis Falls, Swift River Falls, Screw Auger Falls (Grafton), Step Falls.

29

DUNN FALLS
Andover North Surplus, Oxford County

Type: Horsetails and fans
Height: Lower falls is 80 feet; upper falls is 50 feet
Trail Length: 2.0-mile loop
Water Source: West Branch Ellis River
Altitude Gain/Loss: Up 250 feet, down 250 feet

Difficulty: Moderate
Hiking Time: 90 minutes
DeLorme Map: Page 18, D-2
Rating: ★★★★★

DESCRIPTION (HIGHLY RECOMMENDED) The 2-mile loop trail that surrounds Dunn Falls offers more than just one of the highest-rated waterfalls in Maine. As you hike along you will find swimming holes, travel a stretch of the 2,160-mile Appalachian Trail, and discover lower and upper

Dunn Falls as well as half a dozen smaller, unnamed cascades. With so many natural features, we would have to say that a trip to Dunn Falls is sure to leave a lasting impression on everyone. For this reason, this 2.0-mile trail makes a great introduction to the world of the outdoors for anyone not too familiar with what the region has to offer.

Discovering the remote lower Dunn Falls is as surprising as finding any waterfall in Maine. Before you reach the side trail to view Dunn Falls, only miniature horsetails and cascades will be spotted. How shocking and mind-boggling the nearly vertical 80-foot drop of lower Dunn Falls is to the virgin eye! With rock walls up to 100 feet in height on opposite sides of the falls, the area is outstandingly scenic. Take your camera for this waterfall.

After visiting the lower falls, you may feel that the trip could not get any better. Wrong! As if the lower falls are not visually appealing and mentally satisfying enough, more gems lie ahead on the trail. Just before the upper falls lie two lovely rocky-bottomed pools, each with small falls cascading into it. The first pool, about 80 feet in circumference, is surrounded by semicircular rock walls, with the waterfall flowing through a gap in the wall. The second pool has a similar structure and almost equal

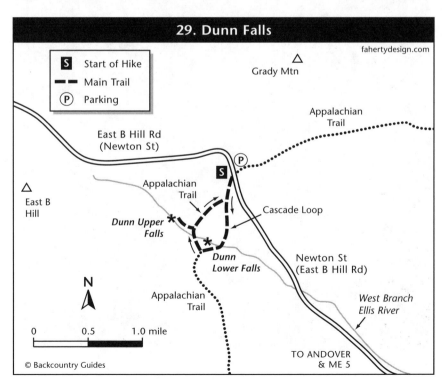

29. Dunn Falls

fahertydesign.com

S Start of Hike
▬ ▬ Main Trail
P Parking

Grady Mtn

Appalachian Trail

East B Hill Rd (Newton St)

P

S

East B Hill

Appalachian Trail

Dunn Upper Falls

Cascade Loop

Dunn Lower Falls

Newton St (East B Hill Rd)

West Branch Ellis River

N

Appalachian Trail

0   0.5   1.0 mile

© Backcountry Guides

TO ANDOVER & ME 5

Dunn Falls

dimensions, but behind the pool lies a 50-foot secret: the elusive upper falls. Although half-hidden by the forest, this fanning horsetail is beautiful and adds a perfect ending to the waterfalls on this trip.

TRAIL INFORMATION From the parking pull-offs, begin descending the Appalachian Trail, heading south toward a brook. Only a few feet from the road, the blue-blazed Cascade Trail will shoot left while the Appalachian Trail will continue straight. The Cascade Trail, which will lead you to lower Dunn Falls, eventually loops back to the Appalachian Trail, soon providing access to the upper falls. Follow the Cascade Trail as it ascends and descends several ridges before reaching a sign directing you to the base of the lower falls with an arrow at mile 0.7. Take a right onto this short, also blue-blazed, 0.2-mile path, which will guide you upstream to Dunn Falls.

After visiting the lower falls, double back to the junction with the aforementioned sign, and this time continue climbing along the Cascade Trail. After 0.2 mile take a right onto the white-blazed Appalachian Trail. Only 50 feet later, cross the West Branch of the Ellis River and take a left at a sign directing you toward the UPPER FALLS. Follow this yet-another-blue-blazed trail to the upper falls and you will see a few other treats along the way, including several pools with rocky beaches and smaller waterfalls. After about 0.1 mile, you will reach the first pool. Continue for 0.1 mile farther for the second pool. You have two options for viewing the upper falls from here: You can either walk along the rocky beach of the pool to spot the upper falls from a gap in the rock wall surrounding them, or continue climbing the trail to its termination at the base of upper Dunn Falls. After absorbing the moment at the upper falls, return and turn left onto the AT. Proceed along the AT north for about 0.7 mile to return to the road and parking area.

DIRECTIONS From the junction of ME 5 and ME 120 in the center of Andover, head west on Newton Street (identified on maps often as East B Hill Road). Follow Newton Street for 8.0 miles and park on either shoulder of the road after spotting a HIKER sign. The areas for parking are also used for the Appalachian Trail. *To get to Andover,* take ME 120 west from Rumford.

OTHER WATERFALLS NEARBY The Cataracts, Screw Auger Falls (Grafton), Step Falls, Ellis Falls, Swift River Falls.

30

EARLEY LANDING FALLS

Willimantic, Piscataquis County

Type: Cascades

Height: 6-foot total drop

Trail Length: Roadside

Water Source: Big Wilson Stream

Altitude Gain/Loss: None

Difficulty: Easy

Hiking Time: Not applicable

DeLorme Map: Page 31, A-5

Rating: ★★★

DESCRIPTION Earley Landing Falls is one of two small waterfalls on Big Wilson Stream classified as a "scenic waterfall" in *DeLorme's Maine Atlas and Gazetteer*. Normally such a diminutive waterfall would be ignored, written off as looking just like a thousand other waterfalls. However, you should add this waterfall to your itinerary for several reasons.

First, the access is quite easy. It is only a few feet off ME 150, minutes

Earley Landing Falls

away from Tobey Falls. Second, the entire picture that is painted at Earley Landing Falls is splendid. From the bridge viewpoint, you get a setting sure to please any artist—a nicely landscaped country house, a patch of hemlock woods, a wide, pretty river, and a segmented set of cascades. The falls are more than 200 feet from the bridge, so bring a telephoto zoom lens for your camera if you have one.

TRAIL INFORMATION The area around the falls is private property, meaning that the only view is from the bridge on Greenpoint Road. Although this may seem like a disappointment, the bridge still affords quite an attractive vista.

DIRECTIONS From the junction of ME 16, ME 6, ME 15, ME 23, and ME 150 in Guilford, take ME 150 north for 12.8 miles. Turn left onto Greenpoint Road, a dirt road that becomes private beginning at the bridge. There is parking 100 feet down Greenpoint Road on your right, and a larger parking area about 150 feet farther up ME 150 on your left. *To get to Guilford,* take ME 150 north from Skowhegan.

OTHER WATERFALLS NEARBY Tobey Falls.

31

ELLIS FALLS
Andover, Oxford County

Type: Horsetails
Height: 22-foot total drop
Trail Length: Roadside
Water Source: Ellis Meadow Brook
Altitude Gain/Loss: None

Difficulty: Easy
Hiking Time: Not applicable
DeLorme Map: Page 18, D-4
Rating: ★★★

DESCRIPTION Minutes away from the spectacular falls of Grafton Notch State Park, and the cataracts off East B Hill Road, Ellis Falls can be either the appetizer or the dessert for your waterfall day trip. Its location, just over 2 miles east of Andover, is likely to be central to the other natural attractions found in your plans for the day.

At the top of the falls is a 5-foot-tall, 5-foot-wide block falling into an oblong-shaped pool. From here the falls horsetail and cascade the ad-

Ellis Falls

ditional 17 feet into a dark tea-colored pool below. The river, which was very flat both up and downstream, surprised us with a drop of this magnitude.

Not nearly as scenic as nearby Dunn Falls, and certainly not world class in beauty like nearby Angel Falls, Ellis Falls is outclassed by the local competition. Waterfall enthusiasts, however, should not shun Ellis Falls for its more impressive neighbors. This waterfall is in a covert location—only noticed if you have specific directions *and* you are looking for it. The parking area is a simple pull-off—the type every road has a dozen of. For this reason, we suggest checking out the falls.

TRAIL INFORMATION The falls are visible from the parking pull-off but difficult to see from the road. To get close to them, you can either walk right up to the ledge overlooking the falls or follow a short path that swings around to the bottom.

DIRECTIONS From the junction of ME 5 and ME 120 in the center of Andover, take ME 120 east for 2.5 miles to a small pull-off on the right side of the road. *To get to Andover,* take ME 120 west from Rumford.

OTHER WATERFALLS NEARBY The Cataracts, Dunn Falls, Swift River Falls.

32

THE FALLS

Sandy Bay, Somerset County

Type: Horsetails

Height: 45-foot total drop

Trail Length: Roadside

Water Source: Sandy Stream

Altitude Gain/Loss: None

Difficulty: Easy

Hiking Time: Not applicable

DeLorme Map: Page 39, A-4

Rating: ★★½

DESCRIPTION If you are traveling in the area of north Jackman, make a quick pit stop at The Falls Rest Area, a small pull-off just off US 201. A fine road stop for a picnic or a break before crossing the Canadian border, the rest area is complete with rest rooms, picnic tables, and a series of drops of Sandy Stream known simply as The Falls.

The Falls is far from spectacular or unique, but it makes up for this with extremely easy road access and a rather original wildflower-lined rest area. To avoid the crowds at this waterfall, visit the other nearby falls, Heald Stream Falls. This waterfall is located in logging territory, accessed by a dirt road only 0.5 mile farther up US 201.

TRAIL INFORMATION Proceed to the north end of the parking lot, where a great view of the falls unfolds. Obvious paths will quickly drop you to the brook below, but unfortunately there really is not much reward in this—no pools for swimming, limited exploring, and the views are not any better. It is better to appreciate the falls while having lunch at one of the picnic tables at the rest area.

DIRECTIONS From the junction of US 201, ME 6, and ME 15 in Jackman, take the combined US 201 north/ME 6 west. After 8.9 miles, pull into The Falls Rest Area on your right. The rest area is located 0.3 mile north of the SANDY BAY TOWN LINE sign. *To get to Jackman,* take US 201 north from Skowhegan.

OTHER WATERFALLS NEARBY Heald Stream Falls, Moxie Falls.

33

FALLS AT FRENCHMEN'S HOLE

Riley Township, Oxford County

Type: Plunge

Height: 10 feet

Trail Length: Less than 0.1 mile

Water Source: Tributary of Sunday River

Altitude Gain/Loss: −20 feet

Difficulty: Easy side of moderate

Hiking Time: Not applicable

DeLorme Map: Page 18, E-1

Rating: ★★★★

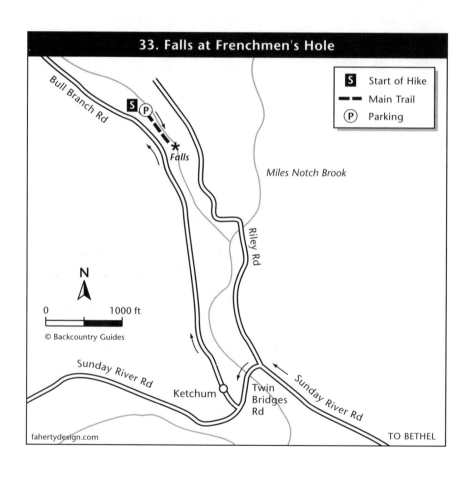

33. Falls at Frenchmen's Hole

S Start of Hike

▬ ▬ Main Trail

Ⓟ Parking

Bull Branch Rd

Falls

Miles Notch Brook

Riley Rd

N

0   1000 ft

© Backcountry Guides

Sunday River Rd

Ketchum

Twin Bridges Rd

Sunday River Rd

TO BETHEL

fahertydesign.com

Falls at Frenchmen's Hole

DESCRIPTION Tucked a few miles beyond the Sunday River Ski Resort access road, the location of the Falls at Frenchmen's Hole has remained a town secret for many generations. The majority of visitors are local residents and their guests; visitors from out of state are unlikely to know about this waterfall and swimming hole.

For months, we had heard rumors of this place. Fellow hikers on the trail told us about a marvelous swimming hole near the town of Bethel. Before long we pieced enough information together to begin looking. It took a few hours of poking around, but eventually we managed to find this special, out-of-the-way waterfall.

Immediately we understood how such a place could remain such a well-guarded secret. The swimming pool created inside a giant pothole below the 10-foot-tall plunge is very deep and inviting for swimmers. Some portions of the pool are too deep to determine the actual depth, but it would not be a surprise if certain sections are often jumped into from the surrounding riverbanks.

TRAIL INFORMATION The main falls and swimming hole can be found by walking 100 feet back up the dirt road and scrambling down one of many paths to the river, where the falls and pool will become obvious. There are also some less-crowded smaller falls and shallower pools lying above the popular spot.

DIRECTIONS From the junction of ME 5, ME 26, and US 2 in Bethel, take the combined ME 5 north/ME 26 north/US 2 east toward the Sunday River Ski Resort and the town of Newry. After 2.7 miles, take a left onto Sunday River Road. Travel on Sunday River Road for 2.1 miles and you will approach a fork in the road. Veer right and continue another 1.0 mile to another fork. Fork right again, and travel an additional 4.3 miles along Sunday River Road. Take a left onto a dirt road that immediately travels over two old bridges. Just after the bridges, take a right and follow this new dirt road for 0.6 mile; the large parking pulloffs will be on your right.

OTHER WATERFALLS NEARBY Step Falls, Screw Auger Falls (Grafton), Snow Falls, Kezar Falls.

34

〰️

GULF HAGAS
Bowdoin College Grant East, Piscataquis County

Type: Plunges, horsetails, and cascades

Height: Varies (see notes)

Trail Length: 8.6-mile loop

Water Source: West Branch Pleasant River and Gulf Hagas Brook

Altitude Gain/Loss: Up 700 feet, down 700 feet

Difficulty: Moderate side of difficult

Hiking Time: 6–8 hours

DeLorme Map: Page 42, D-1

Rating: ★★★★★

DESCRIPTION (HIGHLY RECOMMENDED) In just under 9 miles of hiking a visitor to Gulf Hagas can explore and take pleasure in dozens of natural features, including four officially named waterfalls, plenty of unnamed cascades, tempting swimming pools, a gorge often referred to as the Grand Canyon of Maine, and two scenic rivers—Gulf Hagas Brook and the West Branch of the Pleasant River. Managed through the cooperative efforts of the National Park Service, the Maine Appalachian Trail Club, and KI Jo-Mary, Inc., Gulf Hagas offers an easy-to-follow trail system that allows hours of day-trip enjoyment.

With so many natural features (and so many chances for both exploration and swimming), it is no surprise that the waterfalls of Gulf Hagas rank among the most popular in the state. Luckily for you, the majority of the waterfall crowds remain at Screw Auger Falls, never bothering to venture along the rim of the gorge to the falls that lie upstream. All waterfalls warrant the effort required, as each is beautiful and scenic in its own way.

Screw Auger Falls is our favorite on the hike. Here Gulf Hagas Brook drops 25 feet in a punchbowl formation into a deep, dark pool encircled by a bowl-shaped rock wall. The pool, unfortunately very small in relation to other swimming holes in Maine, still manages to be quite refreshing for a couple of visitors. When visiting the falls, you should be aware that other, unnamed waterfalls lie above and below Screw Auger Falls. These have swimming pools of their own and are recommended in their own right.

Three more waterfalls are accessed by continuing past Screw Auger Falls

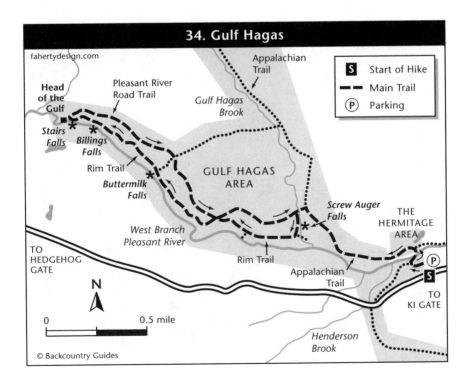

along the rim of the gorge. The first, about 2.8 miles from the parking trailhead, is Buttermilk Falls, a 10-foot horsetail with a portion of its water absconding away down a perpendicular slide to the right of the main route of the water. There is a large pool here, often swum in by several people on any given summer day, but the water has a slightly foamy appearance, forcing us to rate the pool as only somewhat attractive.

Beyond Buttermilk Falls lies Billings Falls, a 15-foot plunge with unobstructed views of the canyon and Stairs Falls, an extensive system of little stairs cascading over jagged steps. Just 4 feet in height, Stairs Falls is still quite interesting and only feet from the main trail.

The final stop of the trip is the Head of the Gulf. At 4.0 miles from the parking lot, the "Head" is a pleasant halfway rest stop. There are several cascades and small pools to admire before you set out on the return trip to the parking lot via the Pleasant River Road Trail.

TRAIL INFORMATION The Maine Appalachian Trail Club, in cooperation with KI Jo-Mary, Inc., publishes the "Gulf Hagas Area" map—one of the finest trail maps we have ever used. This map of the gulf, available at the visitors center on the access road, costs $1 and provides you detailed descriptions on the dozen or so features of Gulf Hagas. We highly

Screw Auger Falls (Bowdoin)

recommend it. If we were to describe the trail in detail, we would most likely confuse you, as other guidebook instructions have confused us. There are simply too many trail junctions and side paths to create an easy-to-follow trail guide.

Instead, here is a summary of the trail. Expect an 8.2- to 9.0-mile loop, depending on the number of side excursions you chosse to take off the main trail. While we have rated the trail moderately difficult, it is very difficult during the wet months of spring, when footing is extremely muddy and crossing the West Branch of the Pleasant River is impossible. The entire trail is rocky and never runs short of attractions. This is a great introductory day hike, but at the same time a moderately challenging venture for any hiker.

DIRECTIONS Take ME 11 south from the center of Millinocket. Take a right onto the KI Road, the dirt road leading to the KATAHDIN IRON WORKS and the KI Jo-Mary Multiple Use Forest. Follow the KI Road for 6.4 miles and you will reach the visitors center, where you must register and pay the day-use fee ($8 per person for out-of-state residents when we visited; cheaper for Maine residents). After registering, continue driving down the dirt road for 0.1 mile and you will reach a fork. Take a right and begin following signs for GULF HAGAS. Continue for 2.2 miles from the first fork and you will reach another. Fork left this time and continue 1.2 miles to yet another fork. Take the left prong for the second time and continue for a final 3.0 miles farther; the large parking area will be on your right. *To get to Millinocket,* take exit 56 off I-95 and take ME 157 east to ME 11 south.

OTHER WATERFALLS NEARBY Hay Brook Falls.

35

HAY BROOK FALLS

Bowdoin College Grant East, Piscataquis County

Type: Horsetails
Height: 28-foot total drop
Trail Length: 0.2 mile
Water Source: Hay Brook
Altitude Gain/Loss: None

Difficulty: Easy (See notes)
Hiking Time: Not applicable
DeLorme Map: Page 42, D-1
Rating: ★★★★½

Hay Brook Falls

DESCRIPTION (HIGHLY RECOMMENDED) Seldom is a natural feature found in New England that is truly still "off the beaten path." Sources have claimed that some of the waterfalls we visited were hidden gems, tucked away from the average traveler and sightseer. In reality, however, there were always at least a few people or traces of recent visitors at these waterfalls. Hay Brook Falls, buried deep in the KI Jo-Mary Multiple Use Forest, is one waterfall exception, remaining as nearly untouched and unspoiled as ever.

Equally magnificent and scenic in low or high water, the falls drop a total of 28 feet in three distinguishable steps. The top drop is of particular interest; the waters of Hay Brook travel down a chute, hit an upward-sloping slide, change direction by 90 degrees, and crash into a small pool. All drops are surrounded by varying species of moss—the colors of yellow, beige, and green are represented—creating a colorful opportunity for photographs.

A friend who joined us on the trip summed up Hay Brook Falls in a simple sentence: "This is definitely one of my favorite waterfalls." We certainly agree, and we believe you will enjoy this remote waterfall as much as we have.

TRAIL INFORMATION The difficulty in reaching Hay Brook Falls lies in the drive to the trailhead. From the trailhead, however, reaching the falls is pleasantly easy. Simply cross the dirt road, pass by the three primitive campsites at Hay Brook, and walk parallel upstream 0.1 mile to the falls.

DIRECTIONS Take ME 11 south from the center of Millinocket. Take a right onto the KI Road, the dirt road leading to the KATAHDIN IRON WORKS and the KI Jo-Mary Multiple Use Forest. Follow the KI Road for 6.4 miles to the visitors center, where you must register and pay the day-use fee ($8 per person for out-of-state residents when we visited). After registering, continue down the dirt road for 0.1 mile and you will reach a fork. Take a right and begin following signs for GULF HAGAS. Continue for 2.2 miles from the first fork and you will reach another. Fork left this time, and continue 1.2 miles to yet another fork. Take the right prong and head toward HAY BROOK. Follow this new dirt road for 2.2 miles to another fork. Fork left, continue 0.2 mile, and take a left at another sign for HAY BROOK. Follow this road for 0.5 mile and take another left. Follow this road for 1.5 miles to the gravel parking area on your left. The parking area is just across the street from the campsites at Hay Brook. *To get to Millinocket,* take exit 56 off I-95 and take ME 157 east to ME 11 south.

SPECIAL NOTE We recommend this waterfall if you have a sport-utility vehicle, truck, or car with high clearance. Low-clearance vehicles may not be able to travel safely on the dirt roads leading to the trailhead of Hay Brook Falls.

OTHER WATERFALLS NEARBY Gulf Hagas.

36

HEALD STREAM FALLS

Bald Mountain Township, Somerset County

Type: Horsetails and cascades	**Difficulty:** Easy
Height: 18-foot total drop	**Hiking Time:** Not applicable
Trail Length: Roadside	**DeLorme Map:** Page 39, A-4
Water Source: Heald Stream	**Rating:** ★★
Altitude Gain/Loss: None	

DESCRIPTION Situated a few miles from the Canadian border, Heald Stream Falls receives only a handful of visitors a month. The falls are not exactly world class in any fashion; most day-trippers are either reluctant to go to this waterfall or simply do not know of its existence. We are including Heald Stream Falls because most waterfalls in this guide are much more popular, and we felt that more remote falls should be included as well.

There are several steps created by the ledges at the waterfall, each visible from the bridge overlooking the waterfall or from its base. The total drop is small, at only 18 feet. There are several dark, private pools for wading or swimming. It should be noted that your odds of encountering an animal are greatly increased at these falls; you are, after all, in moose territory.

TRAIL INFORMATION The falls begin their descent beneath the bridge you just crossed. You have two options. You can either conclude your visit from the bridge or travel down several barely-used paths on either side of the brook to explore the entire area. Expect privacy at this waterfall, especially if you bushwhack to its base.

DIRECTIONS From the junction of US 201, ME 6, and ME 15 in Jackman, take the combined US 201 north/ME 6 west. Travel on this highway for 9.4 miles and take a right onto Bald Mountain Road, a level dirt road marked with a sign for the BALD MTN TRAIL. This road is 0.5 mile north of The Falls Rest Area. Travel on Bald Mountain Road for 2.3 miles, crossing the small bridge over Heald Stream. Parking is just after crossing the bridge on your right. *To get to Jackman,* take US 201 north from Skowhegan.

OTHER WATERFALLS NEARBY The Falls, Moxie Falls.

37

HOUSTON BROOK FALLS
Pleasant Ridge, Somerset County

Type: Horsetails and plunges

Height: 32-foot total drop

Trail Length: 0.25 mile

Water Source: Houston Brook

Altitude Gain/Loss: –75 feet

Difficulty: Easy

Hiking Time: 10 minutes

DeLorme Map: Page 30, D-3

Rating: ★★★★½

DESCRIPTION (HIGHLY RECOMMENDED) Houston Brook Falls is another scenic splendor located minutes off ME 201, allowing for convenient and simple access. An easy, 10-minute walk through woods leads to the star of the show, a 30-foot nearly vertical drop of Houston Brook.

The falls are wild and rugged, with every outcrop of folded rock having a jagged appearance. There are a few notable swimming spots, the best being the shallow rectangular channel just below the falls. During low water, it is a simple task to enter this pool, but in high water the difficulty multiplies. The mist of the falls often makes the surrounding rocks too dangerous to scramble across.

Just downstream, the brook terminates at Wyman Lake, which is visible from the waterfall. The entire area is scenic, with nothing blocking your views. The best time to visit these falls appears to be in the morning, as they have eastern exposure and are lit up by the sun in the early hours of the day.

TRAIL INFORMATION First, approach the roadside sign for the falls. Then be sure to read the sign below outlining two other waterfalls in the area, Mill Brook Falls and Carrying Stream Falls, both accessed by two different short walks off Carry Pond Road. From here, head north as the

Houston Brook Falls

trail descends at a modest rate to the brook. Expect some muddy areas along the trail in springtime, and a few steps up and down near the brook to reach the falls.

DIRECTIONS From the southern junction of ME 16 and US 201 in Bingham, take ME 16 south. Follow ME 16 south for only a few hundred yards as it crosses a bridge over the Kennebec River. Just over the river, only 0.2 mile from US 201, take a right onto Ridge Road. Follow Ridge Road for 3.3 miles and pull into the parking lot on the right at a sign for HOUSTON BROOK FALLS. *To get to Bingham,* take US 201 north from Skowhegan.

OTHER WATERFALLS NEARBY Moxie Falls, Poplar Stream Falls, Tobey Falls, Earley Landing Falls.

38

KEZAR FALLS
Lovell, Oxford County

Type: Cascades

Height: 20-foot total drop

Trail Length: Less than 0.1 mile

Water Source: Kezar River

Altitude Gain/Loss: −25 feet

Difficulty: Easy

Hiking Time: Not applicable

DeLorme Map: Page 10, D-3

Rating: ★★½

DESCRIPTION Lying a few miles southeast of the White Mountain National Forest border, Kezar Falls is an unmarked local picnic spot with a modest-sized gorge and a few small waterfalls. The site used to be a swimming hole, but many fallen trees have long since made jumping off the gorge walls a dangerous activity. Kezar Falls is not really anything out of the ordinary, but it makes a fine place to read, picnic, or simply relax. Locals told us that this is a favorite party spot for young adults during the late hours of the day.

TRAIL INFORMATION The crashing waters of the gorge can be heard from the parking lot. Follow the sound a few feet down to the fence that runs along the rim of the gorge.

DIRECTIONS From Bethel, take ME 35 south; this road will soon join with, and later split from, ME 5. Continue on ME 35 south for 1.2 miles past the spot where ME 5 breaks off. Take a right onto Lovell Road, which is 0.2 mile past the ME 118 and ME 35 junction. Follow Lovell Road for 3.1 miles and you will come to a fork. Head left and travel 0.2 mile farther; the short road to the parking area will be on your right. Take note that the parking area is difficult to spot.

OTHER WATERFALLS NEARBY Snow Falls, Falls at Frenchmen's Hole.

39

MAD RIVER FALLS

Batchelders Grant, White Mountain National Forest, Oxford County

Type: Horsetails

Height: 100-foot total drop

Trail Length: 1.6 miles

Water Source: Mad River

Altitude Gain/Loss: +300 feet

Difficulty: Moderate

Hiking Time: 45 minutes

DeLorme Map: Page 10, C-1

Rating: ★★½

DESCRIPTION From the overlook opposite the falls, you notice that Mad River Falls consists of several horsetails falling into a yellow-tinted pool. Aside from admiring the 100-foot total drop of the falls, there is not much to do here. Exploring is extremely limited, as it would be dangerous to get closer to the falls, and photography is not an option because the falls lie under a heavy tree cover.

To justify a trip to Mad River Falls, add Bickford Slides, another waterfall accessed via a trail from Brickett Place, and Rattlesnake Flume and Pool, a waterfall and swimming hole off the Stone House Trail.

TRAIL INFORMATION (See map on page 41.) The actual trailhead for this waterfall is located not behind Brickett Place but directly across the street. To reach the falls, you are going to follow the yellow-blazed Royce Trail for a total of 1.6 miles. After 0.2 mile you will reach a field clearing, and the trail will suddenly fork right. The trail markers are difficult to spot here, so be on the lookout. After you regain a notion of the trail's direction, the rest of the 1.4-mile walk is fast and simple. Several times, however, you are required to cross the Mad River, which is usually far from *mad* in terms of rushing water. Unless you are hiking in early spring, crossing is easy and straightforward. During really high water the river may be knee-deep or so. There's nothing too difficult, but the crossing is nonetheless certainly worth your attention if you are contemplating this hike. About 1.6 miles from the trailhead, take a left onto a 50-foot-long spur trail to reach the falls. This left is marked by a sign and an arrow for MAD RIVER FALLS.

DIRECTIONS From the junction of ME 113 and US 302 in Fryeburg, take ME 113 north past Chatham and 0.5 mile beyond the posted WHITE MOUNTAIN NATIONAL FOREST BOUNDARY sign. Take a right into the Brickett Place, where the parking lot can be found. *To get to Fryeburg,* take US 302 east from Conway.

OTHER WATERFALLS NEARBY Bickford Slides, Rattlesnake Flume and Pool, Hermit Falls (New Hampshire).

40

MOXIE FALLS

Moxie Gore, Somerset County

Type: Plunge and cascades	**Difficulty:** Easy to first viewpoints; difficult to base of falls
Height: Tallest plunge is 90 feet	
Trail Length: 0.7 mile	**Hiking Time:** 20 minutes
Water Source: Moxie Stream	**DeLorme Map:** Page 40, E-3
Altitude Gain/Loss: −100 feet	**Rating:** ★★★★

DESCRIPTION (HIGHLY RECOMMENDED) Tied for the title of the largest single drop in the state of Maine, Moxie Falls is a scenic waterfall a few miles southeast of the famous whitewater-rafting river, the Kennebec. An equal mix of beauty and grandeur, Moxie Falls is a 30-yard drop of Moxie Stream. Above and below it are several unnamed large, wide cascades with some pools.

The best swimming holes here are 100 feet downstream from the main plunge, while another is just above the main plunge, below a large set of cascades. Both pools require a moderately difficult level of scrambling. Although scrambling down the walls is a tiresome activity, the attempt is easily justified by the rugged, highly scenic gorge and the completely new

Moxie Falls

perspective of the falls from below.

Despite its remote location in midwestern Maine, Moxie Falls is heavily visited, mainly by tourists staying with the nearby whitewater-rafting outfitters. We have visited on multiple occasions during less-than-ideal weather conditions, and there have always been at least a few people either along the trail, swimming in the pools, or resting at one of the many boardwalk vantage points.

TRAIL INFORMATION The trail begins at the center of the parking lot and follows a well-worn path. About halfway to the falls you will approach a sign for the falls and notice the suddenly changing, potentially dangerous currents of the dam-controlled rivers in the area.

The first views of the main plunge are head-on from the top of the gorge on a boardwalk trail. If you are confident in your ability to scramble down the side of a 100-foot gorge, you can reach the base of the falls and a pool suitable for swimming. There are multiple ways to complete such a task, and all of the safest paths lie beyond the head-on boardwalk viewpoints.

DIRECTIONS From Bingham, take US 201 north into the town of The Forks. Once you are in The Forks, take a right onto Old Canada Road just before crossing the Kennebec River Bridge. Follow Old Canada Road for 2.0 miles, and a large sign for MOXIE FALLS will mark the parking area on your left. *To get to Bingham,* take US 201 north from Skowhegan.

OTHER WATERFALLS NEARBY The Falls, Heald Stream Falls, Houston Brook Falls.

41

NESOWADNEHUNK FALLS

Township 2, Range 10, Piscataquis County

Type: Block

Height: 7 feet

Trail Length: Less than 0.1 mile

Water Source: West Branch Penobscot River

Altitude Gain/Loss: –25 feet

Difficulty: Easy

Hiking Time: Not applicable

DeLorme Map: Page 50, D-4

Rating: ★★★½

Nesowadnehunk Falls

DESCRIPTION A classic block-style waterfall (also known as a "horse-shoe" falls), Nesowadnehunk Falls is a 7-foot drop of the West Branch of the Penobscot River. The falls are a well-known portage spot, too steep for canoes, kayaks, and whitewater rafts traveling down the river from the drop-in spot at Ripogenus Gorge.

The powerful 100-foot-wide cascade drowns out the otherwise noisy, Golden Road, which is only yards away. Fly-fishing is also common below the falls, and a decent view of Mount Katahdin can be seen looking downstream. Also, since the falls are controlled by Ripogenus Dam upstream, expect to see a powerful waterfall at any time of year.

TRAIL INFORMATION The trail starts on the opposite side of the road from the parking lot and leads a short distance to the river, where the falls become blatantly obvious. There are limited scrambling opportunities around the falls.

DIRECTIONS From Bangor, take I-95 north to exit 56. Turn left onto ME 157, traveling west toward Millinocket. Just past ME 157's end in the town of Millinocket, take a right onto Katahdin Avenue. Follow signs toward Baxter State Park. As you approach Millinocket Lake on your right, you will need to switch over to the road running parallel to and left of the road you are traveling on. There are several paved lanes to do this, so be on the lookout when you approach Millinocket Lake and Spencer Cove. The road you switched to is called the Golden Road. Travel north on the Golden Road as it eventually crosses the West Branch of the Penobscot River over Abol Bridge. Continue on the Golden Road for 3.1 miles past the bridge and park at the large pull-off on your left.

OTHER WATERFALLS NEARBY Abol Falls, Gulf Hagas, Hay Brook Falls.

42

POPLAR STREAM FALLS
Carrabassett Valley, Franklin County

Type: Horsetails

Height: Upper falls is 24 feet; lower falls is 51 feet

Trail Length: 2.0 miles (see notes)

Water Source: Poplar Stream and South Brook

Altitude Gain/Loss: +250 feet

Difficulty: To upper falls, easy side of moderate; to lower falls, moderate side of difficult

Hiking Time: 60 minutes

DeLorme Map: Page 29, C-5

Rating: ★★½

DESCRIPTION Poplar Stream Falls is located in Carrabassett Valley, a town famous for its ski resort, Sugarloaf USA. The falls lie a few miles east of the resort, accessible by a rough dirt road and a hike through a logging area. They can be accessed by high-clearance vehicles, mountain bicycles, cross-country skis, or hiking.

So remote that nearby residents may not be aware of its existence, Poplar Stream Falls consists of two drops, on two different streams, that are combined under one name. The upper formation, a 24-foot horsetail with a swimming pool below, is on Poplar Stream and just off the trail. The lower drop, a 51-foot horsetail on South Brook, is accessible only by a fairly strenuous amount of bushwhacking.

The swimming hole below the falls lacks the attractiveness of other swimming holes nearby. Although you are likely to enjoy the chilly mountain waters privately, two other swimming holes offer warmer water, more sun exposure, and a general better experience. One is nearby Smalls Falls, which is described elsewhere in this guide, and another hole is located just below the bridge over the Carrabassett River on Carriage Road—the road that you traveled on to reach the falls.

TRAIL INFORMATION After you travel on the dirt road for 1.7 miles, another dirt road will head right (east). You must continue down this new road for 0.2 mile, reaching the end of a logging area. The trail continues to the left down a narrow old road. A few hundred feet farther, you reach a shaky bridge over the stream. The upper falls are just downstream, clearly visible from the bridge. Another, larger set of falls lies downstream. There are no trails, or even old bushwhacking paths, guiding you to the falls. For this reason, only confident explorers should attempt to find the 51-foot lower falls of South Brook.

If you drive the entire 2.0 miles on the carriage road, there is no altitude gain or loss along the trail to the falls. Your hiking time will also be about five minutes.

DIRECTIONS From the junction of ME 142, ME 16, and ME 27 in the center of Kingfield, take the combined ME 27 north/ME 16 west. Travel on this highway for 9.2 miles and take a right onto Carriage Road. After 0.3 mile on Carriage Road, the pavement ends. However you decide to continue traveling up Carriage Road—be it hiking, mountain biking, or driving—the real trailhead to the falls is still 1.7 miles farther along. If you opt to continue driving, there are decent pull-offs beginning 0.8 mile beyond where the road turned to dirt. About 2.0 miles from ME 27/ME 16, a spur road will head right off Carriage Road. The falls are accessible down this road. See "Trail Information" for additional instructions. *To get to Kingfield,* take ME 27 north from Farmington.

OTHER WATERFALLS NEARBY The Falls, Moxie Falls.

43

RATTLESNAKE FLUME AND POOL

Stoneham, Oxford County

Type: Plunge, slides, and a pool
Height: 10-foot plunge
Trail Length: To Rattlesnake Flume, 0.7 mile; to Rattlesnake Pool, 1.1 miles
Water Source: Rattlesnake Brook
Altitude Gain/Loss: +150 feet to pool

Difficulty: Easy side of moderate
Hiking Time: 30 minutes
DeLorme Map: Page 10, C-1
Rating: ★★★½

DESCRIPTION We have a confession to make: The high rating we gave this waterfall is not solely attributable to the cascading waters of Rattlesnake Brook, but rather skewed by the dazzlingly attractive swimming hole created inside a giant pothole commonly known as Rattlesnake Pool.

This pool attracts visitors from all over, not just locals. This is surprising, because the pool is quite small, barely large enough for one family of swimmers. It also offers frigid waters year-round, due to the overhanging hemlock trees above it and the already chilly mountain water. The drawing features are the exceptionally clean, teal-green water and the moss-surrounded slide that feeds the pool. Visualize a lagoonlike pool with a romantic spirit: That's Rattlesnake Pool.

For waterfalls, Rattlesnake Brook offers two small attractions. The first is Rattlesnake Flume, a 10-foot plunge dumping down into narrow gorge walls. The second is a tiny slide that dumps into Rattlesnake Pool. Please take note that the property is private. Do not abuse the private trail system: Stay on the CTA trails and remain at either the flume or the pool. The owners have allowed Rattlesnake Flume and Pool to remain available to the public, and we hope it will always remain that way. Please be respectful of any trails marked NO TRESPASSING.

TRAIL INFORMATION (See map on page 41.) Continue up the dirt road beyond the gate for 0.5 mile and enter the woods on your left at a sign for the STONE HOUSE TRAIL. Follow the Stone House Trail as it slowly gains in elevation for 0.2 mile and you will reach a fork. Veer right; the flume is a few feet down the trail, visible from a wooden bridge and by looking upstream. After the flume, double back to the trail junction and fork left this time if you wish to reach a stunning pool of Rattlesnake Brook. Continue for 0.2 mile past the junction and you will reach a lonely arrow and sign for the STONE HOUSE TRAIL just beyond a small bridge. Take a right here to follow the trail for a final 0.1 mile to the pool. To swim, you must scramble down a moderately steep, although short, embankment.

DIRECTIONS From the junction of ME 113 and US 302 in Fryeburg, Maine, take ME 113 north and continue 6.9 miles past its junction with ME 113B. Take a right onto Stone House Road and follow this to its end, where you will reach a gate. Parking is limited to the right shoulder just before the gate. *To get to Fryeburg,* take US 302 east from Conway.

OTHER WATERFALLS NEARBY Bickford Slides, Mad River Falls, Hermit Falls (New Hampshire).

44

RUMFORD FALLS

Rumford, Oxford County

Type: Cascades	**Difficulty:** Easy
Height: 176-foot total drop	**Hiking Time:** Not applicable
Trail Length: Roadside	**DeLorme Map:** Page 19, E-1
Water Source: Androscoggin River	**Rating:** ★★½
Altitude Gain/Loss: None	

DESCRIPTION Originally referred to as Pennacook Falls or New Pennacook Falls, Rumford Falls is a chain of massive drops of the Androscoggin River. Although the waterfall drops a total of 176 feet, dams have split the once continuously cascading waters into several distinct sections. Noting this, we questioned whether or not to include this waterfall.

The beauty of the scenic upper waterfall ensured it a spot in this guide. Worthy of drawing the attention of any form of artist, Rumford Falls is quite spectacular in strength and setting. The adjacent dam is slowly being concealed by the continuous growth of the trees in front of the structure.

The artificial lake below offers popular fishing for three species of trout and landlocked salmon. The best view of this area is after snowmelt, because the water flow often slowly reduces during the summer months.

TRAIL INFORMATION There is a clear view of the waterfall from the main parking lot. The total drop may be 176 feet, but this is split up among several segments, most of which are inaccessible to the sightseer.

DIRECTIONS Rumford Falls is located 20 feet south of the US 2 and ME 108 junction in Rumford. Pull into the parking lot marked with a sign for SCENIC FALLS VIEWING AND TOURIST INFORMATION. The parking lot is just before the ME 108 bridge over the Androscoggin River.

OTHER WATERFALLS NEARBY Swift River Falls, Ellis Falls.

45

SCREW AUGER FALLS

Grafton Township, Grafton Notch State Park, Oxford County

Type: Plunge and cascades
Height: Plunge is 20 feet
Trail Length: Less than 0.1 mile
Water Source: Bear River
Altitude Gain/Loss: None

Difficulty: Easy
Hiking Time: Not applicable
DeLorme Map: Page 18, E-2
Rating: ★★★★½

DESCRIPTION (HIGHLY RECOMMENDED) One of two Grafton Notch waterfalls described in this guide, Screw Auger Falls—not to be confused with the Screw Auger Falls of Gulf Hagas Brook, also located in Maine—is a 20-foot plunge over the lip of a broad granite ledge into a gorge. Created by the plunge is a transparent curtain of whitewater. Below the main plunge, the Bear River travels through a curvaceous gorge, dropping an additional 30 feet in a series of cascades past giant potholes, shallow pools, and grottoes.

This waterfall is arguably Maine's most heavily visited. On a hot day in early July, we shared the falls and gorge with approximately 100 others. Although the waterfall is far from remote, the countless sunny ledges and sunbathing spots, together with the ability to explore above and below the gorge, will allow you to enjoy this site immensely.

Screw Auger Falls (Grafton)

There are several picnic tables, bathrooms, and a large parking area at the site that is known to fill up on hot sunny days in midsummer. As of 2002 the area is open daily 9 AM–sunset, allowing plenty of time to visit.

TRAIL INFORMATION Begin your walk to the falls by paying the $1.50 honor-system fee per person at the center of the parking lot. The trail first passes a 5-foot-tall cascade and then heads left to the larger drop, several other cascades, and the gorge. It is dangerous, but possible, to scramble into the gorge during periods of low water. We watched as several people waded in the pools inside the gorge on our visit.

DIRECTIONS From the junction of US 2, ME 5, and ME 26 in Newry, take ME 26 north. Continue along ME 26 north for 9.5 miles; the parking area will be on your left shortly after you cross into Grafton Notch State Park. *To get to Newry,* take the combined highway ME 5 north/ME 26 north/US 2 east from Bethel.

OTHER WATERFALLS NEARBY Step Falls, Dunn Falls, The Cataracts, Falls at Frenchmen's Hole.

46

SMALLS FALLS
Township E, Franklin County

Type: Horsetails and cascades
Height: 54-foot total drop
Trail Length: 0.1 mile to top of falls
Water Source: Sandy River
Altitude Gain/Loss: +50 feet

Difficulty: Easy
Hiking Time: 5 minutes
DeLorme Map: Page 19, A-1
Rating: ★★★★★

DESCRIPTION (HIGHLY RECOMMENDED) Just south of the town of Rangeley, the Smalls Falls Rest Area attracts more than just travelers looking for a driving break. Smalls Falls, with its scenic waterfall, colorful gorge, and fine swimming holes, accommodates all, often including visitors from all over New England.

It does not take much water flow to make this waterfall impressive enough to please. Just a tiny stream can create a false sense of white-

Smalls Falls

water power. This is attributable to the fact that the river upstream is considerably wider than the width of water that flows over the four sets of falls at Smalls Falls.

The bottom of Small Falls consists of a 3-foot cascade falling into a 20-foot-wide circular pool. The next waterfall up is a 14-foot fanning horsetail with a deep oblong-shaped pool that people tend to jump into from above—a stunt that is highly dangerous. Even farther up the trail you will find a 25-foot segmented waterfall with a plunge on the left and segmented horsetail on the right. The top waterfall is a 12-foot horsetail and slide. Beyond the final falls of Small Falls lie tiny plunges and cascades with equally clear and beautiful water.

All four sets of falls are found within one of most colorful and beautiful gorges in the region. Its colors consist of beiges, oranges, greens, blacks, browns, gold, and ivory. There are plenty of places to sit along the gorge walls and bask in the beauty of the wide-open area.

Other features that make this waterfall so popular are the pools to swim in and the numerous places to picnic. At the base of each plunge, cascade, and horsetail is a pool to either wade or swim in. Below the lowest fall is a rocky beach leading to the pool. There are also bathrooms, picnic tables, and fire pits—altogether as accommodating a picnic spot as you can find.

TRAIL INFORMATION A short boardwalk trail begins at the far end of the parking lot. After you descend a short set of stairs, the bottom pool and lower falls will come into view. Cross the bridge over the river and climb up the left side of the gorge along a metal fence if you wish to continue exploring upstream. Within 0.1 mile you will observe four distinct sets of falls, and eventually reach the top of the gorge and other popular swimming areas.

DIRECTIONS From the junction of ME 4 and ME 142 just west of the center of Phillips, take ME 4 north for 8.1 miles. Pull into the Small Falls Rest Area parking lot on your left. The rest area is 3.4 miles west of the MADRID TOWN LINE sign. *To get to Phillips,* take ME 4 north from Farmington.

OTHER WATERFALLS NEARBY Angel Falls, Swift River Falls, Rumford Falls.

47

SNOW FALLS
West Paris, Oxford County

Type: Small plunge and cascades
Height: 25-foot total drop
Trail Length: Roadside
Water Source: Little Androscoggin River
Altitude Gain/Loss: None

Difficulty: Easy
Hiking Time: Not applicable
DeLorme Map: Page 11, C-1
Rating: ★★★½

DESCRIPTION The Little Androscoggin River cuts its way through a narrow gorge at Snow Falls in West Paris. At this special rest stop, the state of Maine has constructed a fine picnic area complete with trails on both sides of the gorge, picnic tables, rest rooms, and plenty of parking.

There are four distinctive cascade sets at Snow Falls, with the last being our favorite. It is a thin plunge flowing into a dark pool just below the footbridge over the river. The gorge, with walls up to 30 feet in height, is surrounded by a fence, making this place family friendly and safe for the little ones. The water may be dark and slightly foamy, but the gorge is interesting, and the falls are right off the road, so include Snow Falls if you are close by.

TRAIL INFORMATION This waterfall is only a few feet from the road. There are plenty of log fences, providing many viewpoints of different angles of the gorge. Aside from the boardwalk, there are many picnic tables to sit on and admire the falls, as well as a water pump in case you get thirsty.

DIRECTIONS From the junction of ME 26, ME 117, and ME 119 in South Paris, take ME 26 north for 6.0 miles, heading toward West Paris. Take a left into the Snow Falls Rest Area. *To get to South Paris,* take ME 121 west to ME 26 north from Auburn.

OTHER WATERFALLS NEARBY Kezar Falls, Falls at Frenchmen's Hole.

48

STEEP FALLS

Limington & Baldwin, York County &
Cumberland County

Type: Block

Height: 6 feet

Trail Length: 0.2 mile

Water Source: Saco River

Altitude Gain/Loss: None

Difficulty: Easy

Hiking Time: 5 minutes

DeLorme Map: Page 4, D-5

Rating: ★★★★

DESCRIPTION Steep Falls answers an age-old question: Size really doesn't matter. Only 6 feet in total drop, this still manages to be one of the top-volume waterfalls in Maine. Water flow is strong year-round, powerful even after a two-month dry spell when we visited in the summer.

It may be a local party spot at night, but during the day it is a wide-open area to swim and sunbathe. Being at this waterfall makes you feel like you are at the ocean. There are white sandy beaches, and the sound of the crashing water can lull you to sleep. The water itself has small amounts of foam but is still clean enough to wade or take a dip. Please be careful of the currents if you choose to swim.

As for beauty, this waterfall packs a powerful punch. It is quite scenic and photogenic. Side rocks make nice scenery and frame the waterfall well. The full 75-foot width of this waterfall can only be seen by scrambling up these rocks for a closer look. The currents in the pool near the falls are dangerous, so even though it may look tempting, we ask that you swim downstream by the beaches. While several towns are nearby, this spot still provides the remote and rugged feeling of being encompassed by a waterfall.

TRAIL INFORMATION The quickest way to see the falls is by walking back onto the bridge over the Saco River. The falls can be easily seen upstream.

If you wish to get a more intimate look, head back to the parking area and walk west along a dirt road for 0.1 mile, and you will reach a mound of sand. The falls are less than 0.1 mile farther, reached by a trail that appears after you cross over the sand mound ahead of you. Several paths lead you along the sandy beaches of the riverbank toward the falls.

DIRECTIONS From the junction of ME 11 and ME 125 in the village of North Limington, take ME 11 north for 3.3 miles. Parking lots are on both sides of the road just after you cross the bridge over the Saco River. The parking lot is 0.4 mile south of the ME 11 and ME 113 junction in the village of Steep Falls. *To get to North Limington,* take ME 25 west from Portland.

OTHER WATERFALLS NEARBY None.

49

STEP FALLS
Newry, Oxford County

Type: Horsetails, cascades, and pools
Height: Approximately 250-foot total drop
Trail Length: 0.6 mile
Water Source: Wight Brook
Altitude Gain/Loss: +300 feet

Difficulty: Easy
Hiking Time: 20 minutes
DeLorme Map: Page 18, E-2
Rating: ★★★★½

DESCRIPTION (HIGHLY RECOMMENDED) Step Falls is a spectacular long chain of descending horsetails and cascades—one of the tallest waterfalls in Maine—that lies a few miles outside of the eastern border of Grafton Notch State Park. Situated on a 24-acre property managed by The Nature Conservancy, a million-member organization (2001) dedicated to preserving "the plants, animals and natural communities that represent the diversity of life on Earth by protecting the lands and waters they need to survive," Step Falls was acquired in 1962 and has been a popular attraction for waterfall fanatics and swimming-hole lovers for decades.

At Step Falls, Wight Brook, a wide mountain stream, meanders its way down several hundred feet of sunny granite slabs. During spring runoff, the water volume can supposedly reach up to 500 cubic feet per second. In summer months, however, horsetails and plunges transform into skinny, nearly powerless slides, and dozens of water-sculpted paths that existed in spring often dry up.

As if being one of the tallest falls in Maine is not enough, Step Falls also has numerous shallow pools, many of which offer fine places to wade and, in the slightly deeper pools, swim. The yellow-tinted water appears to be very clean. The largest pool at the site, approximately 40 feet long by 12 feet wide, is surrounded by several moss-covered horsetails that empty into it. Along the edges of the pools are broad, mostly flat, sunny granite slabs that meet every requirement for a relaxing picnic.

TRAIL INFORMATION From the parking area, walk north on the obvious trail into the woods. Soon after entering the woods, The Nature Conservancy has set up a self-registration box with information describing the geology and history of Step Falls. After registering, continue up the yellow-marked trail to all sections of the falls. There are cascades and plunges for a few hundred yards, all easily accessed by many spur paths created by traveling visitors over the years.

DIRECTIONS From the junction of US 2, ME 5, and ME 26 in Newry, take ME 26 north. After 7.9 miles, the parking area will be on your right just before a bridge over Wight Brook. *To get to Newry,* take ME 5 north from Bethel.

OTHER WATERFALLS NEARBY Screw Auger Falls (Grafton), Falls at Frenchmen's Hole, Dunn Falls, The Cataracts, Ellis Falls.

Step Falls

50

SWIFT RIVER FALLS

Roxbury, Oxford County

Type: Cascades

Height: 6 feet

Trail Length: Roadside

Water Source: Swift River

Altitude Gain/Loss: None

Difficulty: Easy

Hiking Time: Not applicable

DeLorme Map: Page 18, D-5

Rating: ★★★½

DESCRIPTION Two sites along the Swift River merit your attention. The first, Coos Canyon, a state-funded picnic area lying in the village of Bryon, is a geologically fascinating granite gorge with precipitous walls, but surprisingly no waterfalls or even small cascades can be found here. The second, just south of the canyon, is a segmented cascade known simply as Swift River Falls.

The powerful, rushing waters of the Swift River cascade over small to large potholes that look as if a giant's fingerprints have created impressions in the rocks. Beyond the falls, the sides of the river are lined with hundreds more potholes and oddly carved granite structures. There is also a natural bridge formation, quite small but still worthy of note.

To our dismay, the area has fallen victim to partygoers and other visitors who have disrespected the land. Spray paint, junk food wrappers, and cigarette butts lie among the potholes. Hopefully the site will one day become a small park or rest area and be cleaned up a bit.

TRAIL INFORMATION The falls are easily accessible by hiking down to the river from the parking lot. There are plenty of opportunities for climbing and exploring the geological features along the riverbank.

DIRECTIONS From the junction of US 2 and ME 17 in Mexico, take ME 17 north and continue for 1.5 miles past the road that leads you to ME 120 (Frye Crossover Road). A circular parking lot will be on your left. *To get to Mexico,* take ME 17 north from Augusta or US 2 east from Bethel.

OTHER WATERFALLS NEARBY Rumford Falls, Angel Falls, Ellis Falls, The Cataracts, Dunn Falls.

51

TOBEY FALLS

Willimantic, Piscataquis County

Type: Horsetail
Height: 8 feet
Trail Length: 0.2 mile
Water Source: Big Wilson Stream
Altitude Gain/Loss: None

Difficulty: Easy
Hiking Time: Not applicable
DeLorme Map: Page 3, A-4&5
Rating: ★★★★

DESCRIPTION After a few local waterfall disappointments and a humid, tiring day, what a pleasant surprise Tobey Falls turned out to be. After nearly two months without precipitation in this region of the state, the rivers and streams around the Monson-Guildford area were either completely waterless or nearly so. Tobey Falls was still running strong, however.

Although in low water, as in our visit, Tobey Falls is classified as a slide waterfall, in high-water months it is a massive cascade falling over a smooth, 45-degree-angled slate rock. Big Wilson Stream is normally a 30- to 50-foot-wide river, but at the waterfall the stream condenses to a fraction of that—about 8 feet under normal conditions. A stream being condensed to such a degree ensures a waterfall with torrents of whitewater, even when other falls of Big Wilson Stream have lost their visual appeal.

Tobey Falls is another waterfall that is much more impressive than its size would indicate. You will be quite surprised, as we were, at just how scenic an 8-foot waterfall can be.

TRAIL INFORMATION Walk straight from the parking lot, passing three boulders, onto the obvious trail that enters the woods. Continue down this short, flat trail for about five minutes; the falls will be on your left as you approach a cleared-out area.

DIRECTIONS From the junction of ME 16, ME 6, ME 15, and ME 150 in Guilford, take ME 150 north for 8.7 miles. When you reach Goodell Corner, ME 150 will swing right. Continue straight instead for 0.1 mile until you reach a stop sign. Take a right here onto Norton Corner Road. Travel on Norton Corner Road for 1.3 miles and take a left onto an unmarked dirt road just after passing Titcomb Road. Follow the dirt road for 0.7 mile, pass through a yellow gate, and park just up ahead on your right just after crossing a bridge over Leeman Brook. The parking area is distinguishable by three boulders that outline the edge of the pull-off. *To get to Guilford,* take ME 150 north from Skowhegan.

OTHER WATERFALLS NEARBY Earley Landing Falls, Houston Brook Falls.

Tobey Falls

III. Massachusetts

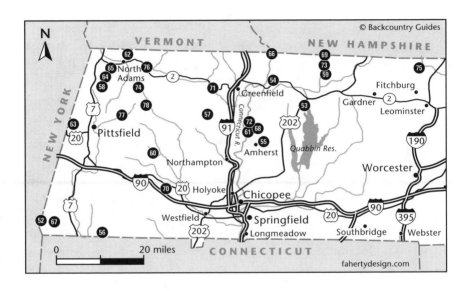

© Backcountry Guides

VERMONT

NEW HAMPSHIRE

N

NEW YORK

62

65 North 76
64 Adams
58 74

2

71

66

54

69
73
59

75

Fitchburg

Gardner
Leominster

77
78

7

63
20

Pittsfield

57

91

Connecticut R.

72 68
61

202

53

2

190

55

60

Northampton

Amherst

Quabbin Res.

Worcester

90
70 20 Holyoke

Chicopee

7

52 67

Westfield

56

202

Springfield

Longmeadow

20

Southbridge

90

395

Webster

0   20 miles

CONNECTICUT

fahertydesign.com

52

BASH BISH FALLS

Mount Washington, Bash Bish Falls State Park, Berkshire County

Type: Plunge

Height: 80-foot total drop

Trail Length: 0.5 mile

Water Source: Bash Bish Brook

Altitude Gain/Loss: −300 feet

Difficulty: Easy side of moderate

Hiking Time: 25 minutes

DeLorme Map: Page 43, I-26

Rating: ★★★★★

DESCRIPTION (HIGHLY RECOMMENDED) Often described as "the state's most dramatic waterfall," Bash Bish Falls is a segmented 80-foot drop of Bash Bish Brook. Worthy of our highest rating, this is perhaps the best-known and most frequently photographed waterfall in Massachusetts. A large boulder splits the falls into two sections, only then to ricochet off a rock wall and rejoin at the base. With a little imagination you could even claim that the falls take on the shape of a diamond. Below the waterfall is a deep pool with clear and inviting water, but unfortunately, dangerous currents have forced state park officials to prohibit swimming.

Bash Bish Falls is one of the most publicized waterfalls in the area, which is what really distinguishes it from other waterfalls in the state. Pictures of the falls have been featured in calendars, in photographic instruction books, and even on the cover of an Appalachian Mountain Club hiking guide to the southern New England states. Just about every hiking guide to Massachusetts, whether online or in print form, mentions this waterfall, although being held in such high regard does have a downside. We have heard accounts of as many as 3,000 people a day visiting the falls on hot weekend summer days. On the upside, Bash Bish Falls sees very few visitors in the cooler days of early spring.

Those looking for more difficult terrain might consider adding nearby Race Brook Falls to complement Bash Bish. Only a few miles apart, the falls combined provide an excellent sampler of the waterfalls Massachusetts has to offer.

TRAIL INFORMATION The trail, marked with blue triangles, travels downhill for its entirety. Full of roots and rocks to maneuver across, the trail crosses two small streams that often dry up during summer, but can

Bash Bish Falls

be very muddy after a heavy rain. As you hike down to the falls, the sound of the crashing waterfall increases. Near the falls there are rock stairways with a handrail, providing an easy access down to the best viewpoint. Altogether the trail is just over 0.5 mile in length, very easy to follow, and requires only a small amount of careful scrambling.

DIRECTIONS From the junction of US 7, MA 41, and MA 23 in Great Barrington, take MA 23 west/MA 41 south into Egremont. After crossing into Egremont, take a left onto MA 41 south. After 0.1 mile, turn right onto a road marked with a sign for MT. WASHINGTON/MT. EVERETT. Follow this road for 7.5 miles until you reach a white sign that says BASH BISH 4. Turn right here; after 4.0 miles, the parking lot for the falls will be on your left. *To get to Great Barrington,* take exit 1 off I-90 and follow MA 41 south.

OTHER WATERFALLS NEARBY Race Brook Falls, Campbell Falls.

53

BEAR'S DEN FALLS

New Salem, Bear's Den Reservation, Franklin County

Type: Cascades
Height: 12-foot total drop
Trail Length: 0.2 mile
Water Source: Middle Branch of the Swift River
Altitude Gain/Loss: –30 feet

Difficulty: Easy
Hiking Time: 5 minutes
DeLorme Map: Page 24, M-6
Rating: ★★★½

DESCRIPTION The Middle Branch of the Swift River drops about 10 feet in a 70-foot-tall gorge while on its way to the Quabbin Reservoir. This drop, formally known as Bear's Den Falls, is a segmented set of cascades. It is split by massive boulders in the middle of the brook, lying between the gorge walls. On the right side of the falls a cascade turns into a fan before landing in a shallow pool.

This area is rich in history and legend. The property was named for a black bear that was shot in the area by a settler. More interesting is the legend of how King Philip met here in 1675 with neighboring chieftains to plan Indian attacks on the white settlers of nearby villages, specifically Hadley, Deerfield, and Northampton. It is believed that these Native Americans celebrated their victories, and hid during their defeats, at the waterfall within the gorge.

Bear's Den Falls is located on property managed by the Trustees of Reservation, a Massachusetts nonprofit, member-supported land conservation organization. This organization also manages the property that Chapel Brook Falls, Glendale Falls, Doane's Falls, Royalston Falls, and Spirit Falls lie on. Members place their focus on "conserving the Massachusetts landscape," and because of them these waterfalls can never be threatened by development.

TRAIL INFORMATION From the parking lot, follow the clearly marked trail 0.2 mile to the falls. There are several spur trails off the main trail, but all eventually lead to the waterfall. Some scrambling is required to get to the base of the falls.

DIRECTIONS From the junction of MA 2 and US 202 in Orange, take US 202 south into New Salem. US 202 will soon join, and later split, with MA 122. Continue traveling on US 202 south for 0.3 mile after US 202 and MA 122 split. Take a right turn onto Elm Street. After 0.7 mile on Elm Street, turn left onto Neilson Road. A small pull-off for the park is 0.4 mile down the road on your right.

OTHER WATERFALLS NEARBY Briggs Brook Falls, Doane's Falls, Spirit Falls, Royalston Falls.

54

BRIGGS BROOK FALLS
Erving, Franklin County

Type: Cascades
Height: 30-foot total drop
Trail Length: 0.3 mile
Water Source: Briggs Brook
Altitude Gain/Loss: +50 feet

Difficulty: Easy
Hiking Time: 10 minutes
DeLorme Map: Page 23, I-29
Rating: ★★

DESCRIPTION A seasonal set of cascades lies on the M&M Trail (Metacomet-Monadnock Trail) just north of MA 2. Although best suited for a trail rest stop (as opposed to a long Sunday drive), the waterfall does offer some exploration opportunities. It is only minutes from a state highway, quite powerful in early spring, and certainly worth the quick stop.

TRAIL INFORMATION The trail begins at the CROSS ST sign, just to the right of a grassy field. Walk up the hill and continue straight past a shed on your right. You will soon see an obvious path into the woods. This is the white-diamond-blazed Metacomet-Monadnock Trail. Follow this trail an additional 0.2 mile to the falls, which will be visible on your left when you reach a footbridge.

DIRECTIONS From Orange, take MA 2 west. When you reach the town of Erving, take a right onto Holmes Street, one of only a few right turns in the town. After about 100 feet on Holmes Street, take another right onto Briggs Street. The parking area is up ahead at the grassy area just before a sign for SEARS WAY. *To get to Orange,* take MA 2 west from Boston or MA 2 east from North Adams.

OTHER WATERFALLS NEARBY Pauchaug Brook Falls, Bear's Den Falls, Shelburne Falls.

55

BUFFAM FALLS

Pelham, Buffam Falls Conservation Area,
Hampshire County

Type: Cascades and slides
Height: 25-foot total drop
Trail Length: 0.5 mile to lowest
falls
Water Source: Buffam Brook
Altitude Gain/Loss: –50 feet

Difficulty: Easy
Hiking Time: 15 minutes
DeLorme Map: Page 35, H-28
Rating: ★★★

DESCRIPTION A trip to Buffam Falls includes a relatively flat and peaceful walk to three main sets of cascades and slides that are no more than 10 feet in height apiece. Buffam Falls is small but still worth the visit, mainly because of the lowermost fall, a fanning slide about 7 feet tall. Buffam Brook takes its last major drop at this fanning slide before connecting with Amethyst Brook a few feet downstream. The town of Pelham maintains the network of trails around the falls, so the area is easy to navigate. Be sure to explore and enjoy the two small brooks.

  TRAIL INFORMATION The trail that begins at the parking lot and immediately climbs a staircase is *not* the trail used to access the falls. The trailhead for Buffam Falls is actually 0.1 mile back up the road. After walking up the road, you will see a trail entering the woods on your right. Enter the woods and, shortly after crossing a bridge, you will see a sign for the BUFFAM FALLS CONSERVATION AREA. Take a right and hike parallel to Briggs Brook past little falls to all three segments of the larger cascades and slides. The trail you are on is actually part of the 117-mile Metacomet-Monadnock Trail (M&M Trail) that runs from Connecticut to southern New Hampshire.

  Once you reach the lowest falls, easily identifiable by the joining of two brooks a few feet farther down the trail, take note of which trail you have been following. The Metacomet-Monadnock Trail becomes quite confusing near these lowermost falls, and it is unsettlingly easy to continue traveling on the M&M Trail, heading south instead of north. Remember to take the trail that runs closest to Briggs Brook, the brook you followed down to the falls originally.

DIRECTIONS From the junction of MA 2 and US 202 in Orange, take US 202 south and continue for 1.8 miles after passing the PELHAM TOWN LINE sign. Take a right onto Amherst Road, follow it for slightly less than a mile, and take a right onto North Valley Road. Follow this road for 2.6 miles, passing a cemetery on your left. The parking area is a paved shoulder to the right of the road. The trailhead can be found by turning around and walking back 0.1 mile up the road you originally arrived on. *To get to Orange,* take MA 2 west from Boston or MA 2 east from North Adams.

OTHER WATERFALLS NEARBY Roaring Falls, Gunn Brook Falls, Slatestone Brook Falls.

56

CAMPBELL FALLS

New Marlborough, Campbell Falls State Forest, Berkshire County

Type: Plunge and cascades

Height: 50-foot total drop

Trail Length: 0.2 mile

Water Source: Whitney River

Altitude Gain/Loss: −150 feet

Difficulty: Easy

Hiking Time: 10 minutes

DeLorme Map: Page 44, M-11&12

Rating: ★★★★★

DESCRIPTION (HIGHLY RECOMMENDED) Within Campbell Falls State Forest, the Whitney River drops 50 feet in a magnificent thundering display. Campbell Falls dumps into a narrow gorge where the direction of the water flow changes twice, first to the right, then to the left. This zigzagging waterfall, as it can best be described, has a rugged appearance not often found in New England waterfalls. Its power in early spring is comparable to waterfalls we have seen in Yellowstone National Park. The rocky gorge is a mind-boggling surprise, considering the gentle terrain of the trail and the surrounding forest.

Make sure to pack all of your photographic equipment when hiking to this waterfall. The falls have both an upper and a lower section, which can be easily framed into one photograph. There is plenty of opportunity

Campbell Falls

to view Campbell Falls because it is open to the public year-round from dawn to dusk.

TRAIL INFORMATION It is slightly difficult to find the trailhead. There is a brown TRAIL sign on a tree with yellow writing and an arrow. Once you find this trailhead, accessing the falls becomes an easy, pleasant walk in the woods. Follow the white-square-marked trail for about 0.2 mile, or 10 minutes, and the falls will be unveiled.

DIRECTIONS From Great Barrington, take MA 23/MA 183, heading toward Monterey. Take a right onto MA 57/MA 183 south when MA 23 continues left. Continue until you reach a right turn for the New Marlborough–Southfield Road, just after arriving in the town of New Marlborough. Travel on New Marlborough–Southfield Road for 1.4 miles, turn left onto Norfolk Road, and continue south to a right onto Campbell Falls Road (a dirt road) just before the Connecticut-Massachusetts border. Take this dirt road for 0.4 mile and park where you can. There is a sign in bad shape that says CAMPBELL FALLS STATE FOREST.

OTHER WATERFALLS NEARBY Buttermilk Falls (Norfolk, Connecticut), Race Brook Falls, Bash Bish Falls.

57

CHAPEL BROOK FALLS

Ashfield, Chapelbrook Reservation, Franklin County

Type: Cascades, slides, and a block
Height: 10 feet, 15 feet, and 20 feet
Trail Length: 0.2 mile to lowest falls
Water Source: Chapel Brook
Altitude Gain/Loss: –50 feet

Difficulty: Easy
Hiking Time: 5 minutes
DeLorme Map: Page 34, A&B-10
Rating: ★★★½

DESCRIPTION Managed by the Trustees of Reservation, Chapelbrook Reservation was a gift of Mrs. Henry T. Curtis in memory of her husband (1964). Within this reservation lie Chapel Brook Falls, a set of three drops totaling about 45 feet, and Pony Mountain, a summit overlooking a nearby valley.

The first waterfall is a 10-foot-tall medium-angled cascade very similar in appearance to Buttermilk Falls in Norfolk, Connecticut. This section of falls is categorized as a fan because Chapel Brook expands from 8 to 15 feet. The next waterfall is slightly wider and travels at a lower angle than the first. The entire formation is more a slide than a cascade, because the waters maintain close contact with the rock as they descend.

The final set of falls at the Chapelbrook Reservation is strikingly comparable to Doane's Falls of Royalston, Massachusetts. This last waterfall drops a total of 20 feet in a block formation. This block waterfall is not as perfectly shaped as Doane's Falls, due to a 5-foot-tall slide that covers its last few feet. For the hearty explorer, smaller pools and cascades can be found downstream.

Also located at Chapelbrook Reservation is Chapel Ledge, a sheer 80-foot granite cliff of Pony Mountain accessible by the Ledges Trail. You can visit the ledge by climbing the trail that begins directly in front of the parking area. A fortunate hiker may be lucky enough to spot a red-tailed hawk, a common visitor to this area.

TRAIL INFORMATION The trail begins on the other side of the road after crossing the bridge. It is about 100 feet farther up the road from the parking lot. The trail is posted; you should be able to hear the falls from the parking lot. Continue 0.2 mile to the lowermost falls.

DIRECTIONS From the junction of MA 2 and I-91 in Greenfield, take I-91 south. Take exit 25 off I-91 and follow MA 116 west toward Ashfield. Continue traveling on MA 116 west for 2.0 miles after passing the ASHFIELD TOWN LINE sign. Take a left onto Creamery Road, and immediately after, take another left onto Williamsburg Road. Travel on this road for 2.2 miles; the parking area will be on your right just before a small bridge. The falls are found by hiking down a trail on the other side of the road.

OTHER WATERFALLS NEARBY Shelburne Falls, Slatestone Brook Falls, Gunn Brook Falls, Roaring Falls.

58

~~~~

DEER HILL FALLS

Williamstown, Mount Greylock State Reservation,
Berkshire County

Type: Horsetail

Height: 30 feet

Trail Length: 0.4 mile

Water Source: Roaring Brook

Altitude Gain/Loss: −150 feet

Difficulty: Easy side of moderate

Hiking Time: 15 minutes

DeLorme Map: Page 20, H-14

Rating: ★★★

DESCRIPTION Deer Hill Falls is one of several highly seasonal, low-volume waterfalls in Mount Greylock State Reservation. When we visited the falls in the middle of June, they looked like a thousand dripping faucets. Resources tell us that in the months of March, April, and May, the falls are a 30-foot-tall curtain of whitewater.

Spring runoff is likely the only time to view the falls during high water. Multiple-day rainstorms may not be enough to fuel this waterfall in summertime. Still, the area is worth a visit: Deer Hill Falls is only a few minutes' walk from the same parking area that accesses our favorite waterfall in the park, March Cataract Falls. By visiting both you can see how different waterfalls can be even when they exist so close to each other.

TRAIL INFORMATION (See map on next page) From the parking lot, follow signs toward the Deer Hill Trail. Begin by walking down a dirt road, passing a few campsites and rest rooms. After walking a few hundred feet on the dirt road, take a left; shortly thereafter you will see a sign for the DEER HILL TRAIL. Follow the obvious path and cross a wooden bridge. In a few more feet you should fork right at a junction and continue hiking for about five more minutes. You will reach another T-junction, where you turn left, and the Deer Hill Trail will soon guide you to the base of the falls.

DIRECTIONS From Pittsfield, take US 7 north and continue for 3.2 miles past the LANESBOROUGH TOWN LINE sign. Take a right onto North Main Street, drive 0.7 mile, and turn right onto a road marked with a sign for STATE RESERVATION. Follow this road for 0.4 mile and take a left onto Rockwell Road; after 6.6 miles, make a left turn onto Sperry Road,

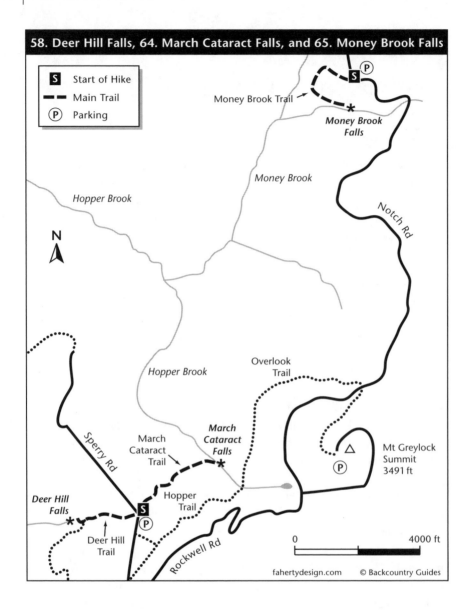

58. Deer Hill Falls, 64. March Cataract Falls, and 65. Money Brook Falls

S Start of Hike
- - - Main Trail
P Parking

Money Brook Trail

Money Brook Falls

Hopper Brook

Money Brook

Notch Rd

N

Overlook Trail

Hopper Brook

March Cataract Falls

Sperry Rd

March Cataract Trail

Mt Greylock Summit 3491 ft

Deer Hill Falls

Hopper Trail

Deer Hill Trail

Rockwell Rd

0   4000 ft

fahertydesign.com   © Backcountry Guides

a dirt road. Follow Sperry Road for 0.1 mile as it passes a small ranger checkpoint. The parking area will be on your left. This parking area also accesses March Cataract Falls.

OTHER WATERFALLS NEARBY March Cataract Falls, Money Brook Falls, Hudson Brook Chasm, Lulu Cascade.

59

DOANE'S FALLS

Royalston, Doane's Falls Reservation, Worcester County

Type: Plunges, cascades, and a block
Height: Approximately 175-foot total drop
Trail Length: 0.3 mile to lowest falls
Water Source: Lawrence Brook
Altitude Gain/Loss: –175 feet

Difficulty: Easy side of moderate
Hiking Time: 15 minutes
DeLorme Map: Page 24, F&G-13
Rating: ★★★★

DESCRIPTION The town of Royalston offers three waterfalls. There is Royalston Falls, a plunge toward the northern end of the town line; Spirit Falls, in the Jacob's Hill Reservation; and Doane's Falls, a nearly 200-foot chain of wide cascades and plunges on a 46-acre preserve managed by the Trustees of Reservation.

Doane's Falls is split into three sections. With a stone bridge as a backdrop, the first section is a pair of plunges. Following a well-marked trail down for a few minutes, you come to the other sections of Doane's Falls. You will pass a few sets of cascades before reaching a 20-foot block waterfall falling over a ledge. The river continues on with small cascades and pools, eventually meeting up with the East Branch of the Tully River.

There are several posted erosion zones at the falls, so be sure to stay on the trail. Several fatalities have occurred here, says an utterly disturbing sign. For this reason, swimming is highly discouraged. If you keep to the trail, admiring the scenery is no more dangerous than viewing any other waterfall. Make sure to visit sometime in summer—the area is open only from Memorial Day through Labor Day, 8 AM–sunset each day.

TRAIL INFORMATION Starting directly in front of the parking lot, the trail descends parallel to the brook. The trail, which should not be deviated from, is marked by yellow blazes. About 0.1 mile from the parking area, a 4-mile round-trip side trail leads to Tully Dam, an extra attraction.

DIRECTIONS From the junction of MA 2 and MA 68 in Gardner,

Doane's Falls

take MA 68 west and continue for 4.7 miles past the ROYALSTON TOWN LINE sign. Take a wide left turn onto Athol Road and continue for 2.0 miles; the parking lot will be on your right. *To get to Gardner,* take MA 2 west from Boston or MA 2 east from North Adams.

OTHER WATERFALLS NEARBY Spirit Falls, Royalston Falls, Bear's Den Falls.

60

GLENDALE FALLS

Middlefield, Glendale Falls Reservation, Hampshire County

Type: Cascades

Height: Approximately 160-foot total drop

Trail Length: 0.3 mile to base of falls

Water Source: Glendale Brook

Altitude Gain/Loss: −160 feet

Difficulty: Moderate

Hiking Time: 15 minutes to base of falls

DeLorme Map: Page 33, I-27&28

Rating: ★★★½

DESCRIPTION Why did we give a high rating to such an unattractive waterfall? As far as picturesque waterfalls go, Glendale Falls would probably receive our lowest rating. There are no vantage points for framing a quality photograph, and the falls have no distinct style. The reason for our rating is this waterfall's sheer size and volume. The drop, which is more than 160 feet, is Massachusetts's third tallest cascade chain. The waters of Glendale Brook crash thunderously and haphazardly over endless ledges and boulders strewn in the brook. Falling into the brook at any point would certainly result in tragedy.

The deep pool at the bottom has some swimming appeal, but its currents may be too dangerous if you visit on the wrong day. This is not really the best place for children, because skilled scrambling techniques are required to access this pool. The Trustees of Reservation, which manages the 60-acre preserve at Doane's Falls, has placed a sign at the parking lot outlining the interesting natural attractions of the area. Be aware that the park is open only sunrise–sunset, so plan your day accordingly.

TRAIL INFORMATION This trail is steep and very slippery when wet; please use caution if you choose to go all the way to the bottom. In places you must use your hands and scramble over wet sections of steep, rocky terrain. There are plenty of trees to hold on to to help pick your way across roots and rocks to get to the base of the falls.

DIRECTIONS From I-90 in Westfield, take exit 3. Follow MA 10/US 202 south. After crossing the Westfield River, turn onto MA 20, which heads toward Huntington. When you arrive in Huntington, take a right onto MA 112. You will soon cross a bridge and take a major left turn immediately after onto Basket Street. After driving on Basket Street for 0.2 mile, you will come to a fork in the road. Take the left prong onto Old Chester Road, continue for 1.3 miles, and you will reach another fork and a sign for the SKYLINE TRAIL. Veer right and continue for 2.5 miles, eventually reaching a third fork in the road. There will be a sign indicating that a right turn will lead you toward North Chester and West Worthington. Take this right fork onto East River Road. Travel on this road for 6.9 miles and take a left onto Clark Wright Road just before crossing a small bridge. Look for a small, green GLENDALE FALLS sign. Follow Clark Wright Road for 0.3 mile; a sign will mark the parking area on your right.

OTHER WATERFALLS NEARBY Sanderson Brook Falls, Wahconah Falls.

61

GUNN BROOK FALLS
Sunderland, Franklin County

Type: Plunges
Height: 30-foot total drop
Trail Length: Roadside
Water Source: Gunn Brook
Altitude Gain/Loss: −40 feet to base of falls

Difficulty: Easy side of moderate
Hiking Time: Not applicable
DeLorme Map: Page 35, A-22
Rating: ★★★★

DESCRIPTION Gunn Brook Falls consists of two plunges, each roughly 15 feet in height and 8 feet in width. The first plunge is a treat. It is possible (and quite easy) to walk right up to the falls, sit down on a rock seat that Mother Nature carved, and savor clean mountain water falling from above.

The second falls are more of the same, except lacking the natural seat. With caution, it is easy to stand on the top of either plunge. These particular falls are heavily covered in moss, especially on the left side of the entire formation. With attentive parenting, this waterfall can be great for children. They will love playing in the chilly waters. Make sure to bring your camera; whether you take pictures of your children playing or of the waterfall and its setting, you will surely bring home some great memories. The green moss surrounding the falls also boosts your chances for a great photograph.

TRAIL INFORMATION An obvious trails lead to the base of the falls. Some scrambling is required, but nothing too difficult.

DIRECTIONS From the junction of MA 47 and MA 116 in Sunderland, take MA 47 north for 1.5 miles. Take a left onto Falls Road, drive for 1.0 mile, and you will come to Chard Pond on your right. Immediately thereafter, take a right onto Gunn Cross Road—a dirt road with no street sign posted. Continue for 0.2 mile to a small parking area on your right. The falls are just off the side of the road on your right. Slatestone Falls are only minutes away, less than a mile farther up Falls Road. *To get to Sunderland,* take I-91 to exit 19 in Northampton. Follow MA 9 east to MA 116 north.

OTHER WATERFALLS NEARBY Slatestone Brook Falls, Roaring Falls, Buffam Falls, Chapel Brook Falls.

62

HUDSON BROOK CHASM

North Adams, Natural Bridge State Park, Berkshire County

Type: Cascades

Height: 25-foot total drop

Trail Length: 0.1 mile (see notes)

Water Source: Hudson Brook

Altitude Gain/Loss: None

Difficulty: Easy

Hiking Time: Not applicable

DeLorme Map: Page 21, C-20

Rating: ★★★½

Gunn Brook Falls in low water

DESCRIPTION Hudson Brook Chasm does not contain any major waterfalls. What it does have is a 100-foot-long chasm. To see all the cascades, the park has constructed a maze of boardwalk trails following chain-link fences that let you see just about every possible viewpoint of the chasm.

The geology of the area is fascinating. The marble rock formations are worth the visit alone, with many circular pools and small caves carved out in the chasm. There is also a natural bridge for which the park is named. The only potential drawbacks are the detractions from the natural features of the area, which include extensive fencing in and around the chasm and the fact that the brook is controlled upstream by a dam.

Although there are no significant waterfalls per se, this site is still worth visiting because it has some small cascades and is a great place for a picnic—and the chasm is fascinating. Definitely bring your children, and a camera, to really enjoy this scenic park in the northwestern corner of Massachusetts. There is a visitors center with rest rooms and wide fields for a picnic in the park, making any visit a great day trip.

TRAIL INFORMATION From the parking lot, follow the easy-to-find trail to the falls. There is a sign for NATURAL BRIDGES. If the gate to the state park is closed, walk up the road for 0.2 mile until you see a staircase leading into some tree coverage. The chasm is just up there, and a viewpoint of the bottom of the chasm lies just to the left of this staircase. If the gate is closed, the trail will be 0.3 mile each way, with an elevation gain of approximately 100 feet.

DIRECTIONS From the junction of MA 2 and MA 8 in North Adams, take MA 8 north. Continue for 0.5 mile and take a left onto McCauley Road. If the gate for the park is open, drive 0.3 mile to the parking lot. If it is not, find a place to park and walk up the road to the falls.

OTHER WATERFALLS NEARBY Twin Cascades, Money Brook Falls, March Cataract Falls, Deer Hill Falls, Tannery Falls.

63

LULU CASCADE

Pittsfield, Pittsfield State Forest, Berkshire County

Type: Plunge and cascades
Height: 10-foot total drop
Trail Length: 0.1 mile
Water Source: Lulu Brook
Altitude Gain/Loss: None

Difficulty: Easy
Hiking Time: 5 minutes
DeLorme Map: Page 32, A-8
Rating: ★★½

DESCRIPTION Pittsfield State Forest, on the western edge of Massachusetts, is a state park with much to offer. There are waterfalls, some of the finest scenic vistas in the state, a large network of trails, as well as low-cost camping.

For waterfalls, Pittsfield State Forest offers two small falls known as Lulu Cascade. Only a short walk from the Lulu Day Use Parking Area, the falls, which lie in a pretty ravine, contain exceptionally clear water. They may not be the most interesting falls in New England, but they are visually charming.

After visiting the falls, however, your trip to the state forest is not complete. Continue down the main park road (Berry Pond Circuit Road) and complete the long loop back to the park entrance. Along the way you will be pleased by vistas, Berry Pond—a natural body of water with the highest elevation in the state—and lots of trailhead parking for the avid hiker. For information on trails, obtain a map at the visitors center. There is a nominal fee for entering the park. Some motorized vehicles are allowed within the park, as are bicyclists and equestrians, allowing every type of outdoor enthusiast the opportunity to enjoy the area.

TRAIL INFORMATION From the Lulu Day Use Parking Area, continue further up the park road and take a right onto a trail just before the small bridge. The falls are 0.1 mile up the trail on your left. The main plunge lies a few feet beyond the first set of cascades.

DIRECTIONS From I-90 in Lee, take exit 2. Follow US 20 west toward Pittsfield. Soon US 7 north will join with, and later split from, US 20 west. Continue on US 20 west for 0.75 mile past the spot where US 7 breaks away. Take a right onto Merrium Street, drive 0.5 mile, and turn left onto West Street. Follow West Street for 1.9 miles and take a right onto Churchill Street. After driving 0.6 mile on Churchill, take a left onto Cascade Street and proceed for 1.5 miles to the contact station for Pittsfield State Forest. Continue straight for 0.6 mile farther and park at the Lulu Day Use Parking Area on your left.

OTHER WATERFALLS NEARBY Wahconah Falls, Tannery Falls, Deer Hill Falls, March Cataract Falls, Money Brook Falls.

64

⌒⌒

MARCH CATARACT FALLS

Williamstown, Mount Greylock State Reservation, Berkshire County

Type: Fan
Height: 30 feet
Trail Length: 0.7 mile
Water Source: Hopper Brook
Altitude Gain/Loss: Up 50 feet, down 125 feet

Difficulty: Moderate
Hiking Time: 25 minutes
DeLorme Map: Page 20, G-14
Rating: ★★★★

DESCRIPTION March Cataract Falls is the must-see waterfall of northwestern Massachusetts. Although it is considered a seasonal waterfall and reduces to a mere trickle in the summer dry months, when it is flowing it is a picturesque horsetail-fan set on the western slopes of Mount Greylock.

In essence, March Cataract Falls is the Arethusa Falls of Massachusetts. Although considerably shorter in length, it is very similar to Arethusa in that the water fans peacefully down a rock wall into very shallow pools. Both falls are also highly exposed to the sun and are moderately difficult to access.

To make a multiple-hour trip out of March Cataract Falls, be sure to check out Deer Hill Falls, a waterfall accessed by the same parking area, as well as Money Brook Falls and the summit of Mount Greylock, all accessible by nearby park roads. At the summit of Mount Greylock are paved parking areas and beautiful views of several New England states and New York.

TRAIL INFORMATION (See map on page 96.) From the small parking area, return to the fork at the ranger station and take the right fork—

March Cataract Falls

not the left one, which you took to pull into the parking area. After passing several campsites on your left, you will reach the trailhead on your right rather quickly. From this point forward the trail is blue blazed, fairly well used, and easy to follow. It can be slippery and steep at times, so try to watch your footing. The falls see very few sightseers during the morning hours, but their popularity can grow as the day progresses.

DIRECTIONS From Pittsfield, take US 7 north and continue for 3.2 miles past the LANESBOROUGH TOWN LINE sign. Take a right onto North Main Street, continue for 0.7 mile, and turn right onto a road marked with a sign for STATE RESERVATION. Follow this road for 0.4 mile and take a left onto Rockwell Road. Follow Rockwell Road for 6.6 miles, then turn left onto Sperry Road when you see several signs listing the park attractions and features. Follow Sperry Road for 0.1 mile and park at the small pull-off on your left just after passing by the small ranger checkpoint station. Be prepared to discuss your trail plans with the ranger on duty.

OTHER WATERFALLS NEARBY Deer Hill Falls, Money Brook Falls, Hudson Brook Chasm, Lulu Cascade, Twin Cascades.

65

MONEY BROOK FALLS

North Adams, Mount Greylock State Reservation, Berkshire County

Type: Cascades

Height: 40-foot total drop

Trail Length: 0.8 mile

Water Source: Money Brook

Altitude Gain/Loss: –200 feet

Difficulty: Moderate

Hiking Time: 30 minutes

DeLorme Map: Page 21, F-16

Rating: ★★½

DESCRIPTION Perhaps the least popular of waterfalls on the slopes of Mount Greylock, Money Brook Falls receives very little attention. In comparison to the other waterfalls of the reservation, Money Brook Falls is typical, seasonal, and littered with boulders and fallen trees. Although less attractive than other waterfalls in the reservation, this staircase of cascades is still worth the visit, provided you allow time for March Cataract Falls, Deer Hill Falls, and the summit of Mount Greylock. With the inclusion of the other features of the park you have created a fully eventful day for you and your family.

TRAIL INFORMATION (See map on page 96.) Follow the trail from the parking area to the blue-blazed Money Brook Trail. You will reach two forks on this trail. Make sure to take a left both times. There are signs pointing toward the falls, but they are hard to spot.

DIRECTIONS From the junction of MA 2 and MA 8A in North Adams, take MA 2 west for 1.3 miles. Take a left onto Notch Road and continue 5.0 miles to a small parking area on your right. The parking area for the falls is 4.0 miles north of the summit of Mount Greylock.

OTHER WATERFALLS NEARBY March Cataract Falls, Deer Hill Falls, Hudson Brook Chasm, Twin Cascades.

66

PAUCHAUG BROOK FALLS
Northfield, Franklin County

Type: Plunges and cascades

Height: 15-foot total drop

Trail Length: Roadside

Water Source: Pauchaug Brook

Altitude Gain/Loss: None

Difficulty: Easy

Hiking Time: Not applicable

DeLorme Map: Page 23, B-29

Rating: ★★★

DESCRIPTION Pauchaug Brook Falls consists of an upper 5-foot-tall, 15-foot-wide cascade and a lower 10-foot segmented waterfall. The upper falls are located only 50 feet from the lower falls. The general area is not really scenic, but it is wide open, close to the road, and somewhat photogenic.

Pauchaug Brook splits into two main routes for the lower falls, the first being a plunge, and the second a cascade. Surprisingly, immediately after the waterfall the river turns into a relatively lazy stream. Farther downstream, Pauchaug Brook tends to be a popular canoe route.

TRAIL INFORMATION There are several routes to the falls. If you park on either MA 63 or MA 10, you will have to do some scrambling down to the falls. A pull-off right at the junction, however, allows you to drive into a parking lot specifically for the falls. It is easy to miss, so pay close attention at the highway junction.

DIRECTIONS From the junction of MA 2 and MA 63 in Erving, take MA 63 north. Travel on MA 63 north for about 10 miles to its junction with MA 10. The park for the falls is accessed by a road that starts directly between the split of the two highways. *To get to Erving,* take MA 2 west from Boston or MA 2 east from North Adams.

OTHER WATERFALLS NEARBY Briggs Brook Falls, Shelburne Falls, Bear's Den Falls.

67

RACE BROOK FALLS

Sheffield, Mount Everett State Reservation, Berkshire County

Type: Horsetails and cascades

Height: Approximately 300-foot total drop

Trail Length: 1.1 miles to upper falls

Water Source: Race Brook

Altitude Gain/Loss: +900 feet to upper falls

Difficulty: To the first falls, moderate; to the upper falls, moderate side of difficult

Hiking Time: 60 minutes to upper falls

DeLorme Map: Page 43, J-30

Rating: ★★★★

DESCRIPTION Visitors seeking additional trail time at Bash Bish Falls often end up at Race Brook Falls. Minutes away from Bash Bish, Race Brook offers five distinct sets of waterfalls. If you choose to create a full day trip out of the area, a nice addition to Race Brook Falls is a hike to the summit of Mount Everett or Mount Race.

Race Brook Falls offers a variety of waterfall environments. The lowermost falls are surrounded by dozens of hemlock trees, creating a nice frame. The upper falls are more exposed to the sun and offer more photographic opportunities. Most waterfall types, including horsetails, plunges, cascades, slides, and fans, can be found by continuing up the steep trail to the upper falls. Our favorite is the second set—a horsetail with a shallow pool below. Discounting the slippery access (use caution, please), it is possible to wade right up and lean against the rugged, nearly vertical wall that the water tumbles down.

The upper three falls consist of cascades and plunges similar to the previous ones, but only experienced hikers should climb farther to see these, as the trail is extremely dangerous. Do not attempt to visit these falls in early spring, when mud is a common peril for hikers. Hiking during this time is an accident waiting to happen.

TRAIL INFORMATION Beginning from the left of the parking lot, the trail, marked with blue triangles, is relatively flat until you reach a fork after 0.3 mile. The left trail, marked with a sign stating TO THE AP-PALACHIAN TRAIL VIA THE FALLS, leads to all five waterfalls. The right trail

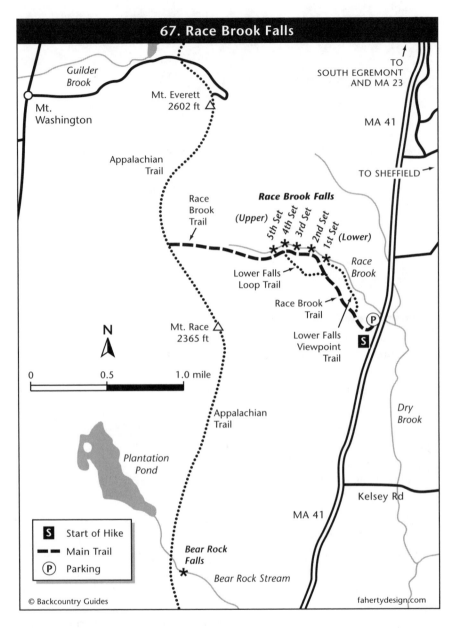

67. Race Brook Falls

Guilder Brook

TO
SOUTH EGREMONT
AND MA 23

Mt. Everett
2602 ft

Mt.
Washington

MA 41

Appalachian
Trail

TO SHEFFIELD

Race
Brook
Trail

Race Brook Falls

(Upper) 5th Set 4th Set 3rd Set 2nd Set 1st Set *(Lower)*

Race
Brook

Lower Falls
Loop Trail

Race Brook
Trail

N

Mt. Race
2365 ft

Lower Falls
Viewpoint
Trail

0   0.5   1.0 mile

Appalachian
Trail

Dry
Brook

Plantation
Pond

Kelsey Rd

MA 41

S Start of Hike
- - - Main Trail
(P) Parking

*Bear Rock
Falls*

Bear Rock Stream

© Backcountry Guides

fahertydesign.com

will lead you to the base of the lowermost waterfall. It is possible to continue from this point to the other four falls, but it is very steep and slippery. It is much safer to take a left at the sign and avoid the treacherous
terrain.

Hike 0.3 mile farther and you will reach the second fork of the trip, marked by a sign for VIEW OF LOWER FALLS LOOP TRAIL. Take a right at this fork. After this point, blue triangles and red squares will guide you to all of the falls. Be aware that the trail is not well marked and it is quite easy to deviate from it, especially as you begin to explore the brook and falls.

After the lower falls, continue climbing parallel to the brook. Soon you will reach the junction with the Lower Falls Loop Trail. You can return to the trailhead by taking this trail.

OPTIONAL HIKE The Race Brook Trail does not come to an end at the upper falls. In actuality, the trail continues west to a junction with the white-blazed Appalachian Trail. By continuing up the Race Brook Trail, you can complement the waterfalls of Race Brook with the peaks of Mount Race and Mount Everett.

At 2.1 miles from the parking area and trailhead, the Race Brook Trail terminates at its junction with the Appalachian Trail. From here you can take a left and follow the AT south for 1.1 miles to the summit of Mount Race, or take a right and follow the AT north for 0.8 mile to the 2,602-foot summit of Mount Everett, the tallest mountain of the Taconic Range. Both summits offer fine views of the surrounding states. If you

Race Brook Falls

are looking for a little privacy, Mount Race is the peak to head to—there is an auto road to the top of Mount Everett.

Another waterfall not described in this guide, Bear Rock Falls, is 1.8 miles south of Mount Race. To reach these falls, continue south on the AT until you reach the Bear Rock Falls Campsite area, where the falls can be found.

DIRECTIONS From the junction of US 7, MA 41, and MA 23 in Great Barrington, take MA 23 west/MA 41 south, heading toward Egremont. After crossing into Egremont, take a left onto MA 41 south and continue for 5.0 miles; you should see a semicircular parking area on your right. There is a sign describing the natural features of Massachusetts. If you are traveling from Connecticut, take CT 44 north to CT 41 north. The parking area for the falls is on your left 2.8 miles after crossing the Connecticut-Massachusetts border. *To get to Great Barrington,* take exit 1 off I-90 and follow MA 41 south.

OTHER WATERFALLS NEARBY Bash Bish Falls, Campbell Falls, Buttermilk Falls (Norfolk, Connecticut).

68

ROARING FALLS

Sunderland, Mount Toby State Forest, Franklin County

Type: Punchbowl and a plunge
Height: 18-foot total drop
Trail Length: 1.2 miles
Water Source: Roaring Brook
Altitude Gain/Loss: +300 feet

Difficulty: Moderate side of difficult
Hiking Time: 45 minutes
DeLorme Map: Page 35, A-24
Rating: ★★★

DESCRIPTION This waterfall is split into two sections by a flat base that contains an oddly placed boulder. The water here is exceptionally clear, and the rock formations and vertical potholes are of great interest. Only agile travelers will be able to jostle their way down the steep, loose-dirt wall to the lower viewpoint of the falls. Combine this waterfall with a trip to the summit of Mount Toby via the dirt road path that led you to the falls (Summit Road).

TRAIL INFORMATION The trail begins at the sign for MOUNT TOBY FOREST. Immediately after passing the sign, a fork appears. Take the left fork, which is a relatively flat, occasionally used dirt road. Follow this road for more than a mile. Eventually the trail will become less wide and steeper. Make sure you do not take any side paths. Stay on this dirt road (called Summit Road).

After a mile or so, you will reach a sign for the ROARING FALLS BYPASS TRAIL on a tree. The trail you want is still farther up the road. Shortly thereafter you will reach a trail on the left side, marked by a sign for ROARING FALLS TRAIL. This is the path that will lead you down a steep embankment to the base of the falls. One warning, however: This trail is hazardously steep and slippery—much too dangerous for children.

Summit Road leads to the summit of Mount Toby, which contains a watchtower with great views of the surrounding area. At the ROARING FALLS TRAIL sign, you are approximately halfway to the summit. The rest of the summit trail is similar to the trail to the falls. Although we do not recommend just visiting the waterfall and returning home, it makes a nice addition to a trip to the summit of Mount Toby.

DIRECTIONS From Northampton, take I-91 north to exit 24. Follow US 5/MA 10 north and take a quick right turn onto MA 116 east. Follow MA 116 east to the junction of MA 116 and MA 47 in Sunderland. Turn left onto MA 47 north and continue for 3.9 miles. Turn right onto Reservation Road just after passing the MONTAGUE TOWN LINE sign. The trailhead will be on your right after 0.5 mile on Reservation Road. The parking lot is on your right just beyond the trailhead and before a building. *To get to Northampton,* take I-91 north from I-90.

OTHER WATERFALLS NEARBY Gunn Brook Falls, Slatestone Brook Falls, Buffam Falls, Chapel Brook Falls.

69

ROYALSTON FALLS

Royalston, Royalston Falls Reservation,
Worcester County

Type: Plunge

Height: 50 feet

Trail Length: 0.5 mile (see notes)

Water Source: Falls Brook

Altitude Gain/Loss: : -150 feet

Difficulty: Easy side of moderate

Hiking Time: 20 minutes

DeLorme Map: Page 24, C-11

Rating: ★★★★

DESCRIPTION The most interesting part of this area is not the waterfall; it is the rock formations created by Falls Brook. A cylinder-shaped gorge created by erosion, or perhaps a retreating glacier from the Ice Age, can best be seen by crossing the brook at the top of the falls. This gorge is a true natural wonder; it is anyone's guess how this gorge could be created by such a calm brook.

Royalston Falls

The falls themselves are also quite a treat. This 50-foot plunge drops off a rock ledge. You can view the falls either from behind safety cable wire fences or by standing on a firmly planted rock at the top of the falls. If you are comfortable with doing so, cross the brook and scramble downstream; you will take in some wonderful new views of the gorge and falls.

Royalston Falls is one of three waterfalls managed by the Trustees of Reservation in the town of Royalston. Be sure to add Doane's Falls to your itinerary, and Spirit Falls if time permits.

TRAIL INFORMATION Yellow markers guide you on this easy-to-follow trail. Although generally a pleasurable and easy walk, the trail becomes steep once you get within 0.1 mile of the falls. Some scrambling is required, but there are many trees to help stabilize you. Although the trail is 1.0 mile round trip, you must add mileage based on how far you travel on the unimproved dirt road that leads to the trailhead. High-clearance vehicles, such as SUVs and trucks, will have no problem with the road, but lower-clearance vehicles must be cautious. For those who must hike up the road, do not despair; the trailhead is obvious and marked with a sign for the falls.

DIRECTIONS From the junction of MA 2 and MA 68 in Gardner, take MA 68 west. Continue for 6.0 miles past the ROYALSTON TOWN LINE sign. Take a right onto Falls Road, which is 1.3 miles north of the town center of Royalston. The distance from the beginning of Falls Road to the trailhead is 3.2 miles. After 2.3 miles, however, the road is unimproved and contains many puddles, rocks, and potholes. A SEASONAL LIMITED USE HIGHWAY sign lets you know right before the road turns really bumpy. Continue as far as you like here, park on the side of the road, and continue walking on the road to the trailhead. A Trustees of Reservation sign for ROYALSTON FALLS marks the trailhead. The parking area is on your right (if you can manage to drive that far), and the trail begins on your left. *To get to Gardner,* take MA 2 west from Boston or MA 2 east from North Adams.

OTHER WATERFALLS NEARBY Spirit Falls, Doane's Falls, Bear's Den Falls.

Sanderson Brook Falls

70

SANDERSON BROOK FALLS

*Chester, Chester-Blandford State Forest,
Hampden County*

Type: Horsetails and cascades   **Difficulty:** Easy
Height: 60-foot total drop   **Hiking Time:** 30 minutes
Trail Length: 1.0 mile   **DeLorme Map:** Page 45, A-28
Water Source: Sanderson Brook   **Rating:** ★★★½
Altitude Gain/Loss: Up 100 feet,
down 30 feet

DESCRIPTION The waters of Sanderson Brook travel down a 60-foot face of a rock wall, called Sanderson Brook Falls. Plunges adorn the top of the wall, followed by cascades of different structures. The force of the plunge smashes into a flat obstructing rock, causing the water to shoot upward before landing into the cascades below. At the base of the falls are pools, small cascades, and plenty of picnic-approved spots. The shallow pools are child safe. Although they may be slightly chilly, children will love splashing around in them on a hot day. There are also large boulders scattered everywhere to climb on, which provide opportunities for exploration.

TRAIL INFORMATION The trail to the falls follows a wide dirt road (Sanderson Brook Road), maintained by the Chester-Blandford State Forest. There is minimal elevation gain, and the road is well marked with blue triangles. It would be nearly impossible to deviate from the trail and miss the waterfall. At 0.9 mile take a right off the road and follow the trail the rest of the way down to the brook, where the scale of the falls will surely surprise you.

DIRECTIONS From Springfield, take I-90 west to exit 3. Turn onto US 202/MA 10 south, then turn right onto MA 20 west, which heads toward Russell and Pittsfield. Drive along MA 20 west for 14.4 miles and you will reach the main entrance of the Chester-Blandford State Forest. Drive 1.6 miles past the main entrance; there will be a small parking lot on your left with a sign for SANDERSON BROOK FALLS. The trail to the falls continues up Sanderson Brook Road, which is usually closed to car travel.

OTHER WATERFALLS NEARBY Glendale Falls.

71

SHELBURNE FALLS

Shelburne, Franklin County

Type: Dam and cascades
Height: 35-foot total drop
Trail Length: Roadside
Water Source: Deerfield River
Altitude Gain/Loss: None

Difficulty: Easy
Hiking Time: Not applicable
DeLorme Map: Page 22, I-11
Rating: ★★½

DESCRIPTION Less than a handful of dams are included in this guide. One reason many of us love waterfalls is because they are some of the last

Slatestone Brook Falls

natural features surviving; their untouched and unspoiled environments are special places of beauty. As such, we are extremely hesitant about describing dams (or the natural features left intact below them) in our guide.

To every rule there are exceptions: Shelburne Falls cannot be left out. The power the dam creates is astonishing, and several of the original cascades and potholes remain despite the construction of the dam. The "glacial potholes," as they are called, are fascinating and scattered everywhere. Therefore, even though this waterfall is intact below a dam and is controlled by a dam, it is still of amazing beauty and worthwhile.

TRAIL INFORMATION Shelburne Falls is located off Deerfield Avenue. Follow the signs to GLACIAL POTHOLES and you will see the falls—they are impossible to miss!

DIRECTIONS Take MA 2 west from Greenfield. When you reach the town of Shelburne, take a left onto MA 2A west and drive 0.6 mile into the town of Shelburne Falls. Once you arrive in town, take a left onto Deerfield Avenue. There will be signs in the area for the GLACIAL POTHOLES—a group of natural features adjacent to the falls. The falls are in the center of town, close by the famous Bridge of Flowers, and several restaurants and local shops.

OTHER WATERFALLS NEARBY Chapel Brook Falls, Briggs Brook Falls.

72

SLATESTONE BROOK FALLS
Sunderland, Franklin County

Type: Fan	**Difficulty:** Easy
Height: 40-foot total drop	**Hiking Time:** Not applicable
Trail Length: Roadside	**DeLorme Map:** Page 23, O-22
Water Source: Slatestone Brook	**Rating:** ★★★
Altitude Gain/Loss: None	

DESCRIPTION There lies a house in the town of Sunderland that either one of us would love to live in. Imagine that you own a small, quaint little house in a town, and in your backyard, only 30 feet from your back door and porch, is a picturesque 40-foot fanning waterfall. How relaxing life must be listening to a waterfall all day long! We admit our jealousy, and you probably will as well once you see Slatestone Brook Falls for the first time.

The entire scene is picture-book perfect, with the Connecticut River on one side and a dazzlingly pretty cascade surrounded by sea-green moss on the other. Complement this roadside attraction with nearby Gunn Brook Falls and you have a fine day of waterfall sight-seeing.

TRAIL INFORMATION Being on private property, the only view to be had of this waterfall is from the road.

DIRECTIONS From the junction of MA 47 and MA 116 in Sunderland, take MA 47 north for approximately 1.5 miles and turn left onto Falls Road. After exactly 2.0 miles on Falls Road, you should see Slatestone Brook Falls on your right as you drive across a small bridge. *To get to Sunderland,* take I-91 to exit 19 in Northampton. Follow MA 9 east to MA 116 north.

OTHER WATERFALLS NEARBY Gunn Brook Falls, Roaring Falls, Buffam Falls, Chapel Brook Falls, Shelburne Falls.

73

SPIRIT FALLS

Royalston, Jacob Hill Reservation, Worcester County

Type: Cascades
Height: 80-foot total drop
Trail Length: 1.0 mile
Water Source: Outflow from
Little Pond
Altitude Gain/Loss: –200 feet

Difficulty: Easy side of moderate
Hiking Time: 35 minutes
DeLorme Map: Page 24, E-12
Rating: ★★

DESCRIPTION Spirits Falls is a two-section waterfall in the Jacob Hill Reservation—yet another waterfall lying on property managed by the Trustees of Reservation. No single part of the falls is more than 10 feet high, but collectively the outflow from Little Pond drops a total of 80 feet. It is not really worthy as a single-destination trip, as this waterfall is seasonal and rather unspectacular, but a trip to Spirit Falls can be combined with visits to other natural features in the area—specifically, Doane's Falls and Royalston Falls, which we do recommend.

You are going to want to leave the children home for this one. The trail is confusing at times, poison ivy can be found in some spots, biting bugs seem to have every inch of trail covered, and steep scrambling is required if the entire falls are to be explored. Do not bother bringing your camera on this hike, either—use up your film at other nearby waterfalls.

TRAIL INFORMATION From the parking lot, follow the trail down the path in front of you. After 5 or 10 minutes you will come to a small and muddy body of water (not exactly a swamp). The trail is confusing here. Simply take a right and start looking for the yellow circles and arrows that will guide you the rest of the way.

The first set of falls is marked with a sign. Many people see this 40-foot section of the waterfall and assume their trip is complete. They are mistaken—you have to continue scrambling to see the other 40-foot section.

It is important to watch the tree markers on this trail. You could easily get confused and take one of the less traveled side paths. When we visited during the muddy season, some rotten logs had been placed to assist us across the mud swamp. Prepare for the worst if you visit in spring—you may end up getting dirty. A little mud is not such a bad thing, but certainly worth noting before you drag your family to this waterfall.

DIRECTIONS From the junction of MA 2 and MA 68 in Gardner, take MA 68 west. Continue for 5.4 miles past the ROYALSTON TOWN LINE sign. Take a left into the parking area for the Jacob Hill Reservation. This parking area is 0.7 mile north of the center of Royalston. The parking area for Spirit Falls is also located 0.8 mile south of Falls Road, which leads to nearby Royalston Falls. *To get to Gardner,* take MA 2 west from Boston or MA 2 east from North Adams.

OTHER WATERFALLS NEARBY Royalston Falls, Doane's Falls, Bear's Den Falls.

Tannery Falls

74

TANNERY FALLS

Savoy, Savoy Mountain State Forest, Berkshire County

Type: Plunges, cascades, and slides
Height: 60 feet, 75 feet, others
ranging 5–20 feet
Trail Length: 0.5 mile
Water Source: Ross Brook and
Parker Brook
Altitude Gain/Loss: –150 feet

Difficulty: Easy side of moderate
Hiking Time: 20 minutes
DeLorme Map: Page 21, H-25
Rating: ★★★★

DESCRIPTION (HIGHLY RECOMMENDED) Tannery Falls is located in an area we would like to call waterfall country. Within a square mile almost a dozen waterfalls, many worthy of their own pages in this guide, lie on the trail network. The main attraction, formally known as Tannery Falls, is a 75-foot series of large plunges and major cascades. The upper 35 feet of these falls is thundering curtain of whitewater, always impressive, even with little water flow. The bottom half of the falls is a series of cascades that end in a pool.

The second largest falls in the area are just off the main trail. They can be seen from the trail as you walk back up, but you have to look carefully. This multisection plunge waterfall descends through an angular gorge. The water remains only 4 to 5 feet wide throughout the long formation. There is also a waterfall seconds from the parking lot, accessible by bushwhacking on a primitive path to the left of the main trail. This trail leads to a segmented waterfall, very similar in structure to that of Bear's Den Falls, only smaller in size and about half as powerful.

Altogether Tannery Falls and the nearly dozen unnamed plunges and cascades that adorn Ross Brook and Parker Brook offer one of the top "off-the-beaten-path" treasures in the region. Try to budget several hours when you plan a trip to this special place.

TRAIL INFORMATION From the parking lot, head straight down the wide trail that is marked with blue blazes. This trail will bring you to the bottom of the largest waterfall, passing many small cascades along the way. After about 8 to 10 minutes, wooden stairs will lead you to metal wire fencing and a view from the top of the falls. Continue right and follow the trail to the bottom of the falls for a much different view. About 100 feet before you reach the bottom, take a right and walk off the main trail for about 50 feet; you will see another 60-foot waterfall, first viewed as you come around a corner.

A small, narrow trail to the left side of the parking lot leads to another waterfall, only 100 feet or so down the trail. This is the waterfall you can hear from the parking lot.

DIRECTIONS From Greenfield, take MA 2 west into the town of Florida. Make a left turn onto Black Brook Road just before you reach the FLORIDA TOWN LINE sign. No street sign is posted, so look for the town line sign. If you are traveling east on MA 2 from North Adams, take a right onto Black Brook Road just after you pass the SAVOY TOWN LINE sign. Travel on Black Brook Road for 2.5 miles, forking right after 1.3 miles, and take a right onto Tannery Road, a dirt road. After 0.7 mile, turn right onto another dirt road; the parking lot, marked by a sign for TANNERY FALLS, will soon appear.

OTHER WATERFALLS NEARBY Twin Cascades, Windsor Jambs, Wahconah Falls, Hudson Brook Chasm.

Trap Falls

75

TRAP FALLS

Ashby, Willard Brook State Forest, Middlesex County

Type: Plunges
Height: 10–12 feet each
Trail Length: 0.1 mile
Water Source: Trapfall Brook
Altitude Gain/Loss: None

Difficulty: Easy
Hiking Time: 5 minutes
DeLorme Map: Page 26, E-9
Rating: ★★★★½

DESCRIPTION (HIGHLY RECOMMENDED) A favorite hangout spot for local residents, Trap Falls is sure to please anyone who ventures into Willard Brook State Forest. Found in an extremely picturesque setting, Trap Falls is much more impressive than its size would indicate. It consists of three plunges lined up side by side. The center fall is slightly higher than the others, and is shaped like a punchbowl. To help visualize the waterfall, picture a minigolf hole with three paths leading to the golf hole below. This waterfall would definitely be one of the attractions on the course.

We suggest spending a few hours here. Bring a picnic (there are plenty of picnic tables near the falls) or start a barbecue in one of the many fire pits. Although probably crowded in summer, this is one waterfall you absolutely cannot miss. Your children will love it as well; remember a camera to capture the smiles on their faces. The park closes daily at 8 PM.

TRAIL INFORMATION From the parking lot, walk parallel to the river on a wooded road for 0.1 mile to the falls. You should be able to hear the falls from the parking lot.

DIRECTIONS From the junction of MA 2 and MA 13 in Leominster, take MA 13 north for 10.3 miles to the town of Townsend, where you will want to take a left onto MA 119 west. Travel on MA 119 west for 3.9 miles; the parking lot for the falls will be on your right. The parking area is 0.2 mile past the Willard Brook State Forest Ranger Station.

OTHER WATERFALLS NEARBY None.

76

TWIN CASCADES

Florida, Berkshire County

Type: Plunges and cascades
Height: 80 feet and 60 feet
Trail Length: 0.3 mile
Water Source: Cascade Brook
Altitude Gain/Loss: +80 feet

Difficulty: Moderate side of difficult
Hiking Time: 15 minutes
DeLorme Map: Page 21, E-25&26
Rating: ★★★★½

DESCRIPTION (HIGHLY RECOMMENDED) This is one of the more popular falls of Massachusetts, due to the other outdoor attractions of the area. Nearby the falls is intense and challenging whitewater kayaking, rock climbing, and hiking. Of particular interest to us are the kayakers. Even on cold, rainy days, such as the day we visited Twin Cascades, there can be a slew of devoted paddlers on the Deerfield River—definitely fun to watch.

Twin Cascades

Twin Cascades, as the name suggests, is composed of two waterfalls. The falls collectively tumble in the shape of a Y. The waterfall on the right is a 60-foot multisection plunge with cascades at the bottom; the waterfall on the left is very similar, except 20 feet taller. Even at the best viewpoints, you cannot see the top of the falls because the water comes from around a corner and the gorge blocks your view. From your relative position it is hard to imagine that a long river lies behind this mammoth rock wall. Even from the trailhead, there is not a mountain to be seen that could possess a brook with such water volume.

Trail dangers prevent this waterfall from receiving a five-star rating. In addition to having difficulty ourselves on the trail, we watched several other hikers with the same problems: The trail is so narrow that your feet often slip, and you begin to slide down the embankment toward the brook. Be sure to bring hiking shoes in good condition, and trekking poles if you have them. If you are confident with your scrambling abilities, this waterfall should not be missed.

TRAIL INFORMATION From the parking lot facing the train tracks, walk over the tracks and take a left. Walk in the woods parallel to the tracks. The area surrounding the tracks is private property, so do not walk along the tracks themselves. The trail, which is a mere 0.3 mile in length, begins to the right of the train tunnel. Take note that the trail is not for amateur hikers: It is steep, often muddy, and very slippery. There are many fallen trees and a rock wall to climb over. At some points the trail is only a foot wide, and directly to its right is a 40-foot cliff falling into the ravine below. Be extra careful if you decide to visit this waterfall.

Also, be particularly careful around the falls themselves. You will be tempted to find alternate viewpoints. If you do, take note that the area is heavily covered with moss and therefore very slippery. Many trees on the mountainside are loosely rooted, ready to be ripped out with a small amount of force; do not trust all of your weight on them.

DIRECTIONS From North Adams, take MA 2 east, heading toward Charlemont. Continue on MA 2 east for 3.0 miles past the CHARLEMONT TOWN LINE sign and take a left onto Zoar Road. This is a wide turn and marked by only a small sign, so look carefully. If you are traveling from Greenfield, take MA 2 west, heading toward Charlemont. Continue on MA 2 west for 1.6 miles past its junction with MA 8A south and take a right onto Zoar Road. Follow Zoar Road for 2.5 miles and turn left onto River Road. Travel on River Road for 4.6 miles; the parking area will be on your left just before a set of railroad tracks. There is plenty of space.

OTHER WATERFALLS NEARBY Hudson Brook Chasm, Tannery Falls, Money Brook Falls, March Cataract Falls, Deer Hill Falls.

77

WAHCONAH FALLS

Dalton, Wahconah Falls State Park, Berkshire County

Type: Cascades
Height: 40-foot total drop
Trail Length: 0.2 mile
Water Source: Wahconah Falls Brook
Altitude Gain/Loss: –30 feet

Difficulty: Easy
Hiking Time: Not applicable
DeLorme Map: Page 33, A-18
Rating: ★★★★½

DESCRIPTION (HIGHLY RECOMMENDED) The state of Massachusetts has several waterfall state parks, including Bash Bish Falls State Park, in the southwestern corner of the state; Campbell Falls State Park, near the Connecticut-Massachusetts state line; and Wahconah Falls State Park, the highlight of this chapter.

Wahconah Falls lies in the heart of the Berkshires, close to the waterfalls of Mount Greylock State Reservation as well as Windsor Jambs, Tannery Falls, Glendale Falls, and Lulu Cascade. Because of its central location, Wahconah's picnic facilities provide for a more-than-suitable lunch stop before finishing out the rest of your day trip. There are picnic tables, restroom facilities, grills, and fields for visitors. As a bonus, the small pools in the clean waters of Wahconah Falls Brook offer refreshing wading and even swimming. We expect this state park to be quite popular on summer weekends, judging by the size of the parking lot.

TRAIL INFORMATION From the parking lot, walk past the gate, head down the embankment, and walk past the picnic area to the falls.

DIRECTIONS From the junction of US 7 and MA 9 in Pittsfield, take MA 9 east. Continue on MA 9 east for 2.2 miles beyond the spot where MA 8A joins in Dalton. Take a right onto North Street, drive 0.1 mile, and fork right onto Wahconah Falls Road. After 0.3 mile, the parking lot will be on your right.

OTHER WATERFALLS NEARBY Windsor Jambs, Tannery Falls, Lulu Cascade, Glendale Falls.

78

WINDSOR JAMBS
Windsor, Windsor State Forest, Berkshire County

Type: Cascades
Height: 50-foot total drop
Trail Length: 0.1 mile
Water Source: Windsor Jambs Brook
Altitude Gain/Loss: –50 feet

Difficulty: Easy
Hiking Time: Not applicable
DeLorme Map: Page 21, N-26
Rating: ★★

DESCRIPTION Windsor State Forest is not known for the cascading waters at Windsor Jambs that travel through an 80-foot-high perpendicular gorge. The state forest is a popular day-use area for swimming in the Westfield River during summer, hunting in fall, and cross-country skiing and snowmobiling in winter. Many visitors do not realize that a powerful set of cascades lies less than a mile away from the main parking lot along the side of the Westfield River.

Although the gorge is interesting and the brook can be very powerful, especially in springtime, Windsor Jambs' natural beauty lies constrained by a green fence that surrounds all vantage points of the gorge. The Jambs area also receives very little sun, and viewing is limited to the top. For these reasons we gave the Jambs a rather low rating. You will enjoy your visit more if you explore what the rest of the state forest has to offer.

TRAIL INFORMATION The trail follows a green chain-link fence that begins at the parking lot. We are not sure whether accessing the falls from the gorge below is possible, but our guess would be that such a hike would be dangerous, and thus most likely prohibited.

DIRECTIONS From the junction of US 7 and MA 9 in Pittsfield, take MA 9 east. Continue on MA 9 as MA 8A joins up with it, then splits off. At 0.5 mile beyond the point where MA 8A splits away, take a left onto West Main Street. After 0.1 mile, turn left onto River Road. Follow

River Road for 2.3 miles and you will pass the WINDSOR STATE FOREST sign. Here is where it gets a little tricky. When you see the headquarters and a large parking area, you need to take a right onto a dirt road. The parking area you will see is not near the falls. Travel on this new dirt road for 0.6 mile, going straight through an intersection at 0.3 mile. At the end of 0.6 mile, you will see a sign pointing right for the JAMBS. Take a right here; the parking area will be just up the road on your right.

OTHER WATERFALLS NEARBY Tannery Falls, Wahconah Falls, Twin Cascades, Chapel Brook Falls.

IV. New Hampshire

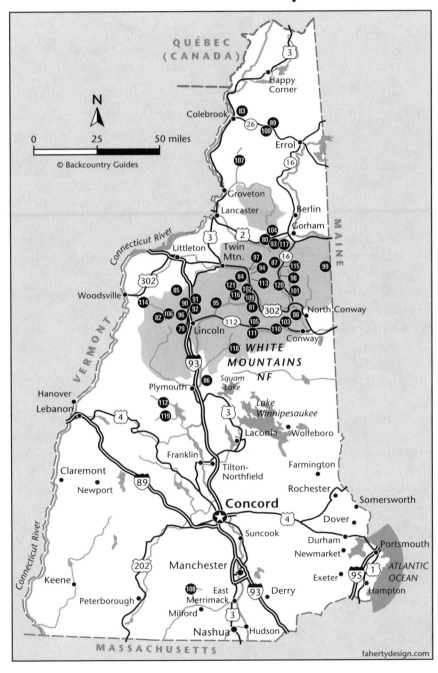

QUÉBEC (CANADA)

N

0   25   50 miles

© Backcountry Guides

Happy Corner

Colebrook
83
26
89
100
Errol

107

16

Groveton
Lancaster
Berlin
Gorham

Connecticut River

104
Littleton
80
93
117
Twin Mtn.
97
16
94
87
115
99
98
84
113
120
101
121
102
116
109
85
90
91
95
81
302
114
92
88
North Conway
Woodsville
82
106
96
112
79
Lincoln
105
110
103
111
Conway

118
WHITE
MOUNTAINS
NF

93

86
Squam Lake

Plymouth

112
Lake
119
Winnipesaukee

3

Hanover
Laconia
Wolfeboro
Lebanon

4
Franklin

Farmington

Claremont
Tilton-
Newport
Northfield

Rochester
Somersworth

Concord

4
Dover

Suncook
Durham
Newmarket
Portsmouth

89
Manchester
95
ATLANTIC
OCEAN

202
Exeter
1

Keene
108
East
93
Derry
Hampton
Peterborough
Merrimack
Milford
3
Nashua
Hudson

MASSACHUSETTS

VERMONT

MAINE

Connecticut River

302

2

3

fahertydesign.com

79

AGASSIZ BASIN

Woodstock, Grafton County

Type: Plunges
Height: 10 feet and 5 feet
Trail Length: Less than 0.1 mile
Water Source: Mount Moosi-
lauke Brook
Altitude Gain/Loss: None

Difficulty: Easy
Hiking Time: Not applicable
DeLorme Map: Page 43, J-11
Rating: ★★½

DESCRIPTION Agassiz Basin is named for Louis Agassiz, a Swiss scientist credited by many with the discovery of the Ice Age. It is located just behind Govoni's Restaurant. Two small falls can be found here. Although the waterfalls are by no means large or of striking beauty, the surrounding area is of historical and geological interest. The waters of the gorge created a gap about 6 feet wide that is known as Indian Leap. There are legends that Native Americans used to jump across the gap as a test of courage. Also of particular interest are the deep, circular potholes and the deep, dark pools in the river.

TRAIL INFORMATION The falls are located behind Govoni's Restaurant. Follow any of the trails that lead behind the restaurant to the brook.

DIRECTIONS From I-93 in Lincoln, take exit 32. Turn onto NH 112 west, heading toward Woodsville. Continue traveling on NH 112 west for 1.7 miles past the junction of US 3 and NH 112. The falls are located behind Govoni's Restaurant. Look for the sign for AGASSIZ BASIN & INDIAN LEAP. Take note that parking at the restaurant is for customers only after 4 PM.

OTHER WATERFALLS NEARBY Beaver Brook Cascades, Paradise Falls, Swiftwater Falls (Bath), Georgiana Falls, Falls on the Flume-Pool Loop.

80

APPALACHIA WATERFALLS

*Randolph, White Mountain National Forest,
Coos County*

Type: Horsetails and cascades
Height: Varies (see notes)
Trail Length: 2.6-mile loop
Water Source: Cold Brook and
Snyder Brook
Altitude Gain/Loss: Up 300 feet,
down 300 feet

Difficulty: Easy side of moderate
Hiking Time: 90 minutes
DeLorme Map: Page 48, I-6
Rating: ★★★★

DESCRIPTION This takes you to four waterfalls fed by two mountain streams that drain waters from Mount Adams and Mount Madison. Gordon Falls is the first stop on this 2.6-mile loop trail. A fanning low-angled cascade about 18 feet tall, Gordon is a well-shaded treat just downstream from where the Maple Walk meets Snyder Brook. There are several shallow pools for wading here.

Next is Salroc Falls. Lower Salroc Falls consists of many small cascades, a long slide, and, finally, a short plunge into a large, cold, and clear pool. Upper Salroc Falls is a few feet upstream. Here Snyder Brook horsetails down moss-covered rocks, then slides into a calm pool. Be sure to rock-hop across the brook to the table rock in front of the falls for the best view and greatest chance for a fine photograph.

Tama Falls, the third waterfall of the trip, is just upstream from Salroc Falls. The final falls on Snyder Brook to be described here, Tama Falls is a 40-foot-tall combination of a block and a set of steep cascades. The view from the trail is not sufficient for this waterfall; be sure to follow one of several paths down to the brook. From here you witness a much more visually appealing waterfall, and as a bonus you can very often find yourself hidden from the crowded trail above.

Cold Brook Falls marks the last stop of the hike, yet is the first and only waterfall of Cold Brook on this trip. Cold Brook crashes down a wide, terraced 30-foot wall into a dark pool. Although there are several modest swimming holes at the other falls of this trip, swimming is prohibited at Cold Brook Falls, as the water is Randolph's water supply.

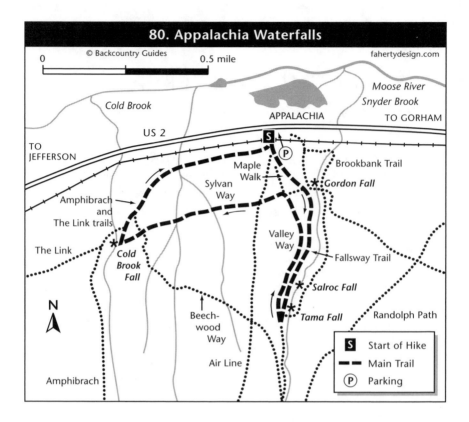

In addition to Gordon, Salroc, Tama, and Cold Brook Falls, more than half a dozen other waterfalls can be found farther up the trails that travel parallel to Cold Brook and Snyder Brook on the way to Mount Madison and Mount Adams. Although these are not described here, many are quite impressive and provide excellent challenges for experienced hikers. For those interested, this route is described more comprehensively in the Bolnicks' *Waterfalls of the White Mountains*.

TRAIL INFORMATION The trail begins at the center of the large parking lot for APPALACHIA. Follow the path beyond the trail information boards, cross the remnants of a set of railroad tracks, and arrive at the Air Line junction. The Air Line Trail will continue right, while you continue straight for a short distance until you reach a sign for the MAPLE WALK. At this junction, the Valley Way Trail forks right and the Maple Walk forks left. Veer left and continue until you reach Snyder Brook and several trail signs.

To reach Gordon Falls, you will need to proceed downstream 100 feet.

After visiting Gordon Falls, backtrack 100 feet upstream to the junction you were just at. From here, proceed upstream on the Fallsway Trail, signed FALLSWAY TOWARD TAMA FALL. Marked yellow, the Fallsway Trail will lead you 0.25 mile to Lower and Upper Salroc Falls. After passing the upper falls, continue climbing along the Fallsway for about 200 feet to another junction. Fork left onto the Tama Fall Loop; Tama Falls will be a short distance ahead.

After visiting Tama Falls, return to the junction you were just at and this time, fork left onto the Valley Way Trail (the right fork would lead you back to Salroc and Gordon Falls). Travel along the blue-blazed Valley Way Trail for 0.3 mile and take a left onto the Sylvan Way. Be sure to stop at each trail junction to spot the inconspicuous trail signs; this one is currently placed on a tree behind you. Continue on the yellow-blazed Sylvan Way, crossing two very skinny brooks and hiking straight through two irrelevant trail junctions. Soon you will reach Cold Brook, and the last waterfall of the trip will be just to your left, a few feet upstream.

To get back to the parking lot from Cold Brook Falls, follow the yellow-blazed trail directly downstream (do not cross Cold Brook at any time). In a few seconds you will reach an oddly constructed half-wooden, half-stone bridge on your left. Instead of crossing the bridge, take a right turn onto the Amphibrach Trail. This trail parallels the highway, which you will hear but not see. After a 15-minute trek along the Amphibrach Trail, you will reach a T-junction. Take a left and, a minute later, another left onto the Valley Way Trail. The parking lot is just ahead and the 2.6-mile loop will be completed.

SPECIAL NOTE The trails used to visit the four waterfalls of Appalachia are located in one of the most complex and confusing trail networks we have found in our travels. We urge you to purchase either "DeLorme's White Mountain National Forest Trail Map" or "AMC Map #1: The Presidential Range" in addition to our trail description and map.

DIRECTIONS From the junction of US 2 and NH 16 in Gorham, take US 2 west and continue for 0.8 mile past the Pinkham B Road (which leads to Dolly Copp Campground and several other waterfalls described in this book). Turn left into a large parking lot marked with a sign for APPALACHIA and several U.S. Forest Service HIKING signs. The parking lot is 2.1 miles east of Lowe's Store on US 2. *To get to Gorham,* take NH 16 north from Conway.

OTHER WATERFALLS NEARBY Mossy Glen, Falls on the Howker Ridge Path, Triple Falls.

81

ARETHUSA FALLS

Harts Location, White Mountain National Forest, Carroll County

Type: Plunge

Height: Approximately 160 feet

Trail Length: 1.5 miles

Water Source: Bemis Brook

Altitude Gain/Loss: +800 feet

Difficulty: Moderate

Hiking Time: 60 minutes

DeLorme Map: Page 44, F-4

Rating: ★★★★★

DESCRIPTION (HIGHLY RECOMMENDED) Discounting the seasonal waterfalls, our research indicates that Arethusa Falls is the single longest drop in New England. Its exact height, however, is of great controversy. We have come across sources stating that Arethusa is anywhere from 125 feet to "well over 200 feet in height." Several other experts believe the falls to be about 160 feet, with which we agree.

This multitiered plunge appears to descend from the sky. From the trail and the bottom viewpoints, you cannot see anything above the falls aside from a few trees on the side of the river. What you do see is a rather graceful expression of Bemis Brook. The streams of water are far from being considered powerful, but their beauty makes this waterfall a must-visit.

Over the years we have seen many people—not ordinarily the hiking type—who struggle on the trail just to have the chance to see Arethusa Falls. They may be exhausted along the trail, but we have never seen anything short of a relieved smile at the waterfall. Everyone appears deeply content when they finally reach the falls. Arethusa Falls becomes, in a nutshell, a job well done for all who witness its graceful beauty.

TRAIL INFORMATION Walk toward the house at the end of the parking lot. Just before you reach it, cross a set of railroad tracks; the trailhead will be on your left. The blue-marked Arethusa Falls Trail will lead you to Arethusa Falls. About 0.2 mile after entering the woods, the Bemis Brook Trail will fork left and lead you past Fawn Pool, Coliseum Falls, and Bemis Brook Falls. This yellow-marked trail rejoins the trail to Arethusa Falls farther up, so it is worth taking either on the way to Arethusa Falls or on your trip back down.

Arethusa Falls

Some visitors have chosen to risk their lives by scrambling up the face of the falls. This is quite foolish and has resulted in tragedy in the past. We remind you that no scramble is worth risking your life.

Arethusa Falls requires a hike of 60 minutes each way, involves crossing over many roots and several brooks, and has muddy sections throughout the year. Do not worry, though; your first sight of the mighty Arethusa Falls is sure to justify your hiking efforts.

DIRECTIONS From the junction of US 302 and NH 16 in the village of Bartlett known as Glen, take US 302 west for 13.4 miles. Turn left onto Arethusa Falls Road and follow it to the parking lot at the end of the road. Arethusa Falls Road is 3.3 miles east of the Willey House Historical Site on US 302. *To get to Glen,* take NH 16 north from Conway.

OTHER WATERFALLS NEARBY Ripley Falls, Nancy Cascades, Kedron Flume, Silver Cascade, Flume Cascade.

82

BEAVER BROOK CASCADES

Woodstock, White Mountain National Forest, Grafton County

Type: Horsetails and cascades

Height: Approximately 400-foot total drop

Trail Length: To lower falls, 0.4 mile; to upper falls, 1.1 miles

Water Source: Beaver Brook

Altitude Gain/Loss: +1,200 feet

Difficulty: Moderate

Hiking Time: 60 minutes to upper falls

DeLorme Map: Page 43, I-9

Rating: ★★★★½

DESCRIPTION (HIGHLY RECOMMENDED) The Beaver Brook Trail runs past set after set of unnamed cascades as it climbs several thousand feet to its termination at the summit of 4,802-foot-tall Mount Moosilauke. As you ascend the steep and moderately difficult trail, the cascades seem to become more impressive, with the final one being our favorite. Nearly every classification of waterfall is represented along this chain, including horsetails, plunges, and slides. For this reason, and more, we highly recommend this hike.

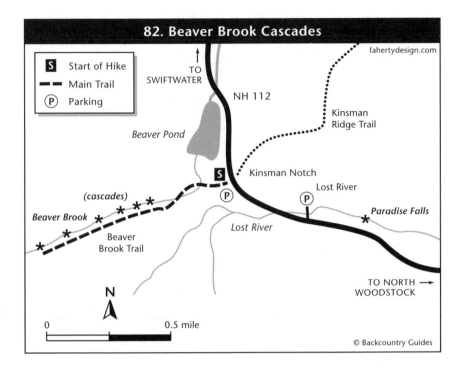

82. Beaver Brook Cascades

fahertydesign.com

S Start of Hike
Main Trail
P Parking

TO SWIFTWATER

NH 112

Beaver Pond

Kinsman Ridge Trail

Kinsman Notch

Lost River

(cascades)

Beaver Brook

Beaver Brook Trail

Lost River

Paradise Falls

TO NORTH WOODSTOCK

N

0   0.5 mile

© Backcountry Guides

With the right combination of ability and time you can venture to the heavily windblown summit of Mount Moosilauke, an 8-mile round trip. If you like the idea of hiking past scenic waterfalls en route to a 4,000-foot-plus mountain summit, check out the Falls on the Falling Waters Trail. That trail will lead you past three waterfalls, with an option to walk the famous Franconia Ridge Trail to the peak of Mount Lafayette, more than 5,000 feet above sea level.

TRAIL INFORMATION Enter the woods behind the White Mountain National Forest billboard and pay station. Within a few feet you approach a T-junction. Take a left and continue along the white-blazed Beaver Brook Trail, which is a rugged, steep stretch of the Appalachian Trail. About 0.1 mile from the parking area you must cross Beaver Brook several times over solidly constructed footbridges. A few minutes farther on you will arrive at a sign outlining the destinations and distances of the Beaver Brook Trail, as well as a notice stating that the TRAIL IS EXTREMELY ROUGH. From this point to the bottom of the falls is 0.3 mile; to the Beaver Brook Shelter, 1.5 miles; and to the summit of Mount Moosilauke, 3.8 miles.

Continue beyond the trail signs to the first major display of cascades at 0.4 mile. The trail crosses a rock platform with many rest-stop opportunities available on flat rock surfaces. Continue climbing, very steeply at times, along the left bank of the brook. About 0.2 mile farther, plus an additional 200 feet of elevation gain, there is another display of cascades.

Do not give up on this killer energy climb quite yet; more falls, with different structures and character, lie ahead. Just past the second set of cascades, at 0.7 mile, you will ascend a 20-foot rock wall. This can be potentially challenging to your upper-body strength, though fortunately you will find nicely placed wooden blocks and a series of metal handrails for climbing assistance. As you step up the last wooden block, the third set of waterfalls unfolds itself.

By now you may want to quit; after all, you have seen hundreds of feet of waterfalls and climbed roughly 700 feet of altitude. We urge you to continue the rest of the way to the charming upper cascades. Our favorite is just ahead, about 0.1 mile beyond the rock wall you just ascended.

The entire trail is quite a calorie burner: In just over a mile of hiking, you gain more than 1,200 feet of altitude. This may sound too difficult for your tastes, but as long as you do not attempt the hike in early spring, when the trail is soaked with waterfall mist and snow runoff, your trip to this waterfall is completely manageable, and not even close to the most difficult hikes described in this guidebook.

OPTIONAL HIKE Instead of just visiting the lovely cascades on Beaver Brook, venture to the summit of Mount Moosilauke, where you can enjoy outstanding views of New Hampshire, Vermont, and even New York on clear days.

Expect rugged, steep terrain for the entire 4.0 miles from the trailhead to the 360-degree views from the 4,802-foot mountaintop. The altitude gain is 3,100 feet, and the expected round-trip time is about six hours for the average hiker. The final stretch of the trail is above tree line, meaning that you will be exposed to potential weather hazards any time of year, including the notoriously strong wind currents. This is another White Mountain National Forest mountain that should only be climbed during good to great weather conditions.

DIRECTIONS From I-93 in North Woodstock, take exit 32. Follow NH 112 west for 6.0 miles beyond its junction with US 3. Pull into the parking lot marked with a TRAILHEAD PARKING sign. This lot is 0.4 mile west of the Lost River Reservation. *To get to North Woodstock,* take I-93 north from Concord, or I-93 south from Franconia.

OTHER WATERFALLS NEARBY Paradise Falls, Agassiz Basin, Swiftwater Falls (Bath), Georgiana Falls, Falls on the Flume-Pool Loop.

83

BEAVER BROOK FALLS

Colebrook, Beaver Brook Falls Natural Area,
Coos County

Type: Horsetail

Height: 50 feet

Trail Length: Roadside

Water Source: Beaver Brook

Altitude Gain/Loss: None

Difficulty: Easy

Hiking Time: Not applicable

DeLorme Map: Page 50, A-2

Rating: ★★★★½

DESCRIPTION (HIGHLY RECOMMENDED) As you are driving along NH 145 past the center of the town in Colebrook, you will travel up and down slight hills, yet no great changes in elevation. The land is flat like the countryside, making it difficult to imagine that a waterfall more than 50 feet in height could be located here. Just as you come around a bend in the road, however, look to your right; you will be instantly mesmerized by the sheer size of the dribbling horsetails at Beaver Brook Falls.

Also surprising is the number of visitors to a waterfall located in northern New Hampshire, well past the White Mountain National Forest region and only a few miles from the Canadian border. The area is popular enough for the state to declare the site Beaver Brook Falls Scenic Area and equip the park with several covered picnic tables and bathrooms.

TRAIL INFORMATION To view this waterfall, you have the option of sitting in your car, relaxing at the picnic tables, or taking a short gravel trail closer to the falls. This trail brings you to a tilted-head view at the base of the falls; steep, loose-dirt trails climb both sides. This can be dangerous, so use caution if you try to reach the top of the waterfall.

DIRECTIONS From the junction of US 3 and NH 145 in Colebrook, take NH 145 north for 2.4 miles, and the parking lot will be on your right. The falls can be easily seen from the road. *To get to Colebrook,* take US 3 north from Lincoln.

OTHER WATERFALLS NEARBY Dixville Flume, Huntington Cascades, Pond Brook Falls.

Beaver Brook Falls

84

BEECHER AND PEARL CASCADES

Bethlehem, White Mountain National Forest, Grafton County

Type: Horsetail, cascades, and a fan
Height: 35-foot horsetail, 20-foot fan
Trail Length: To Beecher Cascade, 0.4 mile; to Pearl Cascade, 0.5 mile
Water Source: Crawford Brook
Altitude Gain/Loss: +200 feet to Pearl Cascade

Difficulty: Easy
Hiking Time: 20 minutes
DeLorme Map: Page 44, C-3
Rating: ★★★★

DESCRIPTION Beecher and Pearl Cascades are two falls located on Crawford Brook, a mountain steam that drains the waters of Mount Field. The first waterfall, Beecher Cascade—a 35-foot horsetail hidden under heavy tree cover—is encompassed by gorge walls of pink-brown Conway granite. Opportunities for exploring and photography are extremely limited here, so be sure to head a few hundred feet farther up the trail to Pearl Cascade, a 20-foot-tall fan. Below the fan, water enters a gorge and becomes trapped in a jagged-edged pothole, creating one of the most delightful small swimming pools in the White Mountains. About 4 or 5 feet deep, this colorful pool—with hues of brown, pink, yellow, green, and black to be found—is the perfect refreshing treat for two or three people.

    TRAIL INFORMATION The trail to both falls begins across the railroad tracks behind the Crawford Depot Station. After entering the woods, you will reach a billboard and a trail junction. The trail to the left climbs Mount Willard and is said to be one of the best short hikes in the area. Continue straight about 200 feet farther and take a left onto the Cascade Loop Trail. About 100 feet up, take a left at the white sign for BEECHER CASCADE. This waterfall will be just ahead, visible through a thick growth of trees. Continue climbing on the Cascade Loop Trail for an additional 0.1 mile and you will reach the white sign for PEARL CASCADE. Take a left and follow a short path down to the brook. Scramble up the brook a few feet for the best view of the falls and to discover a lovely wading spot.

To continue up to the summit of Mount Avalon and Mount Field, climb to the end of the Cascade Loop. The Avalon Trail will proceed upward toward the summits.

DIRECTIONS From the junction of US 302 and NH 16 in the village of Bartlett known as Glen, take US 302 west for 20.5 miles and turn left into the AMC Crawford Depot. This depot is 0.3 mile west of the sign marking the Crawford Notch State Park boundary and 0.3 mile east of Mount Clinton Road. *To get to Glen,* take NH 16 north from Conway.

OTHER WATERFALLS NEARBY Gibbs Falls, Flume Cascade, Silver Cascade, Kedron Flume, Ripley Falls, Arethusa Falls.

85

BRIDAL VEIL FALLS

Franconia, White Mountain National Forest, Grafton County

Type: Plunge and slides
Height: 80-foot total drop
Trail Length: 2.5 miles
Water Source: Coppermine Brook
Altitude Gain/Loss: +1,000 feet

Difficulty: Moderate
Hiking Time: 1 hour, 15 minutes
DeLorme Map: Page 43, E-10
Rating: ★★★★

DESCRIPTION Many visitors may feel they have been to this waterfall before. In actuality, this is one of the most commonly photographed waterfalls in the White Mountains. Pictures of Bridal Veil Falls are scattered across dozens of publications pertaining to the attractions of the White Mountains. Many of these publications hold high praise for this scenic waterfall, and they have reason to.

The major attraction of the falls is the 30-foot-tall main plunge, which does indeed look like a bride's veil. Water elegantly flows at a right angle to a small pool below. The waterfall is transparent, similar to the fabric of a veil. Below this plunge is a large waterslide over flat, polished granite.

With so many other attractions in the White Mountain National Forest requiring only brief access hikes, many will be turned off by the 5-mile round trip that Bridal Veil Falls requires. We encourage you to undertake this healthy hike. Bridal Veil Falls is a fine example of a White Mountain region scenic waterfall, and another great place to relax, sunbathe, and, of course, have a picnic. Perhaps this is why the waterfall is rather highly visited.

TRAIL INFORMATION From any of the parking pull-offs on Coppermine Road, continue up the road on foot until you reach a U.S. Forest Service HIKER sign. Take a left off the road and continue up this trail to the falls. After about 10 minutes of hiking you will reach a sign for the COPPERMINE TRAIL, letting you know you are on the correct path. Although the altitude gain is gradual, the continuous incline of this trail makes it a demanding one for some. It does become slightly steeper and more difficult as you near the falls, especially when you want to advance beyond the first waterslide to the bridal-veil plunge.

DIRECTIONS From Lincoln, take I-93 north to Franconia. Take exit 38 for FRANCONIA/SUGAR HILL. At the end of the off-ramp, turn left, following signs toward NH 116. Continue straight and you will begin to travel on NH 116. After 3.4 miles, take a left onto Coppermine Road (marked by only a COPPERMINE VILLAGE sign). Park on the shoulder before the sign that states NO PARKING BEYOND THIS POINT.

OTHER WATERFALLS NEARBY Falls on the Falling Waters Trail, Falls on the Basin-Cascades Trail, Falls on the Flume-Pool Loop.

86

CAMPTON FALLS
Campton, Grafton County

Type: Block

Height: 15 feet

Trail Length: Less than 0.1 mile

Water Source: Beebe River

Altitude Gain/Loss: −35 feet

Difficulty: Easy side of moderate

Hiking Time: Not applicable

DeLorme Map: Page 39, F-12

Rating: ★★★½

DESCRIPTION Campton Falls is a traditional block waterfall on the

Beebe River. Within a backdrop of several species of pine and hemlock trees, the falls evoke feelings of ruggedness and seclusion, all despite being about 50 feet from the road.

Catch this waterfall if you are ever in the Campton area. You may be surprised to see such a stout and powerful waterfall here, because the road is rather flat and the falls cannot be seen from the road. When you do reach the waterfall, note the two sounds emanating from it: the crash of the block and the gurgling and splashing of the small cascades downstream.

TRAIL INFORMATION The trail begins at the north end of the small parking area. Follow this short trail with caution—it is narrow and can be slippery at times.

DIRECTIONS From Plymouth, take I-93 north to exit 28. Turn onto NH 49 west, heading toward Waterville Valley. Soon you will reach the junction of NH 49 and NH 175. Take a right onto NH 175 south and continue for 3.0 miles, where the unmarked parking area can be found on your left.

OTHER WATERFALLS NEARBY Waterville Cascades.

Campton Falls

87

CRYSTAL CASCADE

Sargents Purchase, White Mountain National Forest, Coos County

Type: Horsetails
Height: 100-foot total drop
Trail Length: 0.3 mile
Water Source: Ellis River
Altitude Gain/Loss: +250 feet

Difficulty: Easy
Hiking Time: 15 minutes
DeLorme Map: Page 44, B-7
Rating: ★★★★

DESCRIPTION Crystal Cascade is an often overlooked waterfall in Pinkham Notch. Too many hikers get caught up tackling Mount Washington to take a break off the Tuckerman's Ravine Trail to view the falls, which are visited by only a fraction of the trail's hikers. Enough traffic is generated, however, for the forest service to post signs prohibiting off-trail hiking.

Directly ahead of a rock-wall outlook, Crystal Cascade drops a total of 100 feet in two uneven steps that are split by a platform with a shallow dark pool. The upper falls are approximately 70 feet in height, and the lower, 30 feet.

Whether you are shopping, dining, staying the night at the AMC Pinkham Notch Visitor Center, or driving along NH 16, stop and give Crystal Cascade a few moments of your time. Your goal in hiking Mount Washington should not be to get to the top as quickly as you can, but to enjoy the beauty of the wilderness.

TRAIL INFORMATION Head past the front entrance of the visitors center and take a right. Directly behind the center are bathrooms and a sign for the TUCKERMAN'S RAVINE TRAIL. Follow this modest uphill trail 0.3 mile to a rock staircase on your right. The only spot to view the falls is just ahead.

OPTIONAL HIKE If you are in decent physical shape, have at least eight hours to spare, and, most importantly, the weather forecast is in your favor, consider continuing the additional 3.7 miles beyond Crystal Cascade to the 6,288-foot summit of the Northeast's tallest peak, Mount Washington. From the waterfall to the summit you will gain approximately 4,000 feet of altitude. This significant climb should not be underestimated.

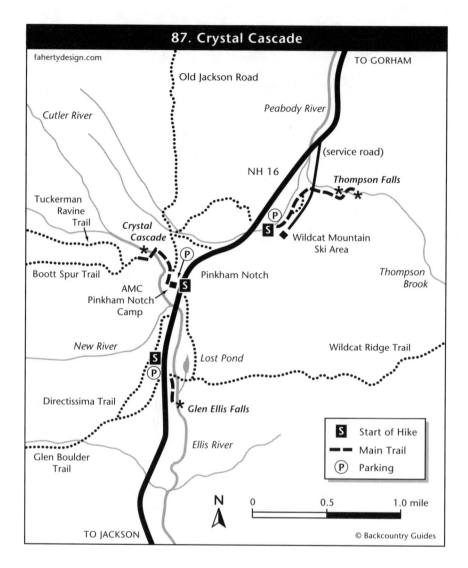

87. Crystal Cascade

fahertydesign.com

TO GORHAM

Old Jackson Road

Cutler River

Peabody River

(service road)

NH 16

Thompson Falls

Tuckerman
Ravine
Trail

Crystal
Cascade

P

S

Wildcat Mountain
Ski Area

Thompson
Brook

Boott Spur Trail

P

S

Pinkham Notch

AMC
Pinkham Notch
Camp

New River

Wildcat Ridge Trail

S

Lost Pond

P

Directissima Trail

Glen Ellis Falls

Ellis River

Glen Boulder
Trail

S	Start of Hike
– –	Main Trail
P	Parking

N

0   0.5   1.0 mile

TO JACKSON

© Backcountry Guides

As a safety precaution, always check with the visitors center for current information regarding the trail and the weather conditions before setting out on this hike.

DIRECTIONS From the junction of US 302 and NH 16 in the village of Bartlett known as Glen, take NH 16 north and continue until you reach the Pinkham Notch Visitor Center on your left. The visitors center is clearly visible from both directions of the highway. The trail to the falls begins behind the center. *To get to Glen,* take NH 16 north from Conway.

Crystal Cascade

OTHER WATERFALLS NEARBY Thompson Falls, Glen Ellis Falls, Winniweta Falls, Jackson Falls.

88

DIANA'S BATHS

Bartlett, White Mountain National Forest, Carroll County

Type: Plunges, cascades, and slides

Height: Tallest plunge is 12 feet

Trail Length: 0.6 mile

Water Source: Lucy Brook

Altitude Gain/Loss: None

Difficulty: Easy

Hiking Time: 20 minutes

DeLorme Map: Page 45, H-9

Rating: ★★★★½

DESCRIPTION (HIGHLY RECOMMENDED) Diana's Baths is a tantalizing mix of potholes, cascades, slides, and small plunges. For many folks the most attractive features of this area are the refreshing pools and potholes. On a hot summer day, plan to see many children (and their parents) relaxing in the swimming holes of Diana's Baths. Do not worry too much about the popularity, though; there is always enough space to relax and get wet.

Depending on the water volume, Lucy Brook can produce either one plunge or many. During high water, the entire area, swimming holes included, can be engulfed with hammering cascades and plunges. In normal conditions, however, there is only one major waterfall, a 20-foot plunge over granite. In addition to being highly photogenic, this plunge is structured in a way that allows you to stand below its falling waters. This plunge can be too powerful for a human head in spring, but in the drier months of the year it becomes much more people friendly.

Parking for the waterfalls is $3 per vehicle; the annual White Mountain National Forest car pass can also be used here. To make the most out of your visit, bring your family, swimsuits, and cameras. As a bonus, check out nearby Cathedral Ledge, where technical rock climbers can often be seen working their way up it's broad face.

TRAIL INFORMATION The trail you will be using to reach the falls, the Moat Mountain Trail, begins at the end of the parking lot. Identified by yellow markers, this easy trail is fairly flat, wide, and very well maintained. There are several benches along the way.

DIRECTIONS From the junction of NH 16 and NH 302 in Conway, take the combined NH 16 north/NH 302 west for 2.7 miles into the village of North Conway. Turn left onto River Road at a set of traffic lights; after 0.9 mile, it will become West Side Road. Continue on West Side Road for 1.4 miles and the parking area will be on your left. *To get to Conway,* take NH 16 north from Rochester.

OTHER WATERFALLS NEARBY Jackson Falls, Winniweta Falls, Lower Falls, Rocky Gorge.

89

DIXVILLE FLUME
Dixville, Dixville Notch State Park, Coos County

Type: Cascades
Height: 18-foot total drop
Trail Length: Roadside
Water Source: Flume Brook
Altitude Gain/Loss: None

Difficulty: Easy
Hiking Time: Not applicable
DeLorme Map: Page 50, C-6
Rating: ★★★

DESCRIPTION Dixville Notch State Park has two waterfall picnic areas. Huntington Cascades is located toward the south end of the park and described elsewhere in this guide. The other waterfall, Dixville Flume, is a set of three drops in a narrow flume whose maximum width is a mere 12 feet.

The total height of the three drops is about 18 feet—considerably smaller than its neighbor. Because the vertical flume walls prevent most sunlight from ever reaching the pools, they appear to be dirty and dark, though in actuality they are quite clean and clear. Perhaps the lack of sunshine is the reason why this area often seems to be bug infested, even when other trails in the area are insect-free.

TRAIL INFORMATION The Dixville Flume is just behind a sign at the parking lot that explains the geology of Dixville Notch. During periods of low water, the scope for exploring in the flume is increased.

DIRECTIONS From the junction of US 3 and NH 26 in Colebrook, take NH 26 east, drive 11.4 miles, and turn left into the Flume Brook Picnic Area; this spot is 0.8 mile east of the ENTERING DIXVILLE NOTCH STATE PARK sign. *To get to Colebrook,* take US 3 north from Lincoln.

OTHER WATERFALLS NEARBY Huntington Cascades, Beaver Brook Falls.

90

FALLS ON THE BASIN-CASCADES TRAIL

Lincoln, White Mountain National Forest, Grafton County

Type: Cascades, slides, and small plunges
Height: Varies (see notes)
Trail Length: 1.1 miles
Water Source: Cascade Brook
Altitude Gain/Loss: +500 feet

Difficulty: Easy side of moderate
Hiking Time: 45 minutes
DeLorme Map: Page 43, F&G-11
Rating: ★★★★½

DESCRIPTION (HIGHLY RECOMMENDED) Imagine a mile-long stretch of a brook with several named waterfalls and dozens of large, unnamed cascades. This is Cascade Brook as seen from the Basin-Cascades Trail. Over a stretch of about 1 mile in length, the wide brook drops a total of 600 vertical feet. Although the trail that runs parallel to the stream is one of the most popular in the White Mountains region, there are enough sun-exposed cataracts, cascades, and slides for everyone to be able to claim a private spot for hours.

The major drawing card here is a small waterfall located in "the Basin." Only a few feet tall, these small falls travel down a narrow chute into a deep whirlpool. There is almost always at least one visitor here during all hours of sunlight, even in winter months. This high visitation is far from surprising. Access to the Basin could not be easier: The area is marked by large signs on a major interstate, there is ample parking, and it is located just south of the other tourist-mobbed features of Franconia Notch State Park, such as The Old Man of the Mountain, the Flume, and Cannon Mountain.

Kinsman Falls, Rocky Glen Falls, and a mile of the Basin-Cascades Trail lie beyond the waterfall at the Basin. Kinsman Falls, a segmented set of cascades split by a large boulder resting in the brook, is the first officially named waterfall of the trail, although before Kinsman the path is blessed with unnamed cascades and plunges, many worthy of recognition. Rocky Glen is the final waterfall of the trip: Here Cascade Brook falls roughly 10 feet between small chasm walls into a deep, yellow-colored pool.

For a complete day in the sun with waterfalls, add the waterfalls of the Basin-Cascades Trail to the falls of the Flume-Pool Loop and the sparsely visited lower and upper Georgiana Falls. All are within several driving minutes of each other. Also consider trekking beyond Rocky Glen Falls for 1.8 miles to Lonesome Lake. This small but beautiful lake is spoken very highly of by the frequent local visitors. The summit of Cannon Mountain is another reasonable day-trip opportunity. Be sure to pick up "DeLorme's Map and Guide to the White Mountains," or another topographic map of the area, to plan your destinations.

TRAIL INFORMATION From the parking area, walk down the paved path to the set of waterslides and a bridge. To view the Basin, take a left before the bridge and follow the crowds a few feet down a flat dirt trail to a staircase. To continue on the trail to the Cascade Brook and the other waterfalls in the area, double back to the bridge, cross it, and take a right at the sign pointing toward the BASIN-CASCADES TRAIL. This blue-marked path will climb steadily past many sets of lovely unnamed cascades to Kinsman Falls at 0.6 mile.

When you reach Kinsman Falls, the trail will cross the brook and continue climbing upstream for an additional 0.5 mile to the last waterfall of the trip, Rocky Glen Falls. Take care at this crossing: During high water, we have seen several people slip into the shallow brook and end up scratched and bruised. While not abnormally difficult, crossing the brook often requires balance and patience. Trekking poles come in handy.

The Basin-Cascades Trail is a popular, well-marked, moderate uphill walk past dozens of cascades. The farther you walk, the less crowded the trail will become, especially along the last 0.5 mile—most visitors turn back after reaching Kinsman Falls.

OPTIONAL HIKE Lonesome Lake and the AMC hut located there are both within reasonable distance of the falls on the Basin-Cascades Trail. To reach these remote places, keep climbing up the Basin-Cascades Trail for 0.4 mile beyond Kinsman Falls to its junction with the Cascade Brook

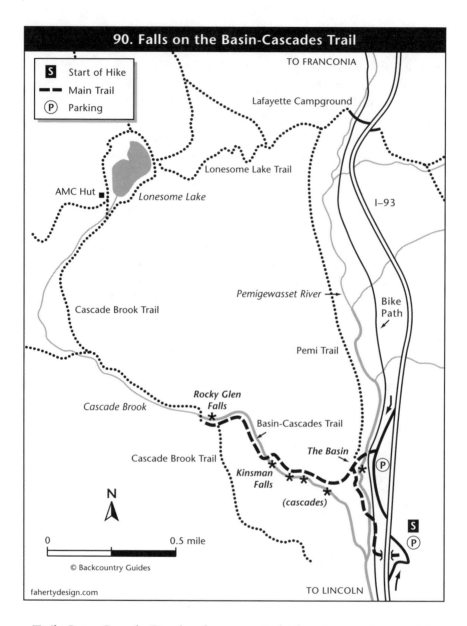

90. Falls on the Basin-Cascades Trail

S Start of Hike
- - Main Trail
(P) Parking

TO FRANCONIA

Lafayette Campground

Lonesome Lake Trail

AMC Hut ■

Lonesome Lake

I–93

Cascade Brook Trail

Pemigewasset River →

Bike
Path

Pemi Trail

Rocky Glen
Falls

Cascade Brook

Basin-Cascades Trail

Cascade Brook Trail

The Basin

(P)

Kinsman
Falls

(cascades)

N
Λ

0   0.5 mile

S
(P)

© Backcountry Guides

fahertydesign.com   TO LINCOLN

Trail. Cross Cascade Brook—dangerous in high water—and turn right. From here it is 1.5 miles to the lake and hut. Once you reach Lonesome Lake, turn left onto the Around the Lake Trail to arrive at the AMC Lonesome Lake Hut, which offers snacks, full meals, and lodging for up to 46 hikers (reservations are recommended).

DIRECTIONS From Lincoln, take I-93 north and continue for 1.5

miles past exit 34A, the exit for the waterfalls at the Flume. Take the exit for THE BASIN. If you are traveling south on I-93 from Franconia, this exit will be 1.2 miles past the Lafayette Place Campground.

OTHER WATERFALLS NEARBY Falls on the Flume-Pool Loop, Falls on the Falling Waters Trail, Georgiana Falls.

91

FALLS ON THE FALLING WATERS TRAIL

Lincoln & Franconia, White Mountain National Forest, Grafton County

Type: Plunges and cascades
Height: 20 feet, 60 feet, and 80 feet
Trail Length: To Swiftwater Falls, 0.9 mile; to Cloudland Falls, 1.4 miles (see notes)
Water Source: Dry Brook
Altitude Gain/Loss: To Swiftwater Falls, +450 feet; to Cloudland Falls, +1,000 feet

Difficulty: To Swiftwater Falls, easy side of moderate; to Cloudland Falls, moderate side of difficult
Hiking Time: 1 hour, 15 minutes to Cloudland Falls
DeLorme Map: Page 43, F-12
Rating: ★★★★★

DESCRIPTION (HIGHLY RECOMMENDED) The Falling Waters Trail is a popular 3.25-mile trail to the summit of Little Haystack Mountain. Along the way are several waterfalls, each with its own personality. Stairs Falls, where Dry Brook plunges down small granite steps into a shallow pool, is the first on this trip. It is also the least crowded, mainly because hikers must venture off the main trail to get a good grasp of this waterfall, whereas the others can be seen directly.

Just a few hundred feet above Stairs Falls is Swiftwater Falls, a 60-foot-high mix of cascades and small plunges. If the trail is crowded, do not count on really enjoying this waterfall. It can be very difficult to navigate around; a visit to Swiftwater Falls is often disappointing because the trail crosses in front of the waterfall. When we visited on Memorial Day week-

Cloudland Falls

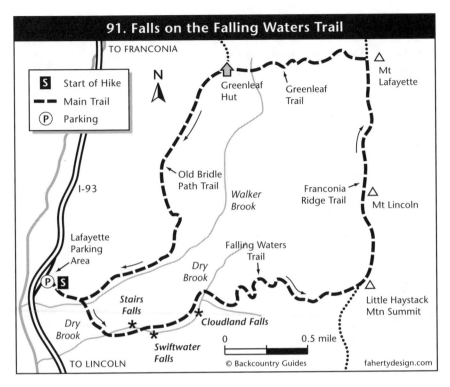

91. Falls on the Falling Waters Trail

TO FRANCONIA

S Start of Hike

--- Main Trail

P Parking

N

Greenleaf
Hut

Greenleaf
Trail

Mt
Lafayette

Old Bridle
Path Trail

I-93

Walker
Brook

Franconia
Ridge Trail

Mt Lincoln

Lafayette
Parking
Area

Falling Waters
Trail

P S

Dry
Brook

Stairs
Falls

Dry
Brook

Cloudland Falls

Little Haystack
Mtn Summit

Swiftwater
Falls

0   0.5 mile

TO LINCOLN

© Backcountry Guides

fahertydesign.com

end, we could barely stop to jot down some notes. Taking out a tripod and snapping a picture was out of the question.

The last waterfall, and by far the main attraction of this trail, is Cloudland Falls, a picturesque fan-type horsetail. Like the other two, this waterfall can be seen from the trail, but the best views are afforded by stepping off the main trail and getting closer. The fanning structure of this waterfall is its most impressive aspect: The width at the top is about 2 feet, while the bottom is about 25 feet across during periods of high water.

TRAIL INFORMATION The Falling Waters Trail begins at the center of the northbound parking area for the Lafayette Campground. Follow the obvious path east into the woods. After 0.2 mile you will reach a fork: On your left is the Old Bridle Path Trail, which leads to the summit of Mount Lafayette via the Greenleaf Trail, while the right fork is the Falling Waters Trail. Follow this blue-marked trail to the three waterfalls.

The first waterfall, Stairs Falls, is approached after 0.8 mile and slightly less than 400 feet of elevation gain. The second, Swiftwater Falls, lies about 75 feet upstream from Stairs Falls. Until now the trail has been an uphill battle with very few trail dangers present. Accessing Cloudland Falls, which is an additional 0.6 mile from Swiftwater Falls, is more challenging. In just over 0.5 mile you will climb nearly 600 vertical feet, cross Dry Brook, and negotiate many steep, muddy sections of terrain.

OPTIONAL HIKE If you are in relatively good shape, the weather forecast is promising, and you have a full day available, follow the rest of the crowd on the Falling Waters Trail to the Franconia Ridge Trail and the 5,260-foot summit of Mount Lafayette for a total round trip of 8.8 miles. Make sure to assess your stamina before considering this optional hike.

If you choose to undertake this extended hike, continue climbing up the Falling Waters Trail beyond Couldland Falls to its terminus at the summit of Little Haystack Mountain. From here, turn left and follow the Franconia Ridge Trail north toward Mount Lincoln and Mount Lafayette. When you reach the summit of Lafayette, 1.8 miles beyond the junction of the Falling Waters and Franconia Ridge Trails, take a left and follow the Greenleaf Trail toward the AMC Greenleaf Hut. At the Greenleaf Hut, take the Old Bridle Path Trail back to the Lafayette parking lot.

Overall the trail is steep and slippery, often for long stretches at a time, and it can remain snowy and icy until late spring. The winds along the ridge can be deadly—be sure the weather forecast is absolutely in your favor before attempting this rigorous hiking loop. With a hefty elevation gain of nearly 4,000 feet, this exhausting endeavor will take the average hiker between six and eight hours to complete.

DIRECTIONS From Lincoln, take I-93 north and continue for 1.5 miles past the parking area for the Basin. Take a right into the parking area for the Lafayette Campground, marked HIKING TRAILS. If you are traveling south on I-93 from Franconia, the Lafayette Campground exit will be on your right approximately 2.0 miles south of the Old Man of the Mountain viewpoints.

OTHER WATERFALLS NEARBY Falls on Basin-Cascades Trail, Falls on the Flume-Pool Loop, Georgiana Falls, Bridal Veil Falls.

92

FALLS ON THE FLUME-POOL LOOP

Lincoln, Franconia Notch State Park, Grafton County

Type: Plunges and cascades

Height: Largest drop is 70 feet

Trail Length: 2.0-mile loop

Water Source: Flume Brook, Cascade Brook, and the Pemigewasset River

Altitude Gain/Loss: Up 200 feet, down 200 feet

Difficulty: Moderate

Hiking Time: 1 hour, 15 minutes

DeLorme Map: Page 43, G-11&12

Rating: ★★★★★

DESCRIPTION (HIGHLY RECOMMENDED) This just may be the most popular waterfall trip in New England. A trip to the Flume-Pool Loop has long been a favorite for families, hikers, photographers, and sightseers. No surprise, considering the variety of natural features offered on the 2-mile loop trail. Along the way you will get your daily dose of waterfalls, covered bridges, glacial boulders, a long flume, and one of the deepest pools below a waterfall around.

The first "waterfall" you visit, Table Rock, is more a slide than a waterfall. Here granite has been weathered by Flume Brook for thousands of years. This waterslide is quite large—about 500 feet long and 75 feet wide.

The next falls is Avalanche Falls, located at 0.7 mile and the climax of the boardwalk within the Flume gorge. Supposedly formed during the great storm of 1883, this waterfall is a major highlight of the hike, and therefore extremely crowded. We had difficultly taking a picture of the falls without fellow visitors in the frame. You will most likely be pushed along the boardwalk trail due to the crowds. If this is so, continue following the trail to the top of the falls, where you can get a less crowded bird's-eye view of this 40-foot-tall plunge.

After Avalanche Falls, continue on the Ridge Path to a short spur trail that leads to a view of Liberty Gorge Cascade—a 70-foot-high, clearwater horsetail. Considerably sunnier than its nearby neighbor, Liberty Gorge Cascade is a more appropriate place for a photograph. Although there is only one viewpoint for the falls, this is a must-see.

Avalanche Falls

The final scenic wonder of the trip is called "The Pool." Very large in size—40 feet deep and 150 feet in diameter—The Pool is located in a deep basin of the Pemigewasset River. Viewpoints from the trail extend around it, offering just about every perspective possible. If swimming were allowed, we would have to consider this one of the top five swimming holes in New England—but "The Pool" is off-limits, probably due both to the intense popularity of the loop and to the difficulty swimmers would have entering and exiting.

TRAIL INFORMATION Begin by paying a modest admission fee at the visitors center and picking up a free trail map.

For the first 0.2 mile of this loop trail, you cross relatively flat, easy terrain. Follow signs toward the GLACIAL BOULDER. Once you reach this fine specimen, take a right onto a trail heading toward THE FLUME. Cross a covered bridge; the Flume boardwalk trail will soon begin. About 0.7 mile past the visitors center, Avalanche Falls will appear just before the Flume boardwalk ends. After relishing the different viewpoint perspectives, continue along the trail to a fork. Veer right here onto the Ridge Path, which will bring you to Liberty Gorge Cascade, The Pool, and finally back to the visitors center. A left here would take you directly back to the visitors center, but you would miss the other attractions of the Flume-Pool Loop.

The Ridge Path will soon take you to a spur path down a 100-foot-long dead-end trail to a head-on view of the Liberty Gorge Cascade. After observing the cascade, continue along the Ridge Path to The Pool. You can then take the Wildwood Trail back to the visitors center.

The entire 2.0-mile trail is meticulously maintained, well-marked, and makes for a pleasant family outing. You should encounter no problems.

DIRECTIONS From Lincoln, take I-93 north to exit 34A. Follow the signs to the FLUME VISITOR CENTER. Both sides of I-93 feature large signs directing you toward THE FLUME.

OTHER WATERFALLS NEARBY Falls on the Basin-Cascades Trail, Falls on the Falling Waters Trail, Georgiana Falls, Agassiz Basin.

93

FALLS ON THE HOWKER RIDGE TRAIL

Randolph, White Mountain National Forest, Coos County

Type: Horsetails, cascades, fans, and small plunges
Height: Stairs Falls is 10 feet; Coosauk Falls, 15 feet; Hitchcock Falls, 30 feet
Trail Length: To Stairs Falls, 0.6 mile; to Coosauk Falls, 0.7 mile; to Hitchcock Falls, 1.0 mile
Water Source: Bumpus Brook
Altitude Gain/Loss: +500 feet to Hitchcock Falls

Difficulty: Moderate
Hiking Time: 45 minutes to Hitchcock Falls
DeLorme Map: Page 48, I-7
Rating: ★★★½

DESCRIPTION The brooks and streams draining water from the northern end of the Presidential Range are rich in cascades and falls, including Triple Falls on Town Line Brook, the waterfalls of Appalachia, and many others not detailed in this book. Three more waterfalls exist just east of Triple Falls, also off Dolly Copp Road, along the Howker Ridge Path: Stairs Falls, Coosauk Falls, and Hitchcock Falls, all of which are accessible via a mile-long trail located in the small town of Randolph.

The authors of *Waterfalls of the White Mountains* discuss Stairs Falls only briefly, mentioning that they have "seen nothing other than the Bumpus [Brook] tumbling through the gorge below." They go on to describe nearby Coosauk Falls as being available in "standard or deluxe versions." When we visited the two falls in June, however, the opposite was true: Stairs Falls was crashing down from the opposite gorge wall into the main path of Bumpus Brook (also referred to as Devil's Kitchen Gorge), while Coosauk Falls had completely dried up.

Perhaps some fallen tree, beaver dam, or shifting of the rocks has blocked the passage of water over Coosauk Falls, in the process igniting Stairs Falls into a frenzy of whitewater. The steps of Stairs Falls are blatantly obvious, increasing the expansion of the fan created as the water travels down. Heavily shaded and located on the other side of the brook from the trail, Stairs Falls is too hidden for a photograph or even a closer inspection.

Coosauk Falls—if water does indeed ever flow here—is a 15-foot-tall set of cascades and slides that dump into the Devil's Kitchen Gorge. Old bumpy paths lead into the gorge for closer views if you happen to see water flowing.

Unlike Stairs Falls and Coosauk Falls, all the waters traveling down Bumpus Brook must pass over Hitchcock Falls, the concluding feature of the trip. Here waters pigtail past boulders in the streambed into clear, green-tinted pools. Located in a secluded ravine that probably sees only a handful of visitors each week, Hitchcock Falls is a place best suited for intimate exploration. Angular boulders are scattered in and around the brook, creating many opportunities to survey the area. Out of the three

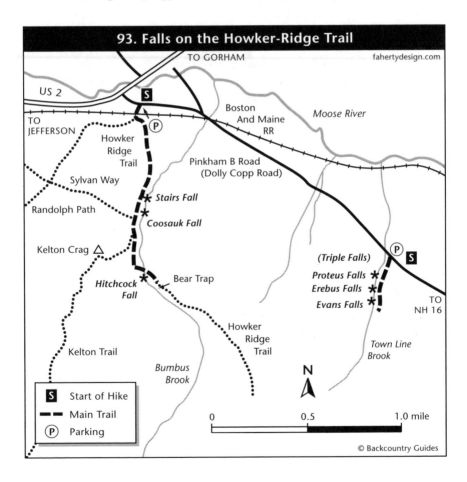

93. Falls on the Howker-Ridge Trail

TO GORHAM

fahertydesign.com

US 2

S

TO JEFFERSON

P

Boston And Maine RR

Moose River

Howker Ridge Trail

Pinkham B Road (Dolly Copp Road)

Sylvan Way

Randolph Path

Stairs Fall

Coosauk Fall

Kelton Crag △

(Triple Falls)

P S

Proteus Falls

Hitchcock Fall

Bear Trap

Erebus Falls

Evans Falls

TO NH 16

Howker Ridge Trail

Town Line Brook

Kelton Trail

Bumpus Brook

N

S   Start of Hike

－ －   Main Trail

P   Parking

0   0.5   1.0 mile

© Backcountry Guides

falls on this trip, Hitchcock is our favorite stop, more for the thrill of being alone in a rocky playground than for the actual impressiveness of the waterfall.

TRAIL INFORMATION From the parking area, follow the combined Howker Ridge Trail/Randolph Path through a field and into the forest. About 0.1 mile from the parking lot, take a left and continue on the Howker Ridge Trail. After another 0.1 mile, cross an old logging road and continue straight. Within a total of about 20 minutes you will reach Stairs Falls, visible across the brook from the trail. Continue climbing upstream along the trail for another 0.1 mile to reach Coosauk Falls. A small, not immediately obvious white sign marks the falls. Up to this point the trail has been an easy-to-follow moderate uphill climb of 0.7 mile. For the rest of the way to Hitchcock Falls, however, things are not so simple. The trail is hardly ever used, very narrow in some stretches, steep, and often muddy in spots.

If you are looking for hours of seclusion at a waterfall in the White Mountains, Hitchcock Falls is your best bet. If you make the decision to continue, fork left just past Coosauk Falls and continue climbing along the Howker Ridge Trail. About 0.1 mile beyond Coosauk Falls, fork left again as the Kelton Trail forks right. The falls are a few minutes ahead and clearly identifiable from the trail.

DIRECTIONS From the junction of US 302 and NH 16 in the village of Bartlett known as Glen, take NH 16 north and continue 3.4 miles past the entrance to the Mount Washington Road. Take a left onto Dolly Copp Road and drive 0.5 mile to a fork, passing the entrance to the campground on your left. Veer left onto Pinkham B Road and continue for 3.8 miles to a U.S. Forest Service parking area on your left. There is a large parking area for the Presidential Range Rail Trail on Dolly Copp Road before the trailhead parking area, so be sure to look for the forest service HIKER sign. The trailhead parking area is 0.1 mile south of US 2 on Dolly Copp Road. *To get to Glen,* take NH 16 north from Conway.

OTHER WATERFALLS NEARBY Triple Falls, Mossy Glen, Appalachia Waterfalls, Thompson Falls, Crystal Cascade.

94

FLUME CASCADE

*Harts Location, Crawford Notch State Park,
Carroll County*

Type: Cascades and small plunges
Height: Approximately 200-foot
total drop
Trail Length: Roadside
Water Source: Unknown
Altitude Gain/Loss: None

Difficulty: Easy
Hiking Time: Not applicable
DeLorme Map: Page 44, C&D-4
Rating: ★★★

DESCRIPTION Flume Cascade is the sister of nearby Silver Cascade, which lies a few hundred feet southeast. It is often confused with "The Flume," which is actually part of the Falls on the Flume-Pool Loop described elsewhere in this guide.

At Flume Cascade, small cascades and plunges end up in the Saco River below the highway. Be sure to scramble up the falls for additional views not seen from the highway.

TRAIL INFORMATION The falls are across the highway from the parking areas. A few worn paths lead their way up Flume Cascade, where new views await you. Increase the scope of your explorations by visiting Silver Cascade, a similar stretch of cascades a few feet down the road.

DIRECTIONS From the junction of US 302 and NH 16 in the village of Bartlett known as Glen, take US 302 west for 19.8 miles; the parking area will be on your left. This lot is 0.4 mile east of the sign marking the CRAWFORD NOTCH STATE PARK BORDER and 2.0 miles west of the Willey House Historical Site. *To get to Glen,* take NH 16 north from Conway.

OTHER WATERFALLS NEARBY Silver Cascade, Beecher and Pearl Cascades, Gibbs Falls, Kedron Flume, Ripley Falls, Arethusa Falls.

95

FRANCONIA FALLS

Lincoln, White Mountain National Forest, Grafton County

Type: Cascades and slides
Height: 30-foot total drop
Trail Length: 3.2 miles
Water Source: Franconia Brook
Altitude Gain/Loss: +300 feet

Difficulty: Easy
Hiking Time: 90 minutes
DeLorme Map: Page 43, G-14
Rating: ★★★★

DESCRIPTION Franconia Falls is located at the end of one of the flat-test long-distance strolls in the White Mountains. In just over 3 miles you will gain a mere 300 feet of altitude, with no ups or downs to speak of. For comparison, consider nearby Beaver Brook Falls, which gains 1,200 feet of altitude in only 1 mile, or the Falling Waters Trail, which gains 1,000 feet in just over 1.4 miles. This lack of elevation gain is the big reason why this waterfall is a favorite hike for families. Another reason is that the falls can be easily accessed year-round by foot, mountain bike, snowshoes, or cross-country skis.

Very similar to Diana's Baths in the town of Conway, Franconia Falls lacks waterfalls of striking natural elegance or style. Both make up for this deficiency with their sunny slabs of rock, swimming pools that widely vary in size, depth, and current, and opportunities for roving around the falls for hours of refreshing pleasure.

The best waterslide in the house is near the base of the falls, very close to the trail that parallels the brook. Roughly 20 feet long, but not continuous, this slide will propel you into a 5-foot-deep pool. Before we began writing in our waterfall notebooks, we felt compelled to chute down the slide!

TRAIL INFORMATION After registering at the Lincoln Woods Visitor Center, proceed down a wooden staircase, cross a wooden bridge, and follow signs to the trailhead for the Lincoln-Woods Trail. A few hundred feet beyond the visitors center, you will cross a wooden footbridge over the East Branch of the Pemigewasset River.

Beyond the bridge, you will reach a trail billboard. Take a right and continue hiking along the rail-trail. After 1.5 miles, look on your left for the Osseo Trail—one gateway to the Franconia Ridge Trail, which many consider the best hike in the Northeast. Continue along the Lincoln-Woods Trail for an additional 1.2 miles and you will reach signs pertaining to the relocated Franconia Brook Campground. A few feet beyond these signs and billboards lies a stone wall; here you will need to take a left and continue down another trail for 0.5 mile to the falls. Before you do so, however, we suggest continuing around the stone wall to another scenic bridge over the East Branch of the Pemigewasset. The cascading blue and green waters of the river are stunning and worth the little extra hiking effort.

SPECIAL NOTE Visitation to Franconia Falls is restricted by the U.S. Forest Service to 60 people per day. Before you begin hiking, you must register at the visitors center. If you are visiting the falls in summer or on a spring or fall weekend, you will want to arrive in the morning hours to reduce the chances of being visitor number 61. If you are traveling on, say, a Monday afternoon in early June, you should have no problem registering and visiting the falls.

OPTIONAL HIKE For a taste of true backcountry falls, you can opt to wander into the Pemigewasset Wilderness, where you will find No. 13 Falls (yes, the name of the waterfall is *No. 13*), a mix of cascades and pools in one of the most remote locations in the region.

From Franconia Falls, return to the Lincoln-Woods Trail. From here it is 5.3 miles (one-way) to No. 13 Falls. Cross the East Branch of the Pemigewasset River and continue on the Wilderness Trail; after only 0.1 mile, turn left onto the Franconia Brook Trail. Follow this trail for 5.1 miles as it gently climbs to the cascades at No. 13 Falls.

Visiting both Franconia Falls and No. 13 can be hard on your feet; the total round-trip hike, at 17.0 miles, is the longest in this guide. You should love both hiking and waterfalls to attempt to bag these two natural treasures in one day. Allot 10 to 14 hours—depending upon your pace and endurance—for this ultimate waterfall expedition. An alternative to a day hike would be to camp at one of the nine hardened tent pads near No. 13 Falls (called Camp 13). Campsites are first come, first served, and the cost per night in 2002 was $8. Check with the Appalachian Mountain Club for backcountry rules and regulations before departing. (Contact the AMC at 603-466-2721, ext. 215, for current information and questions.) The web site for the AMC also offers information on backcountry sites: www.outdoors.org.

DIRECTIONS From I-93 in Lincoln, take exit 32. Head east on NH 112 for 5.2 miles, then turn left into the Lincoln Woods parking area just after crossing a bridge over the East Branch of the Pemigewasset River. This parking area is 2.1 miles west of the Big Rock Campground and 0.3 mile east of the Hancock Campground.

OTHER WATERFALLS NEARBY Georgiana Falls, Agassiz Basin, Falls on the Flume–Pool Loop, Sabbaday Falls.

96

GEORGIANA FALLS

Lincoln, Grafton County

Type: Plunges, cascades, and a fan
Height: Lower falls is 30 feet; upper falls is 60 feet
Trail Length: To lower falls, 0.8 mile; to upper falls, 1.3 miles
Water Source: Harvard Brook
Altitude Gain/Loss: +600 feet to upper falls

Difficulty: To lower falls, easy side of moderate; to upper falls, moderate side of difficult
Hiking Time: 45 minutes to upper falls
DeLorme Map: Page 43, H-11
Rating: ★★★★

DESCRIPTION Many visitors to Georgiana Falls reach only the lower half of this waterfall. They are simply unaware of the quiet isolation provided by the set of falls lying upstream. This is not surprising at all, considering how hidden and poorly marked the trail beyond the lower falls is.

The lower falls consist of a 30-foot-high set of cascades spread across a 20-foot-wide ledge ideal for sunbathing or picnicking; at the base is a deep, dark pool. Although this waterfall is regularly visited, you can still reserve yourself a little space at this highly photogenic, agreeable spot.

The upper Georgiana Falls, which has been referred to as Harvard Falls in the past, has a different personality. Here Harvard Brook splits in two and plunges more than 60 feet into a long chasm below. The plunge on the right is particularly fascinating: It actually fans out then reverse-fans back in before landing, somewhat like the shape of a diamond. The plunge on the left is rather difficult to see from the trail, and we could not find a reasonably safe approach to the bottom of the gorge. It is worth noting that you view the falls head-on from a cliff on the trail, which can be thrilling—and dangerous; watch your footing.

TRAIL INFORMATION From the parking area, follow the yellow-blazed trail that passes through a fence opening then underneath I-93. Shortly beyond I-93, take the right fork at the sign for GEORGIANA FALLS. After about 0.3 mile, you will reach small cascades, and the yellow markers that have guided you thus far will begin to turn red. At first the blazes are both yellow *and* red, but in a few hundred feet the rest of the trail becomes marked only with red blazes.

When you reach the lower falls, keep climbing up the rocks; the trail to the upper falls continues to the right, though it is difficult to follow, with faded and sparse markers. We wandered off the trail several times, constantly peeping into the woods looking for the blazes. Still, if you simply follow the somewhat cleared-looking paths that parallel Harvard Brook just to its right, you will have little difficulty finding both the lower and upper falls.

DIRECTIONS From I-93 in Lincoln, take exit 33. Follow US 3 north for 0.4 mile toward North Lincoln and turn left onto Hanson Farm Road. After 0.1 mile, continue straight onto Georgiana Falls Road to the parking area at its end.

OTHER WATERFALLS NEARBY Falls on the Flume-Pool Loop, Falls on the Basin-Cascades Trail, Falls on the Falling Waters Trail, Agassiz Basin, Paradise Falls, Beaver Brook Falls.

97

GIBBS FALLS

Beans Grant, White Mountain National Forest, Coos County

Type: Horsetail
Height: 35 feet
Trail Length: 0.6 mile
Water Source: Gibbs Brook
Altitude Gain/Loss: +300 feet

Difficulty: Easy side of moderate
Hiking Time: 20 minutes
DeLorme Map: Page 44, C-4
Rating: ★★★½

DESCRIPTION This waterfall flows into a gorgeous, rocky-bottomed clear pool, great for soaking your tired little feet. Due to its sunny southern exposure, this is one of the warmest pools at a waterfall in New Hampshire. Take note that you will need to cross some fallen trees in order to swim.

Gibbs Falls

The waterfall fans out for the last 2 feet of this horsetail. It is in a wide-open area, although a large rock prevents you from seeing the whole falls at one time. The waterfall scoops down around the rock, only to plunge down over the rocky surfaces below. Overall, this is a nice destination away from the nearby crowds of Crawford Notch State Park.

TRAIL INFORMATION Begin your hike to the falls by following the Crawford Connector for 0.3 mile to Crawford Path. When you reach the Crawford Path junction, take a left; after about five minutes you will cross a wooden bridge with some unnamed cascades to your left. These unnamed cascades have yellow-tinted pools and provide a relaxing spot to take a break. Right before the bridge is the path to Crawford Cliff—another great hike to try. Just beyond the bridge, turn left toward the MIZPAH CUT-OFF. About 0.2 mile farther up Crawford Path, a short trail will fork left toward the falls, which you will see and hear shortly.

DIRECTIONS From the junction of US 302 and NH 16 in the village of Bartlett known as Glen, take US 302 west for 20.8 miles. Turn right onto Mount Clinton Road and follow it 0.1 mile to a left into the parking lot. Mount Clinton Road is 0.3 mile north of the Crawford Depot.

OTHER WATERFALLS NEARBY Beecher and Pearl Cascades, Flume Cascade, Silver Cascade, Kedron Flume, Ripley Falls, Arethusa Falls.

98

GLEN ELLIS FALLS

Jackson, White Mountain National Forest, Carroll County

Type: Plunge
Height: 64 feet
Trail Length: 0.3 mile
Water Source: Ellis River
Altitude Gain/Loss: −100 feet

Difficulty: Easy
Hiking Time: 10 minutes
DeLorme Map: Page 44, B-7
Rating: ★★★★★

DESCRIPTION (HIGHLY RECOMMENDED) The most popular waterfall of the Pinkham Notch area is the 64-foot plunge known as Glen Ellis

Glen Ellis Falls

Falls. With a fine spray of water year-round, this waterfall attracts vacationers through all four seasons.

Glen Ellis Falls' location—just minutes from other longtime favorite attractions in the area—and ease of access make this another White Mountain National Forest sight that can be crowded even in the worst weather. Still, as unattractive as a crowded waterfall can be, it is crowded for a reason.

This waterfall is unique in New England with its exceptionally deep green pool and the left-angled flow of its whitewater. It is too bad that Glen Ellis is off-limits to swimming—this would be one of the more enjoyable swimming holes in the state.

Just about anyone who can walk down stairs can visit this waterfall. The trail is short and well worth it. Just do not expect to be alone at this waterfall. Parking is $3, payable at a self-service station, unless you have an annual White Mountain parking pass, which can be purchased at several ranger stations and outdoor sporting goods stores in the area.

TRAIL INFORMATION From the parking lot, follow the Glen Ellis Falls Trail. First you pass underneath NH 16, then proceed down several staircases to the falls. Be sure to check out the upper, middle, and bottom viewpoints, as each offers a different perspective.

DIRECTIONS From the junction of US 302 and NH 16 in the section of Bartlett known as Glen, take NH 16 north for 11.0 miles. Take a left at the sign for GLEN ELLIS FALLS. The parking area will be just up this road. This turnoff is 0.6 mile south of the AMC Pinkham Notch Visitor Center. *To get to Glen,* take NH 16 north from Conway.

OTHER WATERFALLS NEARBY Crystal Cascade, Thompson Falls, Winniweta Falls, Jackson Falls.

99

HERMIT FALLS

Chatham, White Mountain National Forest, Carroll County

Type: Horsetail
Height: 30-foot total drop
Trail Length: 1.3 miles

Difficulty: Easy side of moderate
Hiking Time: 35 minutes
DeLorme Map: Page 45, A-12

Water Source: Basin Brook   **Rating:** ★★★
Altitude Gain/Loss: +100 feet

DESCRIPTION Hermit Falls is located near the North Chatham–Beans Purchase town border. It is hidden a mile northwest of the Basin Campground, which is operated by the U.S. Forest Service.

A seasonal attraction, Hermit Falls is best visited before the end of June or after a substantial rainstorm. In normal wet-weather conditions the waterfall is 30-foot horsetail within a remote, moss-surrounded ravine. In low water it turns into a powerless slide down dark rock. Judging by the size of the broad shelf the water topples off, these falls could grow 10 times as wide in high water.

The falls are an easy walk from either the campground or the picnic area at Basin Pond. They are probably not spectacular enough to go out of your way for—unless, of course, you are a waterfall fanatic. Rather, check out Hermit Falls if you happen to be vacationing at the campground, or if you are visiting other nearby waterfalls. They make a fine addition to other local attractions.

TRAIL INFORMATION The trip to Hermit Falls follows the Basin Trail, a yellow-marked footway that first parallels the southern edge of Basin Pond. The trail begins near the parking area rest rooms behind a brown sign for the BASIN TRAIL. For the first 0.5 mile you will hike along the southern edge of Basin Pond, with several gaps providing scenic views to the north. Soon after you pass the eastern edge of the pond, the trail markers will become less obvious; in several stretches the trail becomes narrow due to overgrown plants. Continue to look aggressively for trail blazes, and the trail will soon return to its original width after crossing several streams. The remainder of this 1.3-mile walk is easy.

DIRECTIONS From the junction of ME 113 and US 302 in Fryeburg, Maine, take ME 113 north, continuing for 7.7 miles past its junction with NH 113B. Turn left into the Basin Recreation Area, follow the access road straight toward the Basin Campground for 0.6 mile, and pull into the Basin Pond parking area on your right. *To get to Fryeburg,* take US 302 east from Conway.

OTHER WATERFALLS NEARBY Rattlesnake Flume and Pool (Maine), Bickford Slides (Maine), Mad River Falls (Maine).

100

HUNTINGTON CASCADES

Dixville, Dixville Notch State Park, Coos County

Type: Horsetails and cascades
Height: Lower falls are 18 feet;
upper falls are 50 feet
Trail Length: 0.3 mile to upper
falls
Water Source: Cascade Brook
Altitude Gain/Loss: +150 feet to
upper falls

Difficulty: Easy side of moderate
Hiking Time: 10 minutes
DeLorme Map: Page 50, C-6
Rating: ★★★½

DESCRIPTION Located in Dixville Notch State Park less than 0.5 mile from the Dixville Flume, Huntington Cascades (often referred to as Huntington Falls) offers two servings of slim horsetails. Lower Huntington Cascades is the formation described in the Bolnicks' *Waterfalls of the White Mountains*. It consists of a segmented horsetail in the center of a ravine, about 18 feet tall and surrounded by the luscious greens of various mosses.

The upper falls are markedly different. With visibility restricted by hemlock trees, the upper falls appear quite small and insignificant from the lower section of cascades. Their true height and beauty can only be seen by continuing up the Huntington Cascades Trail. Although the slender horsetails of the upper falls are mostly hidden under heavy tree cover and surrounding steep gorge walls, this section is the least crowded, and several rock ledges are conveniently located at great vantage points.

TRAIL INFORMATION Travel up the Huntington Cascades Trail from the parking area. About 300 feet after entering the woods, fork right and shortly cross a brook. The falls are 0.1 mile farther up the trail. The lower waterfall can be seen after ascending a short incline; the upper is a few hundred feet beyond. Accessing the upper falls is slightly more difficult, but nothing nearly challenging enough to prevent you from at least getting a satisfying view.

DIRECTIONS From the junction of US 3 and NH 26 in Colebrook, follow NH 26 east. After 11.7 miles, take a right into the Cascade Brook Picnic Area; this area is 1.1 miles east of the ENTERING DIXVILLE NOTCH STATE PARK sign. After you pull in, continue down the road until you reach a trailhead with a sign for HUNTINGTON FALLS. *To get to Colebrook,* take US 3 north from Lincoln.

OTHER WATERFALLS NEARBY Dixville Flume, Beaver Brook Falls.

101

JACKSON FALLS

Jackson, Carroll County

Type: Cascades and small plunges
Height: Approximately 100-foot total drop
Trail Length: Roadside
Water Source: Wildcat Brook
Altitude Gain/Loss: None

Difficulty: Easy
Hiking Time: Not applicable
DeLorme Map: Page 45, E&F-9
Rating: ★★★★

DESCRIPTION The small town of Jackson attracts hundreds of visitors to its swimming holes at Jackson Falls each summer. Although these falls lack any magnificent drops or picturesque formations, they do contain hundreds of small cascades, slides, and plunges. No one piece is alone worthy of a visit or photograph, but Jackson Falls as a whole makes a great place to play underneath a waterfall or splash your feet in a natural pothole.

For generations, this special place has been a favorite for picnics. Families often let their children roam free in the chilly waters for hours. Whether springtime, summer, or even fall, Jackson Falls always has at least a few content visitors.

If you want a part of Jackson Falls to yourself, try the lower half of the falls by walking down the road. Here it is much less crowded, and there are several large plunges to enjoy as well. Pay much more attention to safety, however; the current is stronger and the drops are larger on the lower half of the falls.

TRAIL INFORMATION Follow along the road to reach the upper and lower sections of Jackson Falls. There are many worn trails down and around the falls. There is an altitude loss of approximately 100 feet if you choose to explore the lower falls.

Jackson Falls

DIRECTIONS From the junction of US 302 and NH 16 in the section of Bartlett known as Glen, take NH 16 north for 2.6 miles, past Storyland, and take a right onto NH 16A. (Take note that NH 16A is a loop with two NH 16 junctions—you want to take the northern one.) Follow NH 16A for 0.4 mile to a left onto Carter Notch Road. Follow Carter Notch Road for 0.3 mile; several dirt pull-offs will begin on your right and continue up the road. *To get to Glen,* take NH 16 north from Conway.

OTHER WATERFALLS NEARBY Winniweta Falls, Glen Ellis Falls, Diana's Baths, Crystal Cascade, Thompson Falls.

102

KEDRON FLUME

Harts Location, Crawford Notch State Park, Carroll County

Type: Cascades and slides
Height: Approximately 150-foot total drop
Trail Length: 0.8 mile
Water Source: Kedron Brook
Altitude Gain/Loss: +500 feet

Difficulty: Moderate
Hiking Time: 40 minutes
DeLorme Map: Page 44, E-4
Rating: ★★★

DESCRIPTION Just north of the two famous waterfalls of Crawford Notch State Park—Ripley Falls and Arethusa Falls—lies a third waterfall, Kedron Flume. Here the mountain waters of Kedron Brook surge through a narrow flume, slide for a long distance through a narrow channel, and eventually begin their steep descent toward the highway below.

Exploring the flume is a dangerous business. The rocks on the trail and around the falls are deceptively slippery. Although most of the time the water volume is quite low—perhaps only a few inches deep—enough mist and side drainage make exploring hazardous. If you use extra caution, walk 20 feet downstream from the trail crossing and you can stand atop a waterfall ledge, with views of Mount Webster to the north opening up.

The waters of Kedron Brook can run throughout summer, but we expect you will enjoy the flume more during times of rushing waters. From the beginning of snowmelt season, usually late April to the middle of June, you are pretty much guaranteed a good show.

TRAIL INFORMATION From the picnic area, follow the Kedron Flume Trail to the falls. There is a small sign for the trail above the PIC-NIC AREA roadside sign at the end of the parking lot.

This blue-marked trail is a continuous uphill hike. After about 15 minutes you will cross a set of railroad tracks, just before the halfway mark. From the parking area to this set of tracks, the trail gradually weaves its way toward the flume. From the railroad tracks to the flume, the trail transforms into a rather steep, slippery, muddy experience. About 0.5 mile beyond the tracks, the trail will level out; the narrow flume will appear on your right and continue underneath your feet before dropping again in a horsetail formation.

DIRECTIONS From the junction of US 302 and NH 16 in the village of Bartlett known as Glen, take US 302 west for 17.7 miles. Turn left into the parking area for the Willey House Picnic Area, which is adjacent to the Willey House Historical Site. This picnic area is 0.9 mile west of the road to Ripley Falls and 1.9 mile east of Silver Cascade. *To get to Glen, take NH 16 north from Conway.*

OTHER WATERFALLS NEARBY Ripley Falls, Arethusa Falls, Silver Cascade, Flume Cascade, Beecher and Pearl Cascades, Gibbs Falls.

103

LOWER FALLS

Albany, White Mountain National Forest, Carroll County

Type: Cascades
Height: 10-foot total drop
Trail Length: Roadside
Water Source: Swift River
Altitude Gain/Loss: None

Difficulty: Easy
Hiking Time: Not applicable
DeLorme Map: Page 44, J-7
Rating: ★★★★

DESCRIPTION Located just off the Kancamagus Highway, Lower Falls is another famous White Mountain National Forest attraction. Although the waterfall is not large or particularly powerful, the many cascades and pools of the area are a great place to take a break. There are several small beaches and many places to wade and swim in the river. Be aware, however, that this waterfall is one of the most heavily visited in the White Mountains.

If you do not have a parking pass for the White Mountains, it will cost you $3 to park here. There are bathrooms, drinking water, a covered picnic area, and a grill at the falls. Lower Falls is definitely worth your attention, as it is photogenic and historically one of the most cherished falls of the White Mountains, due to the generations of families that have visited. There are also several other great waterfalls just down the road. Make sure to bring your bathing suit!

Lower Falls

TRAIL INFORMATION From the parking lot, follow the Swift River downstream a short distance. For a complete view of the falls, consider walking down NH 112 about 0.1 mile. An unobstructed picture will unfold.

DIRECTIONS From the junction of NH 16 and NH 112 in Conway, take NH 112 (the Kancamagus Highway) west for 6.9 miles; the marked parking lot for the LOWER FALLS will be on your right. If you are traveling from I-93 in Lincoln, take exit 32 and follow NH 112 east for 28.5 miles; the parking lot will be on your left. The falls are located 2.1 miles east of the Rocky Gorge Scenic Area and 0.6 mile west of the Blackberry Crossing Campground. *To get to Conway,* take NH 16 north from Rochester.

OTHER WATERFALLS NEARBY Rocky Gorge, Sabbaday Falls.

104

MOSSY GLEN

Randolph, Coos County

Type: Cascades and slides
Height: 40-foot total drop
Trail Length: 0.3 mile
Water Source: Carlton Brook
Altitude Gain/Loss: +100 feet

Difficulty: Easy
Hiking Time: 10 minutes
DeLorme Map: Page 48, I-6
Rating: ★★½

DESCRIPTION A short stroll from the road will bring you to Mossy Glen—a series of pools, slides, and cascades set among heavy growth of several moss species. Thin sheets of water drop at low angles here; there is also a pool with a whirlpool current. A nicely crafted pine bridge adds to the visual appeal of the hike.

TRAIL INFORMATION The trail to the falls begins by traveling up a dirt road marked by a sign for the GROVEWAY. After passing by two houses on your left, take a right onto the trail. Soon you will cross a nicely constructed pine bridge. Beyond this bridge, take a left onto a trail marked by a sign for GLENSIDE TO BEE LINE VIA MOSSY GLEN. The upper falls are only 100 feet up this trail. On our visits to Mossy Glen, the trail connecting the lower and upper falls has been very muddy.

Be aware that the trail distance is increased if parking is unavailable near the trailhead. Some have told us of hikers having to park at the Appalachia parking lot on US 2, although we cannot be sure of this.

DIRECTIONS From the junction of US 2 and NH 16 in Gorham, take US 2 west. At 1.3 miles past the RANDOLPH TOWN LINE sign, turn right onto Durand Road East. Take a left after 0.1 mile to continue on Durand Road East; 0.4 mile farther along, the trailhead, marked by a sign for the GROVEWAY, will appear. The trail begins near the Randolph Public Library. There is no official place to park, so you may be forced to park at the Appalachia lot on US 2 and hike back to the Groveway trailhead. *To get to Gorham,* take NH 16 north from Conway.

OTHER WATERFALLS NEARBY Appalachia Waterfalls, Falls on the Howker Ridge Path, Triple Falls.

105

NANCY CASCADES

Livermore, White Mountain National Forest, Grafton County

Type: Horsetails and cascades
Height: Approximately 300-foot total drop
Trail Length: To lower falls, 2.4 miles; to upper falls, 2.8 miles
Water Source: Nancy Brook
Altitude Gain/Loss: +1,500 feet to top of falls

Difficulty: Moderate side of difficult
Hiking Time: 1 hour, 45 minutes
DeLorme Map: Page 44, G-4
Rating: ★★★★★

DESCRIPTION (HIGHLY RECOMMENDED) The sum of the height of the cascades that adorn Nancy Brook is estimated at 300 feet, making Nancy Cascades one of the tallest in New England. Nancy Brook is fed by the waters of Nancy Pond. The cascades and the pond have been held in high regard for more than a century, and rightfully so.

A rust-colored pool below the 45-foot fanning horsetail marks the lowest segment of the formation. The waters of Nancy Brook cascade down gray gneiss bedrock before hopping over a ledge, causing the water to plunge the remaining distance into the pool below. By the time you reach the lower falls, at 2.4 miles, you may be tired of the continuous climbing effort already demanded of you. The spectacular lower falls come as a rewarding relief, worthy of enduring the pains of the trail.

Above the main falls are hundreds of feet of chutes, slides, horsetails, and small plunges equally as stunning and charming as the bottom falls. Just over 0.5 mile above the upper falls, Nancy Pond (also accessed by the Nancy Pond Trail) is a remote, peaceful body of water just southeast of Mount Nancy.

The brook, pond, falls, and nearby mountain are named for a passionate servant woman who entered Crawford Notch during a White Mountain winter, trying to reach the camp where her fiancé was. Failing to catch up with her lover, who had left Nancy to go on a trip without saying good-bye (why he left is not known), Nancy crossed the Saco River and quickly become exhausted by the chilly waters. She was found dead from hypothermia the next day.

Nancy Cascades

TRAIL INFORMATION The Nancy Pond Trail starts from the parking area on US 302 and enters the woods, traveling at first along a yellow-blazed forest road. For the first two-thirds of the way, the elevation gain is modest and the spacious, properly marked trail is simple to follow.

The final third of the trail is markedly steeper, with several brook crossings required. This final section is not as well marked or easy to follow, so you will want to pay attention. One stretch of the upper section has experienced heavy erosion, making for a difficult ramble; take hold of the fallen trees nearby to catapult yourself across the eroded trail.

Once you reach the bottom set of cascades, continue climbing to the left to view the two additional segments of horsetails and cascades above. Beyond the lower falls, expect a steeper, tough trail. It is likely that the trail to the upper falls is extraordinarily slippery in spring, and infested with muddy stretches.

DIRECTIONS From the junction of US 302 and NH 16 in the village of Bartlett known as Glen, take US 302 west for 11.2 miles; the parking area for the Nancy Pond Trail will be on your left. The trailhead is located 2.8 miles west of the sign marking the White Mountain National Forest border and 3.1 miles east of the Crawford Notch State Park border. *To get to Glen,* take NH 16 north from Conway.

OTHER WATERFALLS NEARBY Arethusa Falls, Ripley Falls, Kedron Flume.

106

PARADISE FALLS

Woodstock, Lost River Reservation, Grafton County

Type: Plunge and small cascades	feet, up 125 feet
Height: 20-foot plunge	**Difficulty:** Moderate
Trail Length: 0.8-mile loop	**Hiking Time:** 60 minutes
Water Source: Lost River	**DeLorme Map:** Page 43, I-9
Altitude Gain/Loss: Down 125	**Rating:** ★★★★

DESCRIPTION The first question a visitor to the Lost River may ask is, "Where was this place when I was a child?" Not only does the reserva-

Paradise Falls

tion have a scenic waterfall, but it also offers about a dozen different caves to explore. While some are large enough to walk straight into, others require passing through tight squeezes, where agility and upper-body strength are essential.

The waterfall is the located in the middle of a 0.75-mile boardwalk loop trail from which you can enjoy both a head-on view and a bird's-eye vantage point. Although viewing this waterfall is limited to the boardwalk fencing, there are enough spots to encapsulate the beauty of this waterfall.

This waterfall is one of the most visited in New England, simply because it is seen by all who visit the Lost River. We suggest joining the crowds and getting over to the Lost River Reservation, especially if you (or your children) enjoy caves or waterfalls. The entry fee in 2002 was $9 for adults, $5 for children, and well worth it.

TRAIL INFORMATION (See map on page 139.) The trail begins at the visitors center, follows a boardwalk loop for 0.75 mile past Paradise Falls and caves, and eventually returns to the visitors center. Take note that you will be required to maneuver through one cave to finish the loop. While it is not a tight squeeze, the cave may require you to walk on your knees, or at least remove and carry your backpack or purse. There are about a dozen other small caves to explore along the edges of the trail, but only the one that must be passed through.

DIRECTIONS To get to the Lost River Reservation—where Paradise Falls is located—take exit 32 off I-93 in North Woodstock. Turn onto NH 112 west and proceed for 5.8 miles past its junction with US 3. There are several large signs for the LOST RIVER RESERVATION on the highway, so it's hard to miss.

OTHER WATERFALLS NEARBY Beaver Brook Cascades, Agassiz Basin, Georgiana Falls, Falls on the Flume-Pool Loop, Swiftwater Falls (Bath).

107

POND BROOK FALLS

Stratford, Nash Stream Forest, Coos County

Type: Cascades and slides
Height: 100-foot total drop
Trail Length: 0.1 mile
Water Source: Pond Brook
Altitude Gain/Loss: +200 feet to top of falls

Difficulty: Easy
Hiking Time: 5 minutes
DeLorme Map: Page 50, I-3
Rating: ★★★½

DESCRIPTION Pond Brook Falls is a concealed chain of sparkling cascades and slides in New Hampshire's Coos County. Before the Bolnicks' *Waterfalls of the White Mountains,* this waterfall was absent from all other guidebooks to the area—and while the secret may now be out, Pond Brook Falls remains as private and untouched as it was before.

Just north of the popular day-hike summits of Percy Peaks, the individual cascades of Pond Brook Falls are far from being spectacular, mystifying, or even visually appealing. The attraction is due to broad slabs of rock that nature constructed for your picnicking and sunbathing pleasure. As a bonus, there are plentiful cascades and other nooks and crannies to explore upstream. This is the waterfall for those of you wishing to avoid the crowds farther south in the White Mountains region.

TRAIL INFORMATION At the end of the parking lot, cross a few boulders to enter the woods on soft dirt. After 0.1 mile, you will approach the lower cascades. The official path ends here; you must continue climbing cautiously upstream among rocks and boulders beside the falls.

DIRECTIONS From the junction of US 3 and NH 110 in Groveton, take NH 110 east for 2.6 miles. Take a left onto Emerson Road, continue for 1.4 miles, and you will come to a fork. Veer right to continue on Emerson Road for an additional 0.7 mile. Turn left onto Nash Stream Road, a well-maintained logging road, and proceed 5.7 miles; the parking area will be on your right just beyond a culvert over Pond Brook. Nash Stream Road may be impassible during the early-spring mud season. *To get to Groveton,* take US 3 north from Lincoln.

OTHER WATERFALLS NEARBY Beaver Brook Falls, Dixville Flume, Huntington Cascades.

108

PURGATORY FALLS

Mont Vernon & Lyndeborough, Hillsborough County

Type: Cascades and a small plunge
Height: 25-foot total drop
Trail Length: 1.2 miles
Water Source: Purgatory Brook
Altitude Gain/Loss: Up 100 feet,
down 150 feet

Difficulty: Moderate
Hiking Time: 40 minutes
DeLorme Map: Page 21, E-11
Rating: ★★★

DESCRIPTION If you are in the area of Mont Vernon, jump on over to secluded Purgatory Falls, a short series of cascades through a narrow gorge that is visited most often by horseback. If you do not happen to have a horse, you could also reach the falls via mountain bike or just plain walking. No matter your transportation, expect to get a little muddy, as we did when we visited. Several local residents informed us that for most of the year the trail has giant puddles, often muddy, that must either be traveled through or passed by. Every section is manageable, and could, by all means, be much worse (we have not visited this waterfall in early spring).

The total drop of the falls is short, about 25 feet. Many other waterfalls are more appealing than Purgatory, but many also do not offer the seclusion of this spot. There are two clean picnic tables at the top of the falls for those looking for a private picnic.

TRAIL INFORMATION Begin the trail to the falls by following Upton Road for 0.9 mile. If Upton Road is washed out, which it often is, use the paths on the side to avoid stepping in the large puddles. When you reach a trail junction, Purgatory Brook, and a small swamp, take a left and continue on another old dirt road 0.3 mile farther. The falls are on your right just beyond a picnic table.

DIRECTIONS From the junction of NH 101A and NH 13 in Milford, take NH 13 north for 3.8 miles. Turn onto Purgatory Road, continue for 0.9 mile, and take a right onto Wilton Road. After 0.7 mile, take a left onto Upton Road, an unmarked dirt road. Follow Upton Road for 0.3 mile; the parking lot will be on your left.

OTHER WATERFALLS NEARBY None.

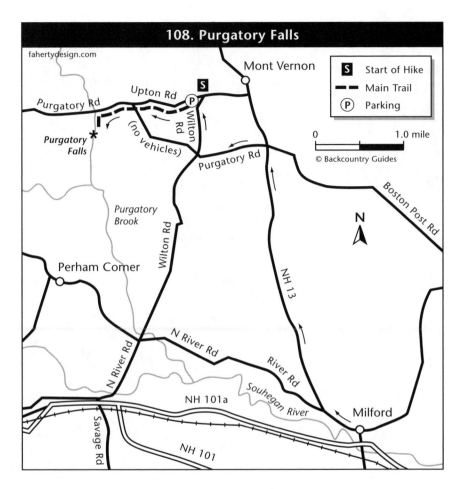

108. Purgatory Falls

fahertydesign.com

Mont Vernon

Upton Rd

Purgatory Rd

Wilton Rd

(no vehicles)

Purgatory Falls

Purgatory Rd

Purgatory Brook

Wilton Rd

Perham Corner

NH 13

N River Rd

N River Rd

River Rd

Savage Rd

NH 101a

Souhegan River

Milford

Boston Post Rd

NH 101

S Start of Hike

– – Main Trail

P Parking

0   1.0 mile

© Backcountry Guides

109

RIPLEY FALLS

Harts Location, Crawford Notch State Park, Carroll County

Type: Horsetail and slides
Height: 100-foot total drop
Trail Length: 0.6 mile
Water Source: Avalanche Brook
Altitude Gain/Loss: +400 feet

Difficulty: Easy side of moderate
Hiking Time: 25 minutes
DeLorme Map: Page 44, E-4
Rating: ★★★★★

Ripley Falls

DESCRIPTION (HIGHLY RECOMMENDED) Crawford Notch State Park is rich with noteworthy waterfalls. Toward its north end are Gibbs Falls, Beecher and Pearl Cascades, and the Flume and Silver Cascades. In the south you will find the popular day-trip destinations of Arethusa Falls (discussed elsewhere in this book) and Ripley Falls.

Ripley Falls is a beautiful 100-foot sheet of whitewater flowing over a smooth rock wall that is set at about a 60-degree angle, causing the rushing mountain water to maintain contact with the rock during its descent. For the best photograph, scramble a few feet downstream and add some scale to your camera's frame, such as a person or rock.

There are only short, temporary periods where the water jumps away from the rock wall. Because of this, Ripley Falls, as an entire structure, is one of the steepest-angled slides in all of New England.

TRAIL INFORMATION The trail is an uphill climb most of the way, at times muddy and moderately steep. From the parking lot, follow the white-blazed Ethan Pond Trail for slightly less than 10 minutes to a junction with the Ripley Falls Trail. Fork left and continue 0.3 mile farther to the falls. The trail will be marked with blue blazes from this point forward.

If you feel more adventurous, you can follow the Ripley/Arethusa Falls Trail to Arethusa Falls. To do this, cross Avalanche Brook and hike this new path for 2.1 miles. Once you reach Arethusa Falls, you can either return to Ripley Falls or walk west on US 302 for 2.4 miles to get back to your car.

For those looking for extended overnight trips, Ripley Falls can be complemented with other waterfalls that sprout from short spur trails off the Ethan Pond Trail. Thoreau Falls and Zealand Falls are two such features that you can add to Ripley to create either a lengthy day trip or an overnight.

DIRECTIONS From the junction of US 302 and NH 16 in the village of Bartlett known as Glen, take US 302 west for 16.8 miles. Turn left onto an unmarked road at a sign for RIPLEY FALLS. This road is 2.3 miles west of Arethusa Falls Road and 1.0 mile east of the Willey House Historical Site. *To get to Glen,* take NH 16 north from Conway.

OTHER WATERFALLS NEARBY Arethusa Falls, Kedron Flume, Nancy Cascades, Silver Cascade, Flume Cascade.

110

ROCKY GORGE

Albany, White Mountain National Forest,
Carroll County

Type: Cascades

Height: 20 feet

Trail Length: Less than 0.1 mile

Water Source: Swift River

Altitude Gain/Loss: None

Difficulty: Easy

Hiking Time: Not applicable

DeLorme Map: Page 44, J&K-7

Rating: ★★★★

DESCRIPTION Along with nearby Lower Falls and Sabbaday Falls, Rocky Gorge is a popular warm-weather attraction for visitors on the Kancamagus Highway. Like any admired waterfall, it can be overrun by persistent shutterbugs, swimmers, and other visitors.

Despite the crowds, this 20-foot plunge is a highly photogenic waterfall set on a sunny river that is worth a stop if you are in the area. A bridge has been constructed to give you a great view. You do not need the bridge to see the falls, though; the river is easy to navigate around.

Although swimming in the gorge is prohibited, you can swim both up and downstream. The river does have a rather fast current, but many rock obstacles create dormant pools perfect for a quick dip.

A pass is required to park at the area. If you do not have a White Mountain National Forest Pass, you can purchase a day pass here. You will also find picnic tables and bathroom facilities, making the area more visitor friendly.

TRAIL INFORMATION From the parking lot facing the river, take the paved path that is followed by a log fence to your right. The falls are just up the path, best viewed from the footbridge that crosses the Swift River.

DIRECTIONS From the junction of NH 112 and NH 16 in Conway, take NH 112 (the Kancamagus Highway) west for 9 miles; the marked parking area will be on your right. If you are traveling from I-93 in Lincoln, take exit 32, follow NH 112 east for 26.4 miles, and look for the parking area on your left. A sign marks the lot for the ROCKY GORGE SCENIC AREA from both sides of the highway. The Rocky Gorge Scenic Area is 2.1 miles west of the parking area for Lower Falls

and 1.6 miles west of the parking area for the Champney Falls Trail.
OTHER WATERFALLS NEARBY Lower Falls, Sabbaday Falls.

SABBADAY FALLS

Waterville Valley, White Mountain National Forest, Grafton County

Type: Punchbowl and plunges
Height: 35-foot total drop
Trail Length: 0.3 mile
Water Source: Sabbaday Brook
Altitude Gain/Loss: +100 feet

Difficulty: Easy
Hiking Time: 15 minutes
DeLorme Map: Page 44, K-4
Rating: ★★★★★

DESCRIPTION (HIGHLY RECOMMENDED) The main gorge at Sabbaday Falls was carved more than 10,000 years ago by large volumes of water from the last melting glacier. This water carried with it sand, gravel, and boulders, which eventually carved out the gorge. Set inside this gorge are two plunges and a punchbowl at the top.

The punchbowl, which is about 5 feet in height, falls peacefully into a circular pool about 4 feet wide. Immediately after, Sabbaday Brook plunges about 22 feet. After landing, the waters of the brook turn right and plunge another 8 feet. There are walking bridges and steps so everyone will be able to see all three parts of this waterfall. Also, be sure to check out the lower pool, which has exceptionally clear water. It is too bad swimming is prohibited, as this pool would be a perfect place to relax!

Since you are already in the area, you may want to check out nearby Champney Falls—a highly seasonal waterfall with good flow only in early spring. The clearly marked trailhead for the falls is only a few miles east of Sabbaday Falls on NH 112. Follow the Champney Falls Trail for 1.7 miles as it continually climbs to the falls. You also have the option of continuing 2.4 miles beyond the falls to the summit of Mount Chocorua, a popular day-trip destination with several routes leading to its summit.

TRAIL INFORMATION The trail to the falls begins directly in front

Sabbaday Falls

of the parking lot. It is wide, well-marked and -traveled, and pretty flat. You will have no problems finding the falls.

Visitors during the winter season can access the falls via cross-country skis or snowshoes; this simple, level trail is quite easy to travel on.

DIRECTIONS From the junction of NH 112 and NH 16 in Conway, take NH 112 (the Kancamagus Highway) west for 15.5 miles; the marked parking area will be on your left. If you are traveling from I-93 in Lincoln, take exit 32, follow NH 112 east for 19.9 miles, and look for the parking area on your right. A sign marks the SABBADAY FALLS PICNIC AREA lot from both directions. This picnic area is located 1.3 miles west of the Passaconaway Campground and 2.0 miles east of the Sugarhill Overlook.

OTHER WATERFALLS NEARBY Rocky Gorge, Lower Falls.

112

SCULPTURED ROCK FALLS

Groton, Sculptured Rocks Natural Area,
Grafton County

Type: Cascades and small plunges
Height: 25-foot total drop
Trail Length: 0.1 mile
Water Source: Cockermouth River
Altitude Gain/Loss: None

Difficulty: Easy
Hiking Time: Not applicable
DeLorme Map: Page 38, J-7
Rating: ★★½

DESCRIPTION This geological wonder is another New Hampshire attraction believed to have been formed by a retreating glacier from the great Ice Age, about 10,000 years ago. Although there are no large drops here, the small cascades and plunges set among the deep curves of a gorge are interesting.

TRAIL INFORMATION From the parking lot, walk back down and cross Sculptured Rocks Road. The trail begins about 50 feet from the parking lot. The falls appear shortly after you enter the woods.

DIRECTIONS From I-93 in Plymouth, take exit 26. Follow NH 3A south into Hebron and continue for 5.0 miles past the junction with NH 25. Take a right onto North Shore Road, drive 2.4 miles, and continue straight onto Groton Road. After 1.7 miles, fork left onto Sculptured Rocks Road. Continue for 1.2 miles; the large parking area will be on your left.

OTHER WATERFALLS NEARBY Welton Falls.

113

SILVER CASCADE

Harts Location, Crawford Notch State Park, Carroll County

Type: Plunges and cascades
Height: 200-foot total drop
Trail Length: Roadside
Water Source: Unknown
Altitude Gain/Loss: None

Difficulty: Easy
Hiking Time: Not applicable
DeLorme Map: Page 44, D-4
Rating: ★★★★½

DESCRIPTION (HIGHLY RECOMMENDED) Silver Cascade is a tall mix of plunges and cascades that hop from left to right down Mount Jackson. The falls continue under US 302, eventually converging with the Saco River below the highway.

Due to the ease of access, this waterfall has dazzled tourists for years, making it one of the most popular in New England. You will understand why once you see the slender ribbon of water tumbling over ledges and through chasm walls. The falls are particularly beautiful during foliage season, and are heavily visited and photographed as a result.

If you are like most visitors, you take a quick look from the road, snap two pictures, and walk back to your car. We suggest venturing beyond the roadside views by climbing up and getting closer to the falls. If you do, you will find some unexpected privacy. Many of the great photographs of this waterfall are taken from such intimate spots.

TRAIL INFORMATION The falls are located across the highway from the parking areas. Flume Cascade, sister to Silver Cascade, is just up the hill on your right.

DIRECTIONS From the junction of US 302 and NH 16 in the part of Bartlett known as Glen, take US 302 west for 19.7 miles; several parking areas will be on your left. Silver Cascade is 1.9 miles west of the Willey House Historic Site and 0.5 mile east of the Crawford Notch State

Silver Cascade

Park border, marked by signs on both sides of the road. *To get to Glen,* take NH 16 north from Conway.

OTHER WATERFALLS NEARBY Flume Cascade, Beecher and Pearl Cascades, Gibbs Falls, Kedron Flume, Ripley Falls, Arethusa Falls.

114

SWIFTWATER FALLS
Bath, Grafton County

Type: Blocks

Height: Tallest block is 8 feet

Trail Length: Roadside

Water Source: Wild Ammonoosuc River

Altitude Gain/Loss: None

Difficulty: Easy

Hiking Time: Not applicable

DeLorme Map: Page 42, F-5

Rating: ★★★★

DESCRIPTION It would be easy to write off Swiftwater Falls as lacking in originality, power, or beauty. Yet this waterfall offers a complete package—a highly worthwhile visit once you consider all the perks.

In the background of these falls is a highly scenic covered bridge, and below them lies one of the largest waterfall swimming holes in New England. With its western exposure, the pool soaks up the sun, often heating the water to tolerable temperatures even in May.

For waterfalls, the Wild Ammonoosuc River drops twice, both structures being block formations. The bottom block is the taller (8 feet) and wider (about 45 feet). You will notice that on the last cascade, only the bottom half is whitewater, which is highly irregular. The Wild Ammonoosuc River slips for the first half then ripples into whitewater, which carries on into the pool, creating a natural waterslide perfect for anyone with strong swimming abilities.

The perfect time to visit this waterfall is the afternoon of a hot, sunny spring day. Although the water will be chilly, it will still be considerably warmer than what you will find at other swimming holes in the region given its hours of sun exposure throughout the day and the pool's lack of current.

TRAIL INFORMATION From the parking lot, walk toward the covered bridge and the river to view the falls. A view of the bridge with the falls set in the foreground can be seen by walking down to the rocky beach outlining the swimming hole.

DIRECTIONS From I-93 in Lincoln, take exit 32 and head west on NH 112. Continue on this road as NH 116 joins and, shortly thereafter, breaks off. At 6.5 miles past the spot where NH 116 breaks off, turn right onto Porter Road. Immediately after, drive through a single-lane covered bridge and pull into the large parking area on your left.

OTHER WATERFALLS NEARBY Beaver Brook Falls, Paradise Falls, Agassiz Basin.

115

THOMPSON FALLS

Pinkhams Grant, White Mountain National Forest, Coos County

Type: Cascades and small plunges
Height: Main plunge is 12 feet
Trail Length: 0.7 mile
Water Source: Thompson Brook
Altitude Gain/Loss: +100 feet

Difficulty: Easy
Hiking Time: 20 minutes
DeLorme Map: Page 45, A&B-8
Rating: ★★★★

DESCRIPTION Three waterfalls are worthy of attention in Pinkham Notch. Glen Ellis Falls and Crystal Cascade, both drops of the Ellis River, are described elsewhere in this guide. Thompson Falls is a scarcely visited sequence of cascades on Thompson Brook, a mountain stream that flows down the west side of the "A Peak" of Wildcat Mountain.

The lowest cascade of Thompson Falls crashes over an overhanging rock ledge that takes on the shape of a gigantic clam. The clam is roughly 30 feet wide, but water flows over only a portion of that. Below, the waters churn slowly around in an inviting, although very chilly, swimming pool. With some careful footwork and a willingness to get wet, it is certainly possible to find a position behind the falling water on the rocks below the overhanging clam-shaped ledge.

Additional cascades can be found upstream, but they lack the personality of the lower falls. The upper cascades do offer the greatest possibility for exploring in solitude. Still, you are likely to have Thompson Falls entirely to yourself as waterfall lovers focus on the other waterfalls in Pinkham Notch.

TRAIL INFORMATION From the Wildcat Ski Area parking lot, walk behind the lodge and cross over a brook on one of several bridges. Take a left after the bridge and walk along the walkway parallel to the brook. Shortly thereafter, you will enter the woods and come to several signs letting you know you are on the Thompson Falls Trail. Continue along the trail for several minutes and you will reach a fork. Take the right fork; the left would bring you to a few stops on the Way of the Wildcat Nature Trail. A few minutes beyond the fork, you will reach another fork. Veer left here at a sign pointing toward the falls. Soon you will reach a dirt road. Walk across the road and continue along the trail for another 0.2 mile to the falls.

DIRECTIONS From the junction of US 302 and NH 16 in the section of Bartlett known as Glen, take NH 16 north and turn right into the Wildcat parking lot. This lot is 0.8 mile north of the Pinkham Notch Visitors Center and 2.0 miles south of the Mount Washington Auto Road entrance. *To get to Glen,* take NH 16 north from Conway.

OTHER WATERFALLS NEARBY Crystal Cascade, Glen Ellis Falls, Winniweta Falls, Jackson Falls.

116

THOREAU FALLS

Lincoln, Grafton County

Type: Cascades and slides
Height: 80-foot total drop
Trail Length: 4.8 miles
Water Source: North Fork of the East Branch of the Pemigewasset River
Altitude Gain/Loss: +400 feet

Difficulty: Easy side of moderate
Hiking Time: 2 hours, 30 minutes
DeLorme Map: Page 44, E-2
Rating: ★★★½

DESCRIPTION Although not as impressive as its neighbor Zealand Falls, the scenic view from Thoreau Falls is magnificent and more than makes

116. Thoreau Falls & 121. Zealand Falls

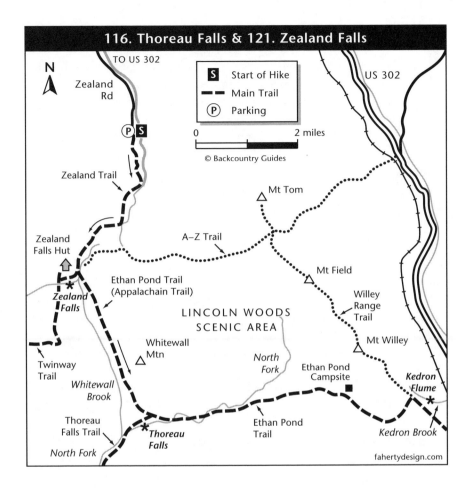

up for the waterfall itself. The rock surfaces are large and flat, creating a fine lunch spot. This spot is also perfectly positioned for admiring the view; make sure to relax for at least an hour here.

The waterfall consists mostly of cascades and slides reaching an 80-foot total drop with no single drop over 15 feet. Decent wading pools lie downstream, hidden from most people at the top of the ledge. This remoteness makes the wading pools very inviting. If the river water is running low, it is safe to scramble down the ledges to the pools below. During high water, however, this should not even be considered.

If you are looking to photograph these falls, we recommend the afternoon hours. During the morning, the sunlight creates a streaking effect on the water that distorts any chance of a good snapshot.

TRAIL INFORMATION From the parking lot, take the trail that continues past the end of the dirt road. This is the blue-blazed Zealand Trail, which covers the first 2.5 miles of this trip. It is rated as easy side of moderate, and grows considerably easier once the muddy spring season ends.

At 2.5 miles you reach the first major trail junction of the hike. If you take a right onto the Twinway Trail, you can visit Zealand Falls and the AMC-run Zealand Hut, both less than 0.3 mile away. To reach Thoreau Falls, you will need to continue straight onto the Ethan Pond Trail (also a section of the white-blazed Appalachian Trail). Follow this new trail for 2.0 miles to its junction with the Thoreau Falls Trail. When you reach the Thoreau Falls Trail, which is clearly marked, take a right and follow the path for 0.2 mile down to the top of the falls. Primitive paths lead you to the base of the falls, but we felt, and believe you will also, that the views from the top of the falls are sufficient.

The variety of hiking environments, plus the smooth and gentle stretches spread across the entire trip, craft quite a pleasant family hike, perhaps one of the best hikes for introducing a hiker to long-distance trekking. The most notable section of the trail includes a walk along the unstable cliffs of Whitewall Mountains, where you are both exposed to the elements and afforded with fine views of Zealand Mountain, Mount Bond, the section of the Zealand Trail that cuts through mountain marshland, and Zealand Pond, where beavers have made their home. A trip to Zealand Falls and Thoreau Falls will forever be one of our favorite day hikes.

DIRECTIONS From the junction of US 3 and US 302 in the village of Carroll known as Twin Mountain, take US 302 east. After 2.2 miles, take a right into the ZEALAND RECREATION AREA. Follow Zealand Road for 3.5 miles to the end of the road, where large parking lots can be found. There is a main parking lot at the end of the road and an overload parking lot just before that. The parking fee in 2002 was $3 per vehicle. *To get to Twin Mountain,* take I-93 north from Lincoln to US 3 north.

OTHER WATERFALLS NEARBY Zealand Falls, Kedron Flume, Ripley Falls.

117

TRIPLE FALLS

Gorham & Randolph, White Mountain National Forest, Coos County

Type: Plunges and cascades
Height: Varies (see notes)
Trail Length: 0.2 mile to top of falls
Water Source: Town Line Brook
Altitude Gain/Loss: +200 feet

Difficulty: Easy side of moderate
Hiking Time: 15 minutes to top of falls
DeLorme Map: Page 48, I-7
Rating: ★★★½

DESCRIPTION In addition to the famous waterfalls of Pinkham Notch, more waterfalls lie within a few miles to the north. Six of these are described in this guide. Three falls—Stairs Fall, Coosauk Falls, and Hitchcock Falls—are described under "Falls on Howker Ridge Trail." The other three falls—Proteus Falls, Erebus Falls, and Evans Falls—are often united together under one appropriate name, *Triple Falls.*

Only minutes from the largest campground in the White Mountains, Dolly Copp, Triple Falls can be conveniently accessed via a short drive, a long walk, or an easy bike ride.

With more than 175 campsites nearby, you would expect that any attractions within walking distance would be popular—but this is not always the case. With only a small sign revealing its location, Triple Falls still lies nearly as untouched as ever. The summit of nearby Pine Mountain, reached via a trailhead that begins just farther down the Pinkham B Road from Triple Falls, attracts a much larger crowd from the campground.

Here is what you can expect to see at Triple Falls: Proteus Falls, the first falls of the hike, is a 20-foot horsetail that falls into moss-covered chasm walls. Erebus Falls, only feet above Proteus Falls, takes on the form of a segmented plunge over a sheath of rock. Just below Erebus is the fastest-traveling waterslide we have seen at a waterfall. Evans Falls, the final feature of Triple Falls, is a small plunge with some cascades and slides varying in size.

The falls are often weak in power—we expect that Town Line Brook dries completely by mid-June—but you do get three waterfalls for the price of one here. To make a day trip out of the area, continue driving along the Pinkham B Road. Spend some time climbing Pine Mountain and visiting the other waterfalls nearby.

TRAIL INFORMATION (See map on page 163.) From the small parking area, cross the road and start up the fairly well-traveled Town Line Brook Trail. After about 0.1 mile, a spur path will lead toward the brook; scramble around a rock wall and the first waterfall, Proteus Falls, will come into view. Continue climbing up the brook for riverside views of Erebus Falls and, shortly thereafter, Evans Falls. The trail is thin and can be extremely slippery and muddy, especially as you advance beyond Proteus Falls to the other cataracts.

DIRECTIONS From the junction of US 302 and NH 16 in the village of Bartlett known as Glen, take NH 16 north. At 3.4 miles north of the entrance to the Mount Washington Road, take a left onto Dolly Copp Road and continue straight for 0.5 mile, passing the entrance to a campground on your left. At a fork in the road here, veer left and follow Pinkham B Road for 2.2 miles to a small parking area on your right just beyond a small bridge over Town Line Brook. *To get to Glen,* take NH 16 north from Conway.

OTHER WATERFALLS NEARBY Falls on the Howker Ridge Trail, Mossy Glen, Appalachia Waterfalls, Thompson Falls, Crystal Cascade.

118

WATERVILLE CASCADES

Waterville Valley, White Mountain National Forest, Grafton County

Type: Horsetail and a fan
Height: 18-foot total drop
Trail Length: 1.2 miles
Water Source: Cascade Brook
Altitude Gain/Loss: Up 300 feet, down 100 feet

Difficulty: Easy side of moderate
Hiking Time: 40 minutes
DeLorme Map: Page 40, A-2
Rating: ★★★★½

DESCRIPTION (HIGHLY RECOMMENDED) If there were ever an award for waterfall beauty per foot of height, Waterville Cascades would certainly contend for the top title. The cascades may be small, at 18 feet

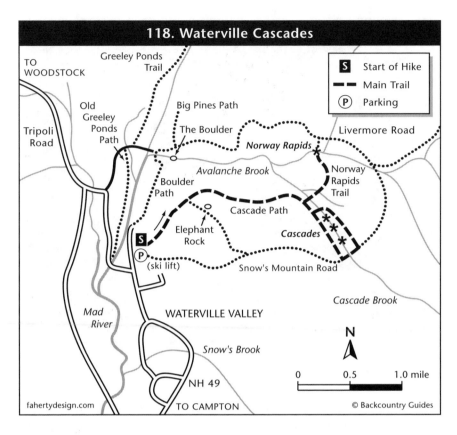

118. Waterville Cascades

TO WOODSTOCK

Greeley Ponds Trail

Big Pines Path

Old Greeley Ponds Path

Tripoli Road

The Boulder

Norway Rapids

Livermore Road

S Start of Hike

— — Main Trail

P Parking

Avalanche Brook

Boulder Path

Norway Rapids Trail

Cascade Path

Elephant Rock

Cascades

S

P (ski lift)

Snow's Mountain Road

Cascade Brook

Mad River

WATERVILLE VALLEY

Snow's Brook

N

0   0.5   1.0 mile

fahertydesign.com

NH 49

TO CAMPTON

© Backcountry Guides

of total drop, but in that short distance Cascade Brook manages to astonish every visitor with its breathtaking flow.

The waterfall begins as a horsetail, quickly descending to a temporary platform of rock at the midway point. From here, the waters converge and fan out in an uprising chute, similar to a ski jump, before landing in an attractive golden pool below. Close to 4 feet deep, the pool is a fine specimen of cold mountain water. Take a dip if you dare, but be warned that the water temperature is not substantially warmer than freezing for most of the year.

Nearby Avalanche Brook has its own splendid natural feature. The Norway Rapids, a short side trip off Cascade Path, is a long chain of cascades of clear whitewater. Although the rapids lack the stunning personality of Waterville Cascades, they are still worth the minuscule effort required to reach them.

TRAIL INFORMATION The trail to the falls begins at the opposite end of the parking lot from the red-colored Snow Mountain Lodge. Begin

Waterville Cascades

by climbing up a grass-covered ski trail for 0.1 mile. Avoid the first few slide paths on both sides of the ski trail. Enter the woods on your left a few hundred feet above the trailhead for Snows Mountain. A sign will let you know you are entering the CASCADE PATH.

After about five minutes, the yellow-blazed Cascade Path will continue straight and the Elephant Rock Trail will spur right. Continue straight on the Cascade Path to a small wooden bridge. This point is about 1.0 mile from the parking lot. Continue right after crossing this 8-foot-long bridge; in 250 feet you will reach the Norway Rapids Trail junction. Continue straight for the Waterville Cascades. The remainder of this walk parallels the brook. The cascades are only 0.2 mile beyond this point.

If you wish to visit the Norway Rapids—more cascades than rapids, if you ask us—return to the Cascade Path and Norway Rapids Trail junction. Follow the Norway Rapids Trail, also yellow-blazed, for 0.4 mile through the woods to Avalanche Brook, where the rapids will be clearly visible.

DIRECTIONS From I-93 in Campton, take exit 28. Turn onto NH 49 north, heading toward Waterville Valley. Continue traveling along NH 49 for 5.7 miles past the WATERVILLE VALLEY TOWN LINE sign. Take a right onto Valley Road, drive 0.5 mile, and turn right again into the parking lot for Snow Mountain. *To get to Campton,* take I-93 north from Plymouth or I-93 south from Lincoln.

OTHER WATERFALLS NEARBY Campton Falls.

119

WELTON FALLS

Alexandria, Welton Falls State Forest, Grafton County

Type: Plunges
Height: 30-foot total drop
Trail Length: 1.2 miles
Water Source: Fowler River
Altitude Gain/Loss: −300 feet

Difficulty: Moderate
Hiking Time: 40 minutes
DeLorme Map: Page 38, K-7
Rating: ★★★★

DESCRIPTION The AMC Cardigan Lodge serves as a trailhead for both the summit of Mount Cardigan and a delightful package of waterfalls of different shapes and sizes, ranging from a staircase of cascades to a 15-foot-tall plunge surrounded by cliff walls on all sides (the lower half of Welton Falls, to be specific). Above the 15-foot plunge, the upper half of Welton Falls consists of an 8-foot-tall cascade, hidden from most vantage points around the falls by curvaceous rocks.

The Fowler River offers swimming for the entire section of the Manning Trail that parallels the brook. There are shallow pools scattered throughout, and a few deep pools below the falls. Always use caution when entering any swimming hole: Slippery rocks and strong currents have been merciless before and will be again. The best opportunity for swimming is directly below the main plunge at Welton Falls. Unfortunately, we scanned the area and could not determine a feasible route out of the pool. (Getting in is not a problem; you could jump off the cliffs!)

TRAIL INFORMATION The trail begins to the right of the AMC Cardigan Lodge. Cross a short, grassy field and enter the woods after passing a sign for the MANNING TRAIL. This yellow-blazed trail is very wide in the beginning, but soon narrows as it begins descending toward the Fowler River. After hiking for about 25 minutes—slightly less than a mile—you will need to cross the river. Beyond this crossing, the markers

become increasingly difficult to locate. The trail waves up and down, and is at times steep and rather narrow. About 0.2 mile past the river, the trail will descend and turn right. Immediately after, fork left and walk toward a green iron fence for a view of the top of the falls from within a bowl-shaped gap in the gorge. To reach the base of the falls, continue back to the trail and head downstream about 100 feet. You may even wish to scramble downstream for pools and small cascades.

DIRECTIONS From I-93 in New Hampton, take exit 23. Turn onto NH 104 west and continue to its junction with NH 3A in Bristol. Turn right onto NH 3A north and follow that highway for 2.1 miles. Take a left onto West Shore Road just before a stone church. Follow West Shore Road for 1.8 miles, then continue straight onto a new road. After 1.3 miles, fork right onto Fowler River Road. Follow Fowler River Road for 3.2 miles and take a left onto Brook Road, marked with a sign for AMC. Follow Brook Road for 1.1 miles and take a right onto

Welton Falls

Shem Valley Road. After 0.1 mile, fork right and head toward the Cardigan Lodge. Continue for an additional 1.4 miles and you will reach the lodge. Parking is on your left, opposite the AMC building. *To get to New Hampton,* take I-93 south from Plymouth or I-93 north from Concord.

OTHER WATERFALLS NEARBY Sculptured Rocks.

120

WINNIWETA FALLS

Jackson, White Mountain National Forest, Carroll County

Type: Cascades and small plunges
Height: 40-foot total drop
Trail Length: 0.9 mile
Water Source: Miles Brook
Altitude Gain/Loss: +100 feet

Difficulty: Easy side of moderate (see notes)
Hiking Time: 30 minutes
DeLorme Map: Page 44, D-7
Rating: ★★½

DESCRIPTION Winniweta Falls is a seldom-visited little waterfall located off NH 16, just south of the Mount Washington Auto Road and Pinkham Notch. At this site there are major cascades, notable plunges, and many slides over rock. Views are usually limited by plant growth, but it is possible to explore some areas of the falls. Be on the lookout for moose here—we have heard some accounts of sightings, and seen plenty of fresh tracks ourselves.

TRAIL INFORMATION From the parking area, walk west toward the Ellis River, which you must cross. Depending on the season, this may be a difficult task. If you are crossing in early spring, you may get wet up to your knees; in midsummer you may only get your feet wet. Beyond the river, take the right fork and look for a small trail sign on a tree. From this point on, the trail is relatively straight and passes through several junctions. Continue straight at each junction to reach the falls.

DIRECTIONS From the junction of US 302 and NH 16 in the village of Bartlett known as Glen, take NH 16 north for 5.4 miles and look for a small parking pull-off on your left, marked by a small, rather inconspicuous trail sign for WINNIWETA FALLS. *To get to Glen,* take NH 16 north from Conway.

OTHER WATERFALLS NEARBY Jackson Falls, Glen Ellis Falls, Crystal Cascade, Thompson Falls.

121

ZEALAND FALLS
Bethlehem, Grafton County

Type: Plunges
Height: 25-foot total drop
Trail Length: 2.8 miles
Water Source: Whitewall Brook
Altitude Gain/Loss: +500 feet

Difficulty: Easy side of moderate
Hiking Time: 1 hour, 15 minutes
DeLorme Map: Page 44, D-2
Rating: ★★★★

DESCRIPTION You get more than just a prized waterfall when you visit Zealand Falls. Along the access hike are scenic marshlands, a mountain body of water known as Zealand Pond, and the Zealand Hut, a convenient hiker facility managed by the Appalachian Mountain Club just above the falls. With drinks (lemonade!), food, and lodging available, the Zealand Hut makes a great trail rest stop or overnight accommodation. Reservations are recommended for those wishing to stay overnight. Be sure to check out the hut if you have not visited one in the region. We are sure you will find the employees friendly and full of great outdoor advice.

During the morning hours on a sunny day, light hits the front of the rock faces of Zealand Falls, illuminating the top of the waterfall. The lower part of the fall is tucked a few feet inside a narrow flume, but is visible upon closer inspection. The roar of the water drowns out any other sounds. A smaller 4-foot waterfall is below the main attraction. At the base of this smaller addition lies a circular pool; it is not very deep, but it makes a fine spot for sitting or wading.

TRAIL INFORMATION (See map on page 201.) Zealand Falls is reached by connecting the Zealand Trail with the Twinway Trail. Walk past the National Forest billboard and continue down the trail that begins at the end of the dirt road. A few feet after you enter the woods, the trail-

Zealand Falls

head sign will appear, as well as information about the Zealand Hut. Follow the Zealand Trail, a relatively flat and easy blue-blazed trail, for 2.5 miles to a major trail junction with the Ethan Pond Trail and the Twinway Trail. From here, take a right onto the Twinway Trail. The falls lie 0.2 mile up this trail, and the Zealand Hut, only a few feet more.

Unless you happen to embark on this trail during the spring muddy season, traveling is extremely easy, with generous sections of flat, smooth hiking. Too add a few hours to your trip, include nearby Thoreau Falls on your itinerary. With Thoreau Falls, the trip grows to a total of 10 easygoing miles. This was one of the most pleasant half-day hikes we encountered while producing this guide. See the chapter on Thoreau Falls for more trail details.

DIRECTIONS From the junction of US 3 and US 302 in the village of Carroll known as Twin Mountain, take US 302 east, continue for 2.2 miles, and take a right into the ZEALAND RECREATION AREA. Follow Zealand Road for 3.5 miles to its end, where large parking lots can be found. There is a main parking lot at the end of the road and an overload parking lot just before that. The parking fee in 2002 was $3 per vehicle. *To get to Twin Mountain,* take I-93 north from Lincoln to US 3 north.

OTHER WATERFALLS NEARBY Thoreau Falls, Beecher and Pearl Cascades, Gibbs Falls.

V. Rhode Island

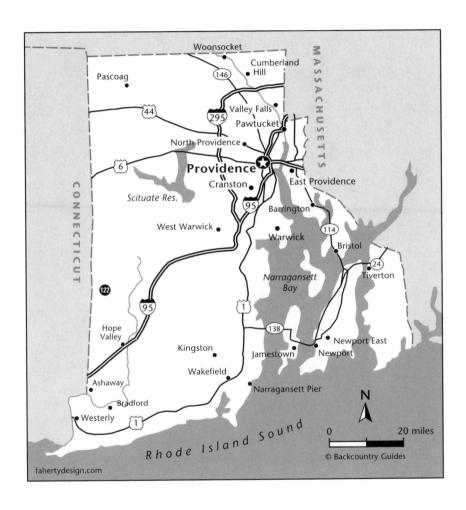

Woonsocket
Cumberland Hill
Pascoag
146
MASSACHUSETTS
44
Valley Falls
295
Pawtucket
North Providence
6
Providence
East Providence
Cranston
CONNECTICUT
Scituate Res.
95
Barrington
West Warwick
114
Warwick
Bristol
24
Tiverton
Narragansett Bay
122
95
Hope Valley
1
Kingston
138
Newport East
Jamestown
Newport
Wakefield
Ashaway
Narragansett Pier
Bradford
Westerly
1
N
Rhode Island Sound
0   20 miles
© Backcountry Guides

faherytdesign.com

122

~

STEPSTONE FALLS

West Greenwich, Arcadia Management Area,
Kent County

Type: Cascades
Height: 10-foot total drop
Trail Length: Less than 0.1 mile
Water Source: Wood River
Altitude Gain/Loss: None

Difficulty: Easy
Hiking Time: Not applicable
DeLorme Map: Page 70, C-3
Rating: ★★½

DESCRIPTION The state of Rhode Island does not sport genuinely mountainous terrain like the five other New England states. In fact, the highest point is Jerimoth Hill—only 812 feet above sea level. Rhode Island is in fifth to last place as far as states with the highest elevations go, behind only Mississippi, Louisiana, Delaware, and Florida.

With such a smooth, gentle landscape covering the majority of the state, it is no surprise that we could only find one notable waterfall. You could surely find other chains of cascades, though probably none that has water flow year-round as Stepstone Falls of West Greenwich does.

Dropping about 10 feet over about 100 feet of distance, the falls are by no means massive or spectacular. Instead, they are peaceful little cascades falling over overhanging ledges. The tallest drop, at only 3 feet, is surprisingly photogenic and charming. The water flows over a broad, flat ledge, creating a long curtain.

For those looking for extra outdoor activities, the Arcadia Management Area offers hiking and horseback riding in some areas. A number of animals reside in the park, including cottontail rabbits, white-tailed deer, foxes, and mink. Fishing is another common activity within the park. Trout can be caught in the Wood River and its tributaries. The ponds within the park offer bass and pickerel.

TRAIL INFORMATION The best view of the falls is found by walking across the bridge beyond the parking area and taking a right onto a white-blazed trail. In just over 100 feet the main cascade can be seen. There are other petite cascades up and downstream from the main falls.

DIRECTIONS From Providence, take I-95 south to exit 5A. Turn onto RI 102 south, drive 0.8 mile, and take a right onto RI 3 south. After

1.2 miles, turn right onto RI 165 west. Follow RI 165 west for 5.1 miles and take a right onto Escoheag Hill Road. After 2.3 miles on Escoheag Hill Road, take a right onto Falls River Road. Continue for 0.6 mile; the pull-off will be on your right just before the bridge over the Wood River.

OTHER WATERFALLS NEARBY None.

VI. Vermont

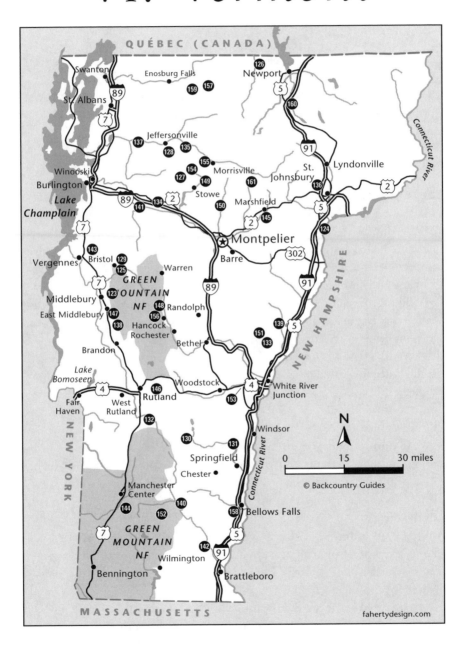

QUÉBEC (CANADA)

Swanton
Enosburg Falls
Newport
126
89
159 157
St. Albans
5
160
7
Jeffersonville
137
91
128 135
Winooski
155
Morrisville
Lyndonville
154
St.
Burlington
127 149
161
Johnsbury
136
Stowe
Lake
89
150
Marshfield
5
Champlain
134 2
141
2 145
124
7
Montpelier
143
Barre
302
Vergennes
Bristol
129
Warren
91
125
GREEN
Middlebury
123
OUNTAIN
89
East Middlebury
147
148
NF
Randolph
138
156
Brandon
Hancock
139
Rochester
Bethel
151
5
133
Lake
Bomoseen
146
Woodstock
4
White River
4
Junction
Fair
West
153
Haven
Rutland
Rutland
132
Windsor
130
131
Springfield
Chester
Manchester
Center
144
140
158
Bellows Falls
152
5
GREEN
MOUNTAIN
142
91
NF
Wilmington
Bennington
Brattleboro

MASSACHUSETTS

NEW HAMPSHIRE

NEW YORK

Connecticut River

Connecticut River

N

0   15   30 miles

© Backcountry Guides

fahertydesign.com

123

ABBEY POND CASCADES

Middlebury, Green Mountain National Forest, Addison County

Type: Horsetails and cascades
Height: 80-foot total drop
Trail Length: 0.2 mile
Water Source: Stream from Abbey Pond
Altitude Gain/Loss: +100 feet

Difficulty: Easy side of moderate
Hiking Time: 10 minutes
DeLorme Map: Page 39, K-10
Rating: ★★★½

DESCRIPTION Powered upstream by Abbey Pond, Abbey Pond Cascades is a sequence of cascades and horsetails that drop 80 feet. From the footbridge that the access trail travels over, you will notice that the area is heavily shaded with little opportunity for a good photograph. To solve this problem, deviate from the trail and hike to the base of the entire falls. There you will notice a completely different perspective, and will be able to pull off a much better photograph. Gravel pits in the background detract from the delightfulness of this waterfall, especially from the bottom, but not enough to stop you from visiting.

TRAIL INFORMATION The trail you will be following to the falls is the blue-blazed Abbey Pond Trail. Begin on a wide gravel path. A short distance from the parking area, you will enter the woods. The cascades are only about 0.1 mile beyond this point. You will reach a short footbridge placed approximately in the center of the cascades. The best view to be had, in our opinion, is from the base of the entire cascade chain, with the bridge serving as the center object. There are several paths to reach the base of the falls, all of which can be slippery and muddy, so use caution. It is also possible to scramble up and explore the area around the top half of the falls.

If time permits, you might want to hike beyond the falls to Abbey Pond, a remote mountain pond frequently inhabited by great blue herons. From the falls, it is about 1.7 miles farther to the pond, and the trail is generally considered moderately difficult.

DIRECTIONS From the junction of VT 116 and VT 125 in East Middlebury, take VT 116 north for 4.3 miles to a right onto a dirt road. Im-

Abbey Pond Cascades

mediately fork left and follow this new gravel road for 0.4 mile to a large parking area. *To get to East Middlebury,* take US 7 south from Middlebury to VT 125 east.

OTHER WATERFALLS NEARBY Middlebury Gorge, Texas Falls, Falls of Lana, Bartlett Falls.

124

BARNET FALLS
Barnet, Caledonia County

Type: Cascades
Height: 50 feet
Trail Length: Roadside
Water Source: Stevens River
Altitude Gain/Loss: None

Difficulty: Easy
Hiking Time: Not applicable
DeLorme Map: Page 42, B&C-5
Rating: ★★½

DESCRIPTION Just before dumping into the Connecticut River, the Stevens River cascades 50 feet in one final magnificent display. A local resident owns the property in front of the waterfall, which must be a real treat for him. Unfortunately for us, this means that views are limited to roadside only. Perhaps one day the town of Barnet will acquire the property and create a lovely small park. This waterfall would definitely be the main attraction in any new park creation; it is worth a visit, if only to view it from the road, as it is a beautiful sight.

TRAIL INFORMATION The views from roadside will have to suffice for this waterfall, which is on private property.

DIRECTIONS Take I-91 south from St. Johnsbury to exit 18. Follow Bartlett Road toward the center of Barnet. When you reach the small town center, take a left onto VT 5. Continue for 0.6 mile and take a right onto Mill Hill Street. The falls are just around the corner on your right.

OTHER WATERFALLS NEARBY Emerson Falls, Marshfield Falls.

125

BARTLETT FALLS

Bristol, Addison County

Type: Block
Height: 15 feet
Trail Length: Less than 0.1 mile
Water Source: New Haven River
Altitude Gain/Loss: None

Difficulty: Easy
Hiking Time: Not applicable
DeLorme Map: Page 39, H-10
Rating: ★★★★★

DESCRIPTION (HIGHLY RECOMMENDED) What makes this waterfall extraordinary is the 40-foot-wide, 120-foot-long sparkling pool that lies below. With its inviting yellow-green waters and depths ranging from ankle height to well over your head, this pool has been known to attract 500 people in a single day.

A favorite Vermont swimming hole for years, Bartlett Falls (also known to local residents as the Falls at New Haven River Gorge) also offers a large block-style waterfall and a sizable gorge. The block, which is 15 feet in height, falls over a broad overhanging ledge. This ledge creates another great feature here: a cave behind the falling water. The flat slabs of rock to the side allow you to get behind the falls with very little effort for a new perspective on waterfalls. There are few spots in New England where this is possible, and none as easy as Bartlett Falls. If the current is not too strong, you can jump through the waterfall and be carried through the swimming pool on the other side.

We strongly suggest when visiting this waterfall that you bring a bathing suit and lunch, and plan to spend a few hours basking in the sun while hearing the laughter of children playing in the water. If the popularity of the falls is too much to handle, more pools, and a quieter atmosphere, can be found farther downstream. Either way, on a hot day this is a must-visit place that you will likely return to many times in your life.

TRAIL INFORMATION Several popular paths lead from the numerous parking areas down to the river. No matter which trail you take, you will eventually come across cascades and potholes for swimming. The main drop is upstream, about 0.3 mile west of the junction of VT 17 and VT 116. Unfortunately, the best view of the main drop is from midriver, because the falls are surrounded by sheer gorge walls. That being said, the

Bartlett Falls

best time to visit is during late spring or summer. If comfortable, be sure to carefully swim up to the falls and explore the cave behind the plunging water. Bartlett Falls is the only waterfall with an easy-access cave in New England that we are aware of.

DIRECTIONS From the western junction of VT 17 and VT 116 in Bristol, take the combined VT 116 north/VT 17 east for 2.8 miles to a right onto Lincoln Road. The parking area is 0.2 mile up the road on your right. *To get to Bristol,* take US 7 north from Middlebury to VT 17 east.

OTHER WATERFALLS NEARBY Bristol Memorial Park Gorge, Abbey Pond Cascades, Little Otter Creek Falls, Middlebury Gorge.

126

BIG FALLS

Troy, Orleans County

Type: Cascades
Height: 40-foot total drop
Trail Length: Less than 0.1 mile
Water Source: Missisquoi River
Altitude Gain/Loss: None

Difficulty: Easy
Hiking Time: Not applicable
DeLorme Map: Page 53, A&B-11
Rating: ★★★★

DESCRIPTION Though simple, the name of this waterfall fits it perfectly. The water rushing through the gorge creates a massive, roaring waterfall. The gorge itself is large with very high walls. The currents are powerful and strong, and the water color is a mixture of mostly ivory, white, and yellow. Considering the volume of the water rushing through the gorge, it is surprising that these falls have never been developed as a hydroelectric project, as have most of the waterfalls with similar strength in Vermont.

The best observation point is from the highest cliff, which is approximately 80 feet higher than the river below. Several segments make up the total waterfall. Before rushing down, the water condenses into an impressive, bubbling rapid. This is where the powerful, almost deadly currents can best be viewed as they swirl around.

TRAIL INFORMATION From the parking lot, enter the woods behind outlying boulders. Walk past some small cascades on your distant left, and a vantage point for the falls will be straight ahead, on top of a soaring gorge wall. From this cliff, you will be able to admire the deadly power of the Missisquoi River at Big Falls, and the giant gorge walls that continue downstream.

DIRECTIONS From Newport, take VT 105 west and continue for 9.0 miles past the TROY TOWN LINE sign to a left onto River Road, an unmarked dirt road. This road is about 1.0 mile east of the center of North Troy. Follow River Road for 1.4 miles to a small parking area on your right. *To get to Newport,* take I-91 north from St. Johnsbury to exit 27. Take VT 191 west to US 5 south.

OTHER WATERFALLS NEARBY Trout River Falls, West Hill Brook Falls, Willoughby River Falls.

Big Falls

127

BINGHAM FALLS

Stowe, Lamoille County

Type: Plunges and cascades
Height: Tallest plunge is 25 feet
Trail Length: 0.3 mile to lower-most plunge
Water Source: West Branch Waterbury River
Altitude Gain/Loss: −150 feet

Difficulty: Easy to first falls; difficult thereafter
Hiking Time: 20 minutes
DeLorme Map: Page 46, F-3
Rating: ★★★★★

DESCRIPTION (HIGHLY RECOMMENDED) This waterfall is a secluded geological wonder. There are lots of curvaceous rocks, which create a deep rumbling, thunderous sound as the powerful high volume of water is forced into the small slice between the two gorge walls. This is one of the greatest gorges we have seen on our many hikes. The water is a beautiful clear teal color and even remains that color as it plunges and cascades over the rocks.

The first waterfall flows into a very deep pool before a cascade continues over another ledge. The second waterfall is a 25-foot block that fans out just before flowing into yet a third waterfall—perhaps the most beautiful of all as it plunges into still another pool of a vibrant teal color. These third falls are also impressive because the water shoots away from the rocks at an angle and falls into the sexiest pool we have ever seen: deep, clean, beautiful, and completely private, practically begging to be swum in. The right side of the pool has dangerous currents that would trap you underneath large boulders in the river, while the left side has little to no current at all. The center of the pool is more dangerous as the currents push onward down the river; if you choose to swim, please note this as you cool down in the refreshing water.

Although this waterfall is a great one, we do ask that you be careful when scrambling down to the last falls. The gorge walls are high, and the water is powerful. There is a cross and a plaque on a tree in memory of people who have died there. Hike responsibly, do not get too close to the edges, and please, if you do not feel comfortable, do not scramble down the high gorge walls.

Bingham Falls

TRAIL INFORMATION From the unmarked dirt pull-offs, continue down the only trail on the northbound side of the state highway. After an easy 0.2-mile walk, you will reach the first falls. From here you can follow the trail right to discover more wonders, more pools, and increasingly difficult footing. The trail can be very difficult due to its steepness and the amount of scrambling required to get to the base of the third plunge, but it is well worth the effort. We advise that you do not attempt to visit the final plunge alone; bringing a rope in case of emergency is not a bad idea, either.

DIRECTIONS From the junction of VT 100 and VT 108 in Stowe, take VT 108 north for 6.3 miles to parking areas on both sides of the road. *To get to Stowe,* take I-89 north from Montpelier to exit 10. Follow VT 100 north.

OTHER WATERFALLS NEARBY Brewster River Gorge, Moss Glen Falls (Stowe), Sterling Brook Gorge, Terrill Gorge.

128

BREWSTER RIVER GORGE

Cambridge, Lamoille County

Type: Horsetails
Height: 45-foot total drop
Trail Length: 0.3 mile
Water Source: Brewster River
Altitude Gain/Loss: None

Difficulty: Moderate
Hiking Time: 20 minutes
DeLorme Map: Page 46, B-1
Rating: ★★★★

DESCRIPTION Given its short access trail, reaching Brewster River Gorge—known as Jefferson Falls or Jeff Falls to some—takes a surprisingly long time. You may need upward of half an hour to get to the waterfall, due mostly in part to a river crossing about 0.1 mile from the parking area.

You are going to have to take off your shoes and partake in a balancing act as you rock-hop across the stream. Then you must locate the continuation of the trail. These requirements make accessing Brewster River Gorge moderately difficult, especially in spring when the water levels of the river are up.

At the falls, the water picks its way through and around boulders that appear to have fallen on top of one another through the years. There are small greenish-tinted pools at the base of the falls. The river itself is quite wide, with an extended riverbank. There are places where the banking is sandy, and others where it is grassy or covered with small pebbles. There are also lots of rocks to scramble over and play on if you choose. The well-worn area looks like many people have chosen to spend some time here, enjoying the soft sound of the water and relaxing on the bank.

TRAIL INFORMATION The trail begins at the end of the parking lot. Easy and flat for the majority of the time, the only complication for visiting this waterfall is a crossing of the Brewster River. Depending on the season, accessing the other side of the river can be ridiculously easy or a nuisance. In spring expect to remove your shoes and get wet up to your knees or so. In summer, when the Brewster River's volume diminishes, you may perhaps get away with only scuttling across small rocks. Once you have reached the other side of the river, the falls will be a few hundred yards farther up the trail.

DIRECTIONS From the junction of VT 108 and VT 15 in the cen-

Brewster River Gorge

ter of Jeffersonville, take VT 108 south for 0.6 mile and turn left onto Canyon Road. After a couple of hundred feet, turn right at a sign for the BREWSTER RIVER GORGE PARK just before going through a covered bridge. *To get to Jeffersonville,* take VT 15 east from Burlington.

OTHER WATERFALLS NEARBY Bingham Falls, Fairfax Falls, Dog's Head Falls, Terrill Gorge.

129

BRISTOL MEMORIAL PARK GORGE

Bristol, Addison County

Type: Plunges

Height: 10 feet and 15 feet

Trail Length: 0.1 mile

Water Source: Baldwin Creek

Altitude Gain/Loss: −50 feet

Difficulty: Easy

Hiking Time: 5 minutes

DeLorme Map: Page 39, G-11

Rating: ★★½

DESCRIPTION The best view of this waterfall is from the bridge at its base. You will see a side view of the upper plunge and the lower horsetail, but if you stand on the bridge a small thin stream of water deviating from the larger waterfall will be directly visible. The last horsetail falls into an oyster-shaped rock surface, which has obviously been carved by the force of the water during early spring when runoff passes through the gorge. Considering how the main portion of the waterfall twists around these large rocks, the small stream alongside almost speaks to the other water, saying, *I am going to take my own route and sneak down inside this rock crevasse.*

The water has worn away the rocks through the years, so the rough surface surrounding the waterfall is quite different from the smooth wet rock surface directly next to and under the waterfall itself. There is a 50-foot gorge below the main attraction and the bridge. Only a thin stream of water passes through. Bristol Memorial Park Gorge may not be highly recommended for the waterfall, but it is still worth the visit if you make a duo-waterfall day out of it by also visiting Bartlett Falls.

TRAIL INFORMATION From the parking lot, follow an easy boardwalk trail for a few minutes until you reach the falls and gorge.

DIRECTIONS From Bristol, follow the combined VT 116 north/ VT 17 east. Turn right onto VT 17 east when it breaks away from VT 116 north, drive 2.2 miles, and pull into the parking lot marked with a sign for the MEMORIAL FOREST on the right. *To get to Bristol,* take US 7 north from Middlebury to VT 17 east.

OTHER WATERFALLS NEARBY Bartlett Falls, Abbey Pond Cascades, Little Otter Creek Falls.

130

BUTTERMILK FALLS

Ludlow, Windsor County

Type: Horsetails and cascades
Height: Lower falls is 20 feet; upper falls is 15 feet
Trail Length: 0.1 mile
Water Source: Branch Brook
Altitude Gain/Loss: None

Difficulty: Easy
Hiking Time: Not applicable
DeLorme Map: Page 30, J-3&4
Rating: ★★★★

DESCRIPTION The majority of the top-rated swimming holes in Vermont—in both our opinion and that of the general public—lie in the northern half of the state. This waterfall is one of the few great swimming holes in southern Vermont. There is a large pool below both the lower and upper falls, each being deep enough for complete submersion. The lower falls flow into a deep 25-foot-wide pool of clear, olive-green water. Later in the season a quaint twist of water wraps itself around a slightly wetted rock, adding character to what is usually a typical plunge throwing itself over the ledge during high-water-volume times.

The upper falls is a segmented horsetail, with the right fall being predominant. The left horsetail is strong only in spring or after a heavy rain. In general this horsetail is steeper and slightly taller—it is 15 feet high, whereas the right horsetail is about 12 feet. Both streams of water flow into another large swimming pool with clear water and a pebble-covered bottom. This waterfall should be visited both in spring and later on in summer—it really looks like two different waterfalls with different water flow in the respective seasons.

TRAIL INFORMATION Many trails lead to the falls from the road; follow any of these paths a few feet and you will reach the brook. You can scramble your way up or downstream to many smaller, although equally enjoyable, cascades and pools.

DIRECTIONS From Ludlow, take the combined VT 100 /VT 103 north. Continue on VT 103 for 0.2 mile after VT 100 breaks off. Take a right onto Buttermilk Falls Road. Follow this road for 1.3 miles and park on any of the shoulders on your right. *To get to Ludlow,* take I-91 south

Buttermilk Falls

from White River Junction to exit 8. Follow VT 131 west to VT 103 north.

OTHER WATERFALLS NEARBY Clarendon Gorge, Cascade Falls.

131

CASCADE FALLS

Weathersfield, Windsor County

Type: Horsetail

Height: 80 feet

Trail Length: 1.1 miles

Water Source: Ascutney Brook

Altitude Gain/Loss: +700 feet

Difficulty: Moderate

Hiking Time: 45 minutes

DeLorme Map: Page 31, J-9

Rating: ★★★½

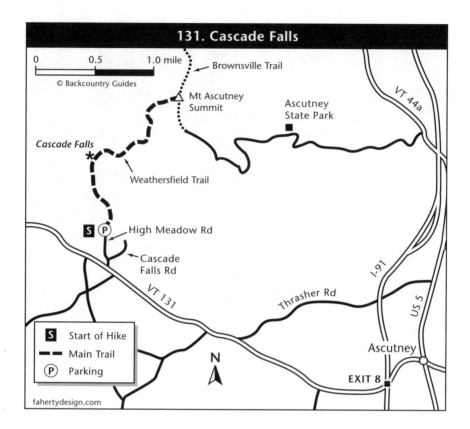

131. Cascade Falls

0   0.5   1.0 mile

© Backcountry Guides

Brownsville Trail

Mt Ascutney
Summit

Cascade Falls

Ascutney
State Park

VT 44a

Weathersfield Trail

High Meadow Rd

Cascade
Falls Rd

VT 131

Thrasher Rd

I-91

US 5

Ascutney

EXIT 8

S Start of Hike

Main Trail

P Parking

N

fahertydesign.com

DESCRIPTION This waterfall is best in springtime—it dries up quite quickly after all the snow melts. About halfway to Cascade Falls is another, smaller, rumored waterfall, named Little Cascade Falls. We suspect that this structure may not even be a real waterfall; it appears to be much too seasonal, completely dried up by June most years. If water were flowing, it would be an 80-foot total drop. In early July when we visited, however, the site looked as though it had not seen water in more than a month.

After crossing over the smaller falls, continue up the trail to the bigger formation, which is even impressive when mostly dry. You will be standing at the top of the falls, where a large ledge will cause the water to steeply and rapidly drop. This ledge is 30 feet wide, but the falls are no more than a few feet wide at the maximum. We suggest sitting close to the ledge and admiring the fall and the panorama unfolded before you. A perfectly placed boulder makes for a great seat just before the ledge.

TRAIL INFORMATION From the parking area, begin ascending

Mount Ascutney via the white-blazed Weathersfield Trail. The distance from the lot to Little Cascade Falls is only 0.4 mile, and the elevation gain is about 250 feet. When you reach Little Cascade Falls, continue climbing along the Weathersfield Trail to a trail ladder. Ascend the sturdy ladder; the first scenic vista of the trail is to your left. There is a nice rock outcropping for a quick rest. After admiring the view, continue climbing the moderately steep trail to Cascade Falls. A little over 1 mile from the parking lot, you will reach a sign directing you left to the falls and right toward the rest of the 1.8 miles of the Weathersfield Trail needed to reach the summit of Mount Ascutney. Take a left at this sign and begin walking toward the clearing. As you start walking down the large, flat rock toward the ledge over which the brook tumbles, you will be blown away with another scenic vista. This one has views of approximately 80 miles away, or perhaps more, especially on exceptionally clear days. A perfectly placed boulder overlooks the waterfall and the panorama near the ledge of the fall.

As a whole, the trail is a continuous climb with many reenergizing flat stretches. There is nothing particularly difficult or steep on this trail, but once again, it does eventually reach the tall summit of Mount Ascutney.

DIRECTIONS Take I-91 south from White River Junction to exit 8. Take VT 131 west for 3.1 miles and turn right onto Cascade Falls Road. After 0.1 mile, take a left onto High Meadow Road. Follow this road for 0.4 mile to the parking lot at its end.

OTHER WATERFALLS NEARBY Buttermilk Falls, Quechee Gorge & Mill Pond Falls.

132

CLARENDON GORGE
Clarendon, Rutland County

Type: Cascades

Height: 8-foot total drop

Trail Length: 0.1 mile

Water Source: Mill River

Altitude Gain/Loss: −25 feet

Difficulty: Easy

Hiking Time: 5 minutes

DeLorme Map: Page 29, G-13

Rating: ★★½

DESCRIPTION What makes this waterfall special is a 30-foot-long shaky suspension bridge over the gorge. This gorge is a popular swimming hole with deep yellow-green pools. Ten feet of small cascades underneath the bridge are best seen by walking down the many paths beyond the bridge. There are many potholes and plenty of large rocks to sit on and bask in the sun. The river is beautiful due to its width, with surprisingly low volume given its size. The main reason you might come to this waterfall is to enjoy the scenic river, crossing the bridge, and to spend some time with your family picnicking and swimming. As a waterfall it is not too impressive, but the surroundings add to the overall appeal of this visit.

TRAIL INFORMATION The trails used to access the gorge are the combined Appalachian Trail and the Long Trail. From the parking area, walk past the trail billboard and immediately descend into the woods. Follow the white-marked trails for 0.1 mile to a shaky suspension bridge over the gorge. From here you can see all the small cascades and the deep gorge walls. It is possible to scramble down to the base of the gorge to the popular swimming hole under the bridge.

DIRECTIONS From Rutland, take US 7 south to VT 103 east. Follow VT 103 east for 2.3 miles to a right into the APPALACHIAN/LONG TRAIL parking lot. Take note that the VT 103 sign on US 7 is marked EAST, while the highway is marked SOUTH once you begin traveling on it.

OTHER WATERFALLS NEARBY Buttermilk Falls, McLaughlin Falls.

133

COVERED BRIDGE FALLS
Thetford Center, Orange County

Type: Cascades
Height: 25-foot total drop
Trail Length: 0.1 mile
Water Source: Ompompanoosuc River
Altitude Gain/Loss: None

Difficulty: Moderate
Hiking Time: 5 minutes
DeLorme Map: Page 35, G-14
Rating: ★★★

DESCRIPTION Covered Bridge Falls is, as the name could suggest, a waterfall that neighbors a covered bridge. The bridge, which is approximately

50 feet in length, sits just above the 25-foot chain of cascades in the town of Thetford. Covered Bridge Falls is often referred to as Thetford Center Falls.

Although the bridge is only a few yards above the falls, accessing any view of the falls, other than from the road or bridge, is surprisingly difficult—but do not leave the area without a closer look. If its location were more publicly disclosed, it would certainly receive more attention from painters and photographers: The waterfall and covered bridge create one artistic frame.

TRAIL INFORMATION The falls begin 50 feet downstream from the covered bridge, accessible by barely used trails on either side of the river. If you are visiting in spring, the trail should be obvious; only moderate bushwhacking is required. In summer, undergrowth will increase the bushwhacking difficulty significantly. In either case, bushwhacking is required for only a few yards, and the cascades are quite worth it in our opinion.

DIRECTIONS Take I-91 north from White River Junction to exit 14. Take VT 113 west for 2.4 miles, then turn left onto Tucker Hill Road. Follow this road for 0.3 mile and park before or after the covered bridge.

OTHER WATERFALLS NEARBY Old City Falls, Glen Falls, Quechee Gorge & Mill Pond Falls.

Covered Bridge Falls

134

DEVIL'S POTHOLES

Bolton, Chittenden County

Type: Plunges and cascades
Height: 45-foot total drop
Trail Length: Less than 0.1 mile
Water Source: Joiner Brook
Altitude Gain/Loss: None

Difficulty: Easy
Hiking Time: Not applicable
DeLorme Map: Page 45, K-14
Rating: ★★★★★

DESCRIPTION (HIGHLY RECOMMENDED) This is a waterfall that fits everyone well. It is perfect for children, teens, and adults alike. There are plenty of flat rock surfaces for picnickers and sunbathers, pools for swimmers, and a stunning set of waterfalls sure to please anyone.

Or actually, three sets of waterfalls. The first plunge drops into a small, round pool about 5 feet wide by 5 feet long. The second plunge falls into an almost perfectly circular pothole about 25 feet in diameter. The surrounding cliff walls are also arched accordingly. Each pool is filled with the deep, emerald-green water so common to Vermont swimming holes. The third cascade falls into a river channel. Just ahead, the water becomes much shallower, creating knee-deep pools ideal for younger children.

The beaches at the base of the falls are part sandy, part loose rocks; the remainder is the base of the ledge the waterfall flows through. Certainly some of the coldest of all the swimming holes in New England, Devil's Potholes should be visited only during hot days in summer for the swimming. Year-round, however, the waterfall remains quite scenic itself and worth visiting for more than just swimming.

TRAIL INFORMATION From any of the parking areas, walk east toward the brook. There are almost a dozen short paths leading to the upper, middle, and bottom sections of the falls from the road. It is also possible to slowly scramble down from the upper viewpoints to the base of the falls without returning to the road to take another path.

DIRECTIONS From Burlington, take US 2 east. Continue on US 2 for 0.4 mile past the BOLTON TOWN LINE sign and take a left onto Bolton Valley Road. After 0.2 mile you can park on the shoulder on either side of the road.

OTHER WATERFALLS NEARBY Huntington Gorge, Moss Glen Falls (Stowe), Bingham Falls, Brewster River Gorge.

Devil's Potholes

135

DOG'S HEAD FALLS

Johnson, Lamoille County

Type: Cascades
Height: 6 feet
Trail Length: 0.1 mile
Water Source: Lamoille River
Altitude Gain/Loss: None

Difficulty: Easy
Hiking Time: Not applicable
DeLorme Map: Page 46, B-5
Rating: ★★★

DESCRIPTION The best view of this waterfall is actually from the road, River Road East, before you reach the path to the water. From the road, a massive profile of a canine quickly indicates the source of this waterfall's name. A topic of controversy is the breed of dog; in our opinion, it is a Saint Bernard!

This waterfall is known as Upper Dog's Head Falls to some. After taking the trail you will be standing on the actual formation of the head to view the cascade. It is about 6 feet in total drop, yet has a large volume of yellowish water. Very strong currents prevent swimming in the deep pools below. The Lower Dog's Head Falls consists of two sections of 5-foot cascades and rapids, and is found just back down the road you came. It is said that during low water, the entire volume of the Lamoille River travels through a natural bridge formation at Lower Dog's Head Falls, although we have yet to see such a natural wonder.

TRAIL INFORMATION The waterfall and the "Dog's Head" are both visible off in the distance after traveling 0.7 mile on River Road. The trail to the falls begins 0.1 mile farther at the pull-off described in the directions below. From the pull-off, walk through a short field, cross a set of railroad tracks, and go through a short stretch of wooded area. The falls will be just ahead, accessed by some fairly easy rock scrambling.

DIRECTIONS From the junction of VT 108 and VT 15 in Jeffersonville, take VT 15 east and drive 0.6 mile past the JOHNSON TOWN LINE sign. Please note that this is not actually the town's border. Take a right onto Railroad Street and follow it for 0.3 mile. Immediately beyond an old iron bridge, turn left onto River Road. Continue for 0.8 mile to a small pull-off on your left. *To get to Jeffersonville,* take VT 15 east from Burlington.

Dog's Head Falls

OTHER WATERFALLS NEARBY Brewster River Gorge, Terrill Gorge, Sterling Brook Gorge.

136

EMERSON FALLS

St. Johnsbury, Caledonia County

Type: Cascades
Height: 20-foot total drop
Trail Length: Roadside
Water Source: Sleepers River
Altitude Gain/Loss: None

Difficulty: Easy
Hiking Time: Not applicable
DeLorme Map: Page 48, I-5
Rating: ★★★

DESCRIPTION Controlled upstream by a hydroelectric project, Emerson Falls is a low-angled cascade that always has some water flow. As the water jumps down over jagged bedrock, some small pools are created, and these little potholes of water attract the majority of visitors to this waterfall.

The site is quite urban; there are businesses and other buildings directly behind the waterfall. This distracts from the natural beauty of Emerson Falls. Luckily, if you hike down to the base of the waterfall, you quickly forget that you are in a developed area. The waterfall, with its rugged, irregular nature, still manages to drown out the human-made structures just downstream.

TRAIL INFORMATION The trail to the falls is located adjacent to the Emerson Falls Business Center and is very short. The falls are immediately visible from the business center and the road.

DIRECTIONS From I-91 in St. Johnsbury, take exit 21. Take US 2 west for 0.8 mile to a right onto Town Highway 7. Take an immediate right onto Emerson Falls Road. Follow this road for 0.3 mile; the falls will be on your left. There is no official parking area, so you may have to park back up the road.

OTHER WATERFALLS NEARBY Barnet Falls, Marshfield Falls.

137

FAIRFAX FALLS
Fairfax, Franklin County

Type: Cascades

Height: 80-foot total drop

Trail Length: Roadside

Water Source: Lamoille River

Altitude Gain/Loss: None

Difficulty: Easy

Hiking Time: Not applicable

DeLorme Map: Page 45, A-12

Rating: ★★

DESCRIPTION Once an untouched, high-volume waterfall, Fairfax Falls has now become controlled by the dam above it and the ever-increasing demand for electricity. Since 1918, this waterfall has been dammed and used for hydroelectric power. Although the power plant next door detracts from the natural setting, the waterfall retains much of its original beauty.

Spring runoff guarantees a powerful show at Fairfax Falls. Yet even in times of low water, this waterfall is still of interest; small streams pick their way down the 86-foot-tall structure into the wide river below. A bonus is a nice flower-lined path that continues down to the stream from the roadside vantage points: The power plant has made a conscious effort to retain some of the original beauty this waterfall possessed.

TRAIL INFORMATION Fairfax Falls is another Vermont waterfall visible from the road. Also, since the area around it is the fenced-in property of a power station, there is no trail to the falls. You will, however, find a flower-lined walk along the fence from which to snap a few pictures of the falls if you so please.

DIRECTIONS From Burlington, take VT 15 east to VT 128 north, then turn right onto VT 104 south. After 1.0 mile, you can park on the pull-offs on your left before the power station.

OTHER WATERFALLS NEARBY Brewster River Gorge, Bingham Falls, Dog's Head Falls.

138

FALLS OF LANA
Salisbury, Addison County

Type: Horsetails and cascades
Height: 100-foot total drop
Trail Length: 0.2 mile
Water Source: Sucker Brook
Altitude Gain/Loss: +150 feet

Difficulty: Moderate side of difficult
Hiking Time: 15 minutes
DeLorme Map: Page 33, E-10
Rating: ★★★★★

DESCRIPTION (HIGHLY RECOMMENDED) Have you ever seen one of those waterfalls in romance movies where the leading characters fall in love? The upper section of the Falls of Lana certainly qualifies as one of those waterfalls; if directors in Hollywood were briefed on this spot, Falls of Lana could become a star.

The top horsetail at the Falls of Lana curves down through a gorge into a stunning and deep swimming pool. This pool has little to no current at all, and with minimal tree coverage overhead, it is highly exposed to the sun's rays. Yet even with the sun beating onto the surface of the pool, the water is cooler than most swimming holes. This is mostly due to it being a mountain stream, replenished as warmer water flows downstream. It is very clean and hidden when you look up at it from the absolute base.

The lower sections of this waterfall are equally beautiful, but it is much more difficult to get closer to them. The lower falls consist of horsetails and cascades winding down through a gorge, with a 50-foot drop (out of the 100-foot total drop) within 0.1 mile. At the base of the falls this middle section is hard to see due to a rock ledge. By hiking a little farther around the corner you will notice that despite its height this section is very slim, traveling more through a flumelike formation than a gorge. After rounding the corner you will start the ascent to the upper falls, which really are the star of the show. The area is great for waterfall enthusiasts, hiking groups, and technical rock climbers. Plan to spend some time exploring and admiring the beauty around you.

TRAIL INFORMATION The trail starts at the parking lot. In 100 feet you will exit the forest and walk under a large black drainage pipe. The first set of cascades is straight ahead; a few feet beyond, the trail reenters the forest. Once you reach the first cascades, you must make a decision. To this point, the trail has been easy and reasonably safe for just about anyone. From here on, however, you must begin climbing up a moderately steep and slippery trail to the more interesting horsetails and cascades above. If you accept the task, continue upstream to the right of the brook on a well-used and obvious trail to the top of the major horsetail. When you reach the crest of the horsetail, you will be rewarded with two additional waterfalls and a lovely swimming pool. You may also continue climbing to explore the other small cascades above. Be prepared to wade across the pool, with the ever-present risk of slipping and falling down the tallest horsetail waterfall in the area. This danger is a reality, so take extra care if you choose to continue beyond this middle pool to the top of the Falls of Lana.

DIRECTIONS From Middlebury, take US 7 south to a left onto VT 53. Follow VT 53 for 3.8 miles; the parking area will be on your left, 0.25 mile south of the Branbury State Park entrance.

OTHER WATERFALLS NEARBY Middlebury Gorge, Texas Falls, Abbey Pond Cascades.

Falls of Lana

139

GLEN FALLS
Fairlee, Orange County

Type: Plunge and cascades
Height: 80-foot total drop
Trail Length: To plunge, 0.2 mile;
to upper cascades, 0.3 mile
Water Source: Glen Falls Brook
Altitude Gain/Loss: +50 feet

Difficulty: Easy to plunge; moderate side of difficult thereafter
Hiking Time: 10 minutes
DeLorme Map: Page 36, D-2
Rating: ★★★★

DESCRIPTION What makes this waterfall so exceptional is how narrow the plunge is. It pours through a small opening cut between the gorge walls. This is one of the few plunges that make a splashing sound instead of a roar. Yet it is a surprisingly large plunge for such a small and weak stream. When you hike up toward the waterfall, the meager stream is quite deceptive. The waterfall is enclosed between two giant ledges of fractured rock. It is set back from the road, completely hidden, and heavily shaded, but just enough sunlight forces its way through to allow for a decent picture. The plunge drops into an almost perfectly circular pool.

Downstream from this plunge is a smaller yet equally pretty waterfall below. It almost tricks you into not going farther, but we do encourage you to do so. Above the plunge are even more cascades and plunges, which are only slightly less attractive. One of the cascades is just below the remains of an old dam, which detracts from these upper sets of falls. Leaves and ground cover will cause your hike to the falls to be slippery, but it really is well worth the total effort.

TRAIL INFORMATION From the Department of Fish and Wildlife parking area, walk back up Lake Morey Road until you see a tennis court on your left. Across from the tennis court are two converging paths that lead you on a flat trail past several unnamed cascades and plunges to the star of the show, Glen Falls. After hiking about 0.1 mile, you will reach a 12-foot segmented plunge with a clear moss-surrounded pool. Continue hiking upstream to the right of the brook to Glen Falls. When you reach the main falls, you can choose to hike the moderately difficult trail to less attractive cascades above.

DIRECTIONS Take I-91 north from White River Junction to exit 15 in Fairlee. Follow signs to LAKE MOREY ROAD. Follow Lake Morey Road west for 1.5 miles and leave your vehicle in the Vermont Department of Fish and Wildlife parking area on your right.

OTHER WATERFALLS NEARBY Covered Bridge Falls, Old City Falls.

140

HAMILTON FALLS

Jamaica, Hamilton Falls Natural Area,
Windham County

Type: Horsetails and slides
Height: Approximately 125-foot total drop
Trail Length: 0.2 mile to base of falls

Water Source: Cobb Brook
Altitude Gain/Loss: −125 feet to base of falls

Difficulty: Easy side of moderate
Hiking Time: 10 minutes
DeLorme Map: Page 26, I-3
Rating: ★★★★½

DESCRIPTION (HIGHLY RECOMMENDED) A short distance northeast of Jamaica State Park is the final mile of Cobb Brook, a water source renowned for one of Vermont's tallest waterfalls, 125-foot Hamilton Falls. Although the waterfall itself does not have much power during the year, it is unique. The waters of the brook literally slice their way sideways through deeply cut gorge walls before landing in popular wading pools below the entire formation. At the top of the falls is a deep pool and rock ledges that people often jump from. For your own safety, swimming is not permitted here, and for good reason: A sign at the falls states that 10 people have died in this exact location. *The currents in this pool are deadly and should not be tested.*

Jamaica State Park also offers hiking, camping, hunting, fishing, whitewater kayaking (one weekend in spring and fall, the Ball Mountain Dam releases high levels of water, and kayakers and canoeists have made events out of these dates).

The area inside Jamaica State Park also has some history of particular interest. In 1748, the last year of King George's War, the borders between New France and the British colonies were still hotly disputed. On the night of May 31, 1748, two Frenchmen and nine Indians crept up the West River in what is now the town of Londonderry and attacked British troops, killing five and wounding another. This massacre occurred at Salmon Hole, a popular fishing spot during that time period on the West River (it is now known more as a popular swimming hole).

Hamilton Falls is an amazing place to bring children and have a picnic. There are sunny areas for tanning, but still enough shade along the side to keep cool. You will find that this waterfall is very popular, and other people will be relaxing here as well; you have little chance of seclusion. Most visitors tend to be from outside the area, which is rather surprising, because most refreshing waterfalls in Vermont are yet to be commonly known to outsiders.

TRAIL INFORMATION Two different trails will lead you to the falls. Follow the Switch Road Trail for 0.1 mile as it gradually decreases in altitude to a sign for the falls. Take a right at the sign and continue climbing down to the base of the falls. A shorter trail, accessed by parking a few feet farther down Windham Road and walking down the trail on your left, leads to the top of Hamilton Falls. However, we feel that by reaching the base first, it will be easier to determine whether or not you wish to view the other sections of the falls. We prefer to hike up the wall, rather than down it. Hiking up the side of this waterfall is still moderately difficult, due in part to the degree of steepness, but more so to the lack of anything stable to hang on to as you climb. For purposes of safety, it is much less dangerous to take the original trail from the parking lot to the top of the falls.

DIRECTIONS From the junction of VT 35 and VT 30 in Townshend, take VT 30 north for 4.5 miles into the village of West Townshend. Take a right onto Windham Hill Road and follow that for 4.2 miles to a left onto Burbee Pond Road. Follow this road for 0.8 mile to a left onto West Windham Road. Follow West Windham Road for 2.8 miles; the parking lot will be on your left, marked by a sign for the SWITCH ROAD TRAIL. *To get to Townshend,* take VT 30 north from Brattleboro.

OTHER WATERFALLS NEARBY Pikes Falls.

Hamilton Falls

141

HUNTINGTON GORGE
Richmond, Chittenden County

Type: Horsetails and cascades
Height: Main horsetail is 15 feet
Trail Length: Less than 0.1 mile
Water Source: Huntington River
Altitude Gain/Loss: –40 feet

Difficulty: Easy
Hiking Time: Not applicable
DeLorme Map: Page 45, K-12
Rating: ★★★★

DESCRIPTION Huntington Gorge is equally famous for its swimming holes and the frightening death toll racked up here in the last half century. A sign at the falls indicates the tragic fates of 18 visitors between 1950 and 1994. With some common sense, and some careful scouting, you can bypass the obvious dangers to enjoy the popular swimming holes and marvel at the gorge and falls.

The gorge attracts some crazy personalities. We have seen many young adults leaping off its sloping walls, and others diving into swimming pools not nearly deep enough to warrant safe diving practices. We have even read that Huntington Gorge is a nudist hot spot, although we have not encountered anything of the sort.

For falls, the gorge has many small treasures, approximately half of which can be seen at each vantage point. There is also one main horsetail falling into the pool at the end of the gorge. The currents between the falls continue through the popular swimming pools within the gorge. We urge you to bypass these dangerous spots and restrict swimming to the large channel below the bottom falls.

The area also happens to have a little history. By 1802 a gristmill opened at the site, operating continuously for more than a century. The Richmond Light and Power Company converted the mill in 1903 to generate electricity for the nearby villages. Nowadays the gorge lies in its natural state, with evidence of past use nearly nonexistent. Make sure to plan on spending hours at Huntington Gorge, and many more if you visit Devil's Potholes nearby, another must-see waterfall and popular swimming place.

TRAIL INFORMATION Several trails begin at the parking area and descend about 20 yards to the river and gorge. Once you reach the gorge, it is fairly easy to explore the entire area, including the large pool at the base of the lowermost falls.

DIRECTIONS Take I-89 south from Burlington to exit 11. Take US 2 east into Richmond and turn right onto Bridge Street. Follow Bridge Street for 0.5 mile to a left onto Huntington Road. After 3.5 miles, make a left onto Dugway Road. Follow this road for 1.5 miles and park at the pullouts on your right.

OTHER WATERFALLS NEARBY Devil's Potholes, Moss Glen Falls (Stowe), Bingham Falls.

142

JELLY MILL FALLS
Dummerston, Windham County

Type: Cascades

Height: 30-foot total drop

Trail Length: Roadside

Water Source: Stickney Brook

Altitude Gain/Loss: None

Difficulty: Easy

Hiking Time: Not applicable

DeLorme Map: Page 22, F-6

Rating: ★★

DESCRIPTION A favorite bathing and party spot for locals for years, Jelly Mill Falls is a petite little formation on a mountain stream in Dummerston. The waterfall consists of a series of step falls and miniature cascades carrying the water downstream a few feet south to the mouth of the brook.

The total drop may be 30 feet, but no individual fall is really more than a yard in height. As such, the falls are not really visually appealing, or impressive for that matter. They are included in our guide because they still manage to draw a significant number of visitors to their shallow pools and broad, flat slabs of rock, which provide ideal tables for picnics.

TRAIL INFORMATION The falls are to the right of the road and are clearly visible. There is no official trail or path to follow. The flat rocks around the falls can be quite slippery, so use caution when stepping in the heavy moss-growth areas surrounding the falls.

DIRECTIONS From I-91 in Brattleboro, take exit 2. Take VT 9 east a short way to VT 30 north. Follow VT 30 north for 5.0 miles and take a left onto Stickney Brook Road (which is often confused with Pleasant Valley Road). Take this road for 0.1 mile; the pull-off will be on your right.

OTHER WATERFALLS NEARBY Hamilton Falls, Pikes Falls.

143

LITTLE OTTER CREEK FALLS
Ferrisburgh, Addison County

Type: Block	**Difficulty:** Easy
Height: 8 feet	**Hiking Time:** 5 minutes
Trail Length: 0.1 mile	**DeLorme Map:** Page 38, F-7
Water Source: Little Otter Creek	**Rating:** ★★½
Altitude Gain/Loss: −20 feet	

DESCRIPTION Little Otter Creek is a shallow lowland stream that travels across agricultural lands at a very small angle of descent. At Little Otter Creek Falls, the waters of the creek abruptly drop 8 feet in a wide block-style form. During peak snow runoff, the entire creek cascades over the bedrock at the site. Low-water times create several passageways through which the water flows.

The water is too shallow and muddy to make swimming appealing. The area is very exposed to the sun and, being only feet from the road, hardly remote. You will also spot some algae on the rocks, signifying potential pollution or agricultural runoff. Besides the stunning fact that a slow-traveling, lowland water source such as Little Otter Creek actually has a waterfall, there is not much to draw you to this place. But as we have mentioned before, for those who are waterfall enthusiasts—like us—every waterfall, including this one, deserves to be visited, because every waterfall is distinct and unique in its own right.

TRAIL INFORMATION From the parking area, continue down an old dirt road for 0.1 mile and take a left down a path just before crossing a covered footbridge. This short path is quite easy to miss, so be on the lookout. There is limited exploring at the falls. We have seen pictures of this waterfall taken from its base, but we were unsuccessful at locating any paths that led downstream. We suppose a little bushwhacking could bring you safely to the base of the falls.

DIRECTIONS From Middlebury, take US 7 north and continue for 4.5 miles past its junction with VT 17 in New Haven Junction. Take a right onto Monkton Road, follow this for 1.2 miles, and take a left onto Middle Brook Road. Follow Middle Brook Road for 1.4 miles to a right onto Wing Road. Follow this road for 0.7 mile; the one-car-sized pull-off will be on your right. The pull-off is actually an old, unused road.

OTHER WATERFALLS NEARBY Bristol Memorial Park Gorge, Bartlett Falls, Abbey Pond Cascades.

144

LYE BROOK FALLS

Manchester, Green Mountain National Forest, Bennington County

Type: Horsetail
Height: Approximately 100-foot total drop
Trail Length: 2.3 miles
Water Source: Lye Brook
Altitude Gain/Loss: 600 feet

Difficulty: Moderate
Hiking Time: 90 minutes
DeLorme Map: Page 25, I-10
Rating: ★★★★½

DESCRIPTION (HIGHLY RECOMMENDED) Lye Brook Falls is a steeper, taller version of Money Brook Falls of Massachusetts. Both are seasonal, drying up often by the end of June. When we arrived at Lye Brook Falls in July, only dribbles of water were cascading down the rocks. It was still intriguing as the water dropped in sheets of thin veils, and we assume it will have a much different and more powerful look during parts of the season with high water volume. Some hiking friends of ours have suggested that the elegance of low water flow is more picturesque at Lye Brook Falls. We recommend that you try visiting it during both times and form your own opinion.

Near the top of the waterfall, portions of the falls are somewhat hidden by rocks and trees. Sunlight penetrates this waterfall because of its western exposure. At the top, larger step cascades start out narrow and spread as the water finds its way down over the rock surfaces. About halfway down, most of the water condenses into a strong angular horse-tail, while other trickles of water hop down the smaller steps alongside the horsetail.

In summary, this is a great hike for the family—the longest waterfall hike for Vermont in this guide, as a matter of fact—and it is definitely worth every footstep required in order to reach it.

TRAIL INFORMATION To reach Lye Brook Falls, you must follow the Lye Brook Trail for 1.8 miles until you come to a fork. The Lye Brook Trail veers left and continues climbing. You should fork right and continue on a new, gently downsloping trail for 0.5 mile to the falls.

The steepness of the first third of this walk in the woods is gradual and manageable. The second third is a moderate uphill fight for many vis-

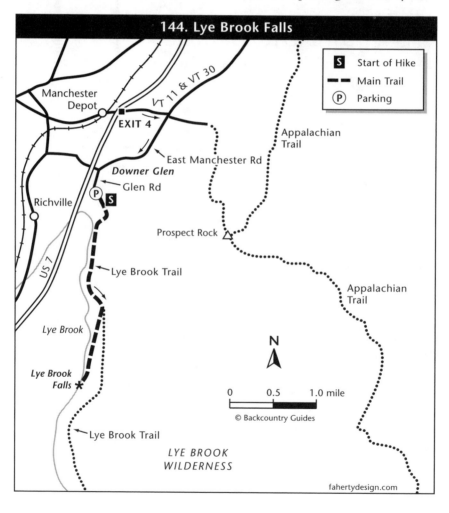

144. Lye Brook Falls

S	Start of Hike
- -	Main Trail
P	Parking

Manchester Depot

VT 11 & VT 30

EXIT 4

Appalachian Trail

East Manchester Rd

Downer Glen

Glen Rd

Richville

Prospect Rock

Lye Brook Trail

US 7

Appalachian Trail

Lye Brook

Lye Brook Falls ✶

N

0   0.5   1.0 mile

© Backcountry Guides

Lye Brook Trail

LYE BROOK WILDERNESS

fahertydesign.com

Lye Brook Falls

itors. The final part of the trail, the last 0.5 mile, follows the spur trail to the falls from the Lye Brook Trail. This segment is very easy and enjoyable, much less demanding than your earlier climb. In summary, this is the longest and greatest altitude-gain waterfall hike in the state. It is not the most difficult, however; the trail is well-marked and well-used. It is just constant climbing for most of the way. The end will certainly justify the means with this treasure in southern Vermont.

DIRECTIONS From US 7 in Manchester, take exit 4. Take the combined VT 11/VT 30 east for 0.4 mile and turn right onto East Manchester Road. Follow this road for 1.1 miles to a left onto Glen Road. A few hundred feet down this road, fork right and follow this new road to its end, where you will find the parking area.

OTHER WATERFALLS NEARBY Pikes Falls, Hamilton Falls.

145

MARSHFIELD FALLS

Marshfield, Washington County

Type: Cascades	**Difficulty:** Easy
Height: 100-foot total drop	**Hiking Time:** Not applicable
Trail Length: Roadside	**DeLorme Map:** Page 41, A-12
Water Source: Marshfield Brook	**Rating:** ★★★½
Altitude Gain/Loss: None	

DESCRIPTION Years ago this waterfall stood alone in the woods. Today Marshfield Falls is split into an upper and lower section by a paved road. The lower formation is a fan that travels down and splits into plunges on the left side and a staircase of cascades on the right. The total drop of the lower falls reaches about 40 feet.

The upper section of Marshfield Falls is taller, but there is no parking pullout to stop and admire the waterfall. It is narrow with a less apparent staircase of cascades than the lower falls have. The water is thicker and spreads out below at lower sections. It is more shaded, preventing any photograph, with only the absolute top of the waterfall being exposed to the sun. Yet as a combination, the waterfall—upper and lower—is still quite beautiful.

TRAIL INFORMATION There is no formal trail network or even somewhat used paths around the falls. This waterfall is best suited for a quick glimpse from the road. If you only have time to visit either the bottom or the top viewpoints, skip the top and enjoy the bottom.

DIRECTIONS From I-91 in St. Johnsbury, take exit 21 and follow US 2 west for 1.4 miles past the MARSHFIELD TOWN LINE sign. Take a left onto School Street. If you are traveling from Montpelier via US 2 east, School Street will be on your right 0.3 mile after the town line sign (this is actually not the town border). Follow School Street straight for 0.2 mile and you will come to a fork. The right fork, Lower Depot Road, will lead to the bottom of the cascades after 0.1 mile; they will be on your left. The left fork, Upper Depot Road, leads to the remaining portion of the falls.

OTHER WATERFALLS NEARBY Barnet Falls.

146

MCLAUGHLIN FALLS

Mendon, Rutland County

Type: Plunge and cascades
Height: 25-foot total drop
Trail Length: 0.1 mile
Water Source: North Branch
Eddy Brook
Altitude Gain/Loss: None

Difficulty: Easy
Hiking Time: Not applicable
DeLorme Map: Page 29, D-14
Rating: ★★★

DESCRIPTION Both the upper and lower sections of McLaughlin Falls are plunges, with the upper dropping 15 feet and the lower, 10 feet. At the top plunge the waters of Eddy Brook fall into a shallow yellow pool, with lots of bubbling whitewater, although the bottom plunge is more of a visual treat. Water flows over a flat ledge, creating a plunge with very little water deviating from the rest of the river's path. Below is a large dark green pool about 25 feet in diameter, edged by a rocky beach perfect for a picnic or for setting up the tripod and composing a photograph.

As enticing as the pool below can be, the lower plunge is not for swimming; this is marked as a watershed area, and so swimming and wading are illegal. The beautiful dark green color of the pool almost makes us wish the town could find another water source.

TRAIL INFORMATION From the parking area, follow the trail that runs parallel and to the left of the river. A short distance from the parking area, a small spur path will lead right to the top of the falls. Do not assume that the bottom plunge is not worth the extra effort of scrambling down. Continue down the trail to the pool at the base of the falls for a nicely structured plunge. Getting to the base requires moderate effort, as the dirt is quite loose and could make you slip if you are not careful.

DIRECTIONS From the junction of US 7 and US 4 in the center of Rutland, take US 4 east for 5.1 miles to a right onto Wheelerville Road. Wheelerville Road is 2.4 miles east of the MENDON TOWN LINE sign. Follow this road for 5.3 miles to a pullout on the left, just before a bridge.

OTHER WATERFALLS NEARBY Buttermilk Falls.

147

MIDDLEBURY GORGE
Middlebury, Addison County

Type: Cascades
Height: 8-foot total drop
Trail Length: Roadside
Water Source: Middlebury River
Altitude Gain/Loss: –25 feet

Difficulty: Easy
Hiking Time: Not applicable
DeLorme Map: Page 33, C-9&10
Rating: ★★

DESCRIPTION In the process of deciding which waterfalls were to be selected for this guide, we had to debate whether Middlebury Gorge should be included. Should we include a waterfall if there is actually no cataract of any significant size? There are small cascades that total less than 10 feet in total drop here, but no cascade is more than a yard tall.

There is nothing wrong with Middlebury Gorge—it offers fine swimming, and the gorge itself is quite interesting—it is just that this place does not offer much of a waterfall. Still, because it is a popular swimming hole in Vermont and centrally located among a wealth of other higher-rated waterfalls, we chose to include it. Given the popularity of this gorge and stream of small cascades, we felt you should be able to form an opinion for yourself.

TRAIL INFORMATION Middlebury Gorge is another location with no official trail—just several paths created by locals heading to the swimming hole below the VT 125 bridge. While it is easy to view the cascades from the bridge, moderate scrambling is required to reach the swimming channels and pools within the gorge.

DIRECTIONS From Middlebury, take the combined US 7 south/ VT 125 east. Take a left onto VT 125 east when it breaks away from US 7. Continue on VT 125 east for about a mile past its junction with VT 116; the pullout will be on your right, just after crossing over the brook.

OTHER WATERFALLS NEARBY Abbey Pond Cascades, Falls of Lana, Texas Falls.

148

MOSS GLEN FALLS (GRANVILLE)

Granville, Green Mountain National Forest, Addison County

Type: Horsetail

Height: 45 feet

Trail Length: Less than 0.1 mile

Water Source: Deer Hollow Brook

Altitude Gain/Loss: None

Difficulty: Easy

Hiking Time: Not applicable

DeLorme Map: Page 34, A-1

Rating: ★★★★★

DESCRIPTION (HIGHLY RECOMMENDED) Two of the most charming waterfalls in Vermont have the same name. There is Moss Glen Falls in the town of Stowe, and there is Moss Glen Falls of Granville, a roadside attraction featured in just about every photographic portrait of Vermont ever published. The second is the focus of this chapter. It is a gorgeous horsetail with thin streams of water that choose their own paths over the large boulders. It starts out bubbling down over some steps before spreading out to playfully jump down sections of the underlying rock. As the water glistens off the wet rocks, it rains into a light teal pool about 20 feet wide.

The best viewpoint is on the boardwalk, due to the fact that the falls are in a wide-open area. The green foliage adds some great color around the falls. Black and white butterflies on the scene create a mystical atmosphere.

Moss Glen Falls is a quick stop for many highway travelers, but if you take the time to admire it fully you will see how indescribably beautiful it really is. There is even a waterfall bonus if the season is right: In spring look for a thin horsetail about 50 feet tall, often referred to as Little Moss Glen Falls. You will find this just short of the boardwalk trail as you walk toward the star of the show.

TRAIL INFORMATION The waterfall is located at the end of the boardwalk that begins at the parking pull-off. You may notice Little Moss Glen Falls to your right as you walk along the boardwalk if water is currently flowing down the structure.

DIRECTIONS From Middlebury, take US 7 south to VT 125 east, then follow VT 125 into Hancock. Turn left onto VT 100 north and follow this highway for 7.0 miles. You will see the falls on your left and a small parking lot immediately after. This lot is 4.3 miles north of the LOWER GRANVILLE TOWN LINE sign.

OTHER WATERFALLS NEARBY Texas Falls, Middlebury Gorge.

149

MOSS GLEN FALLS (STOWE)
Stowe, C. C. Putnam State Forest, Lamoille County

Type: Plunge, slide, and fan
Height: 100-foot total drop
Trail Length: 0.2 mile to middle viewpoint
Water Source: Moss Glen Brook
Altitude Gain/Loss: +50 feet to middle viewpoint

Difficulty: Easy to middle viewpoint; easy side of moderate to enter gorge
Hiking Time: 10 minutes
DeLorme Map: Page 46, G-6
Rating: ★★★★★

DESCRIPTION (HIGHLY RECOMMENDED) Every year a class of local artists convenes at this waterfall to draw, paint, and sketch a portrait of Moss Glen Falls in an attempt to capture the beauty that can only be

Moss Glen Falls (Granville)

found here. This formation is worthy of their attention because it consists of three different types of falls. Starting out as a 20-foot plunge, very thin and powerful, Moss Glen Brook tumbles, pausing momentarily in a dark pool. From here a 20-foot-thick blanket of whitewater plummets into a segmented fan before landing at the base of the waterfall.

There are a few different standpoints with which to view the falls, each magnificent in its own way. The upper viewpoints, from high above the brook, are approximately two-thirds the distance to the top of the falls. From the lower viewpoint, accessed by wading your way upstream into the gorge, you can see the formation in its entirety.

Add Moss Glen Falls to other waterfalls in the town of Stowe, specifically Bingham Falls and Sterling Brook Gorge, for an amazing waterfall day trip.

TRAIL INFORMATION Follow the skinny path in front of the parking lot as it winds its way through several fields before entering the woods. Seconds after you enter the woods, you will begin climbing a steep 50-foot-tall ridge. As you climb, you will hear the falls on the other side. At the top of the ridge, the incredible 100-foot drop is unveiled.

After serious consideration, we have decided to let you in on Moss Glen Falls' biggest secret. Not many are aware of this, but you can backtrack on the trail and wade your way upstream along the riverbed into the gorge. Inside, you will be surrounded by tall gorge walls—and a totally secluded view of the falls awaits you. While the rest of Moss Glen Falls is nearly overrun with visitors, you may find solitude here inside the gorge. The best part of this whole side trip is that the walls and the splashing of the waterfall filter out any noise coming from above.

DIRECTIONS From the junction of VT 100 and VT 108 in Stowe, take VT 100 north for 3.0 miles to a right onto Randolph Road. After 0.4 mile on Randolph Road, turn right onto Moss Glen Falls Road. Follow Moss Glen Falls Road for 0.5 mile; the parking area will be on your left. *To get to Stowe,* take I-89 north from Montpelier to exit 10. Follow VT 100 north.

OTHER WATERFALLS NEARBY Bingham Falls, Sterling Brook Gorge, Terrill Gorge, Dog's Head Falls.

Moss Glen Falls (Stowe)

150

NORTH BRANCH FALLS
Worcester, Washington County

Type: Block

Height: 10 feet

Trail Length: Roadside

Water Source: North Branch
Winooski River

Altitude Gain/Loss: None

Difficulty: Easy

Hiking Time: Not applicable

DeLorme Map: Page 47, I-8

Rating: ★★½

DESCRIPTION Clearly visible from VT 12, the North Branch of the Winooski River flows over giant boulders and jagged rocks in one massive block-style waterfall formation into a large, dark pool. Although this waterfall is nothing spectacular in terms of style, history, or geology, with its easy access it makes this a nice rest stop. There is no better place around to stretch your legs on the way to your destination. For the enthusiast, even the smallest waterfall is worth the stop.

TRAIL INFORMATION The only view of North Branch Falls is from the road. We observed no trails or paths leading to the falls. The view from the road is clear enough to take in the entire waterfall and the cascades above anyway.

DIRECTIONS From I-89 in Montpelier, take exit 8 and follow VT 12 north for 4.1 miles past Calais Road, which is on your right. The falls will be visible from the highway on your left.

OTHER WATERFALLS NEARBY Terrill Gorge, Sterling Brook Gorge, Moss Glen Falls (Stowe).

151

OLD CITY FALLS

Strafford, Orange County

Type: Plunge and cascades
Height: 45-foot total drop
Trail Length: 0.3 mile
Water Source: Old City Brook
Altitude Gain/Loss: –125 feet

Difficulty: Moderate
Hiking Time: 15 minutes
DeLorme Map: Page 35, E-12
Rating: ★★★★½

DESCRIPTION (HIGHLY RECOMMENDED) When we informed two local residents that we had come from Massachusetts to see Old City Falls, they were shocked; for as long as they had enjoyed this waterfall it had remained a local secret, far from a tourist attraction that drew visitors from all over.

There are two sets of falls at Old City Falls– an upper plunge and a set of cascades, both of which flow into refreshing pools. Although they are not deep enough to dive into, they are waist-deep—enough to cool you down on a hot day. At the upper pool the waterfall splashes on top of your head as you lean against the rocks.

When viewing this waterfall from the base, it is very attractive because you cannot see the middle pool that the plunge falls into. We only discovered it after a man climbed up the steep ravine walls to swim up there. It is also attractive because the plunge lies to the left of the cascade below it: A large flat boulder causes the water to curve around to the right before falling down into the series of cascades.

Before hiking down to the falls you will notice picnic tables, trash barrels, and a shelter from the rain. Old City Falls offers hours of enjoyment, so be sure to bring the bathing suit, towels, and a picnic. Visitors will surely love eating their peanut butter and jelly sandwiches with a crashing waterfall in the distant background.

TRAIL INFORMATION The trail to the falls begins at the end of the parking area and soon enters the forest. Although the trail to the base of the falls is rather easy, with only a few short stretches of steep terrain to climb down, exploring the area around the falls is more of a challenge. The official trail ends at the brook. From here to the falls, you must rock-hop carefully, making sure not to fall into the brook's chilly waters.

Old City Falls

There is plenty of exploring to do around the falls, most of which is challenging and sometimes highly dangerous. Technically, you could stand underneath the upper plunge or swim in the midlevel pool. Accessing the midlevel pool is done by making use of your upper-body strength to climb the roots to the left of the waterfall. This trail is quite difficult, but it is manageable. The trail that allows you to stand in the upper plunge is extremely dangerous and not recommended.

DIRECTIONS Take I-89 north from White River Junction to exit 2. Take VT 132 east into the village of South Strafford. In South Strafford, take a left onto Tunbridge Road. Follow this road for 2.2 miles and fork right. Follow this road for 0.8 mile and take a right onto Old City Falls Road. After 0.9 mile, turn left into a dirt road that leads to the parking area. There is a sign for the park just down this dirt road.

OTHER WATERFALLS NEARBY Covered Bridge Falls, Glen Falls.

152

PIKES FALLS

*Jamaica, Green Mountain National Forest,
Windham County*

Type: Cascades and slides

Height: 20-foot total drop

Trail Length: 0.1 mile

Water Source: North Branch
Brook

Altitude Gain/Loss: –40 feet

Difficulty: Easy

Hiking Time: Not applicable

DeLorme Map: Page 26, J-1

Rating: ★★★

DESCRIPTION Children enjoy Pikes Falls more than any other age group. On hot summer days they can be seen sliding down a 10-foot-long rock slide into a pool here. The looks of pure pleasure on their faces confirm their love for this place.

Is it the slide they love, or the fact that below this waterfall is one of the largest swimming holes in the state? About 40 feet wide, 25 feet long, and up to 10 feet deep, this pool, with its clear, olive-green tinted water, is complemented by a large rocky beach running along its edges. With such a large pool and a suitable beach for relaxing or eating a snack, you might imagine that Pikes Falls would be crowded. That is simply not the case, however. It may have a few friendly swimmers on a hot day, but not nearly the crowds of other swimming holes in the state.

TRAIL INFORMATION The trail begins at the parking pull-off. Enter the woods and, in approximately 20 feet, fork left to descend a set of stairs to the base of the falls and the swimming pools. Fork right if you wish to visit the top of the falls. Either approach is short and easy.

DIRECTIONS From the center of Brattleboro, take VT 30 north. Follow VT 30 north past Townshend into East Jamaica, where VT 100 north will join. At 3.2 miles after this juncture, make a left onto South Hill Road directly across from the Jamaica Country Store. Immediately after this turn, fork right onto Pikes Falls Road and continue for 2.3 miles. Here, Pikes Falls Road will continue right and cross a bridge. Drive for an additional 2.4 miles on this road; you will find a wide shoulder on your left to park.

OTHER WATERFALLS NEARBY Hamilton Falls, Lye Brook Falls.

153

QUECHEE GORGE & MILL POND FALLS

Hartford, Quechee Gorge State Park, Windsor County

Type: Mill Pond Falls is a horsetail; inside Quechee Gorge are cascades
Height: Mill Pond Falls is 30 feet
Trail Length: 1.6 miles total trip
Water Source: Ottauquechee River
Altitude Gain/Loss: –200 feet to base of gorge

Difficulty: Easy
Hiking Time: 60 minutes
DeLorme Map: Page 31, C-11
Rating: ★★★½

DESCRIPTION *Vermont's Little Grand Canyon* is the phrase thrown around to describe the mile-long Quechee Gorge. While you really cannot compare the gorge here to the mile-deep, 277-mile-long Grand Canyon in Arizona, it is impressive compared to all others in New England.

You can overlook the entire gorge from the VT 4 highway bridge. From there, it is 165 feet to the river below. This provides quite a scenic and wild view of the shallow valley that the Ottauquechee River has cut its way through. As for a waterfall, you cannot really see one from the bridge without a pair of binoculars.

By following the South Trail as it parallels the river downstream, however, you can get a closer inspection of the small cascades within the gorge. If you are looking for major waterfalls, you will not find any within the gorge—you have to hike to the top, where you will find an artificially created waterfall flowing over a dam, called Mill Pond Falls. This is a horsetail that very few visitors to the gorge bother to find. It is neither powerful nor scenic, but it helps end a rather fine trip to Queechee Gorge, Vermont's longest and most famous gorge.

TRAIL INFORMATION The two trails that lead to both the gorge and the waterfall begin behind the Quechee Gorge Gifts & Sportswear store. Walk down a wooden staircase and you will see a TRAILHEAD sign. If you take a left, it is a 0.5-mile walk to the bottom of the gorge. Based on our opinion and those of people we have talked with at the gorge, there is not much to see or do down there. Instead, take a right for a 0.3-mile walk to Mill Pond Falls and the dam above. These falls are more interesting than the bottom of the gorge. When you return from Mill Pond Falls, do make sure to see Quechee Gorge from the highway bridge.

DIRECTIONS Take I-89 north from White River Junction to exit 1. Take US 4 west for 2.6 miles and park on your right just before the Quechee Gorge Gifts & Sportswear store.

OTHER WATERFALLS NEARBY Cascade Falls, Covered Bridge Falls, Old City Falls.

154

STERLING BROOK GORGE

Stowe, Lamoille County

Type: Plunges and cascades
Height: 105-foot total drop
Trail Length: 0.2 mile to end of gorge
Water Source: Sterling Brook
Altitude Gain/Loss: –125 feet

Difficulty: Easy side of moderate
Hiking Time: 15 minutes
DeLorme Map: Page 46, E-4
Rating: ★★★

DESCRIPTION This waterfall—reached by following a self-guiding interpretative trail—is the perfect place to take a class for a field trip. You will notice many small tablets describing the history, geology, and lore of Sterling Brook Gorge. You learn at one of the "stops" that there are three falls, six cascade sets, and eight pools within the gorge.

No falls or cascades are greater than a few yards tall, and none of the pools is really accessible without constant danger. Only about half the drops or cascades are fully visible in summer, when the fresh young leaves on the trees hinder your view. There is a quiet picnic spot at the base of the falls, great for a snack or a light lunch. At the beginning and end of the hike, a nice-sized grass field would be a fine place to gather your class and discuss what they have learned.

TRAIL INFORMATION From the parking lot, cross the bridge marked with a RESIDENT VEHICLES ONLY sign. The trailhead is just after the bridge on your left, marked with a billboard describing the gorge's rules and geology. The trail you are about to embark on is an interpretative one with several "stops" along the way outlining key geological features and facts from the beginning to the end of the gorge. The falls begin shortly after the trail. Continue along the trail for more plunges, cascades, pools, and the gorge. If you continue down the trail past where the interpretative signs end—about 0.3 mile from the road—you will eventually arrive at the brook well beyond the end of the gorge. To our surprise, we found the most unexpected picnic table we've ever seen. It turns out to be a truly secluded place for a picnic.

DIRECTIONS From the junction of VT 108 and VT 100 in Stowe, take VT 100 north for 1.7 miles to a left onto Stage Coach Road. Follow this road for 1.7 miles to a left onto Sterling Valley Road. After 1.6 miles on Sterling Valley Road, you will come to a four-way intersection. Take the right-hand fork that does *not* pass through a covered bridge (there are two right turns here). Continue 2.9 miles farther and take a left at a sign for STERLING FOREST PARKING. Continue down this road for 0.1 mile and leave your vehicle in the parking area. *To get to Stowe,* take I-89 north from Montpelier to exit 10. Follow VT 100 north.

   OTHER WATERFALLS NEARBY Terrill Gorge, Moss Glen Falls (Stowe), Bingham Falls, Dog's Head Falls.

155

TERRILL GORGE

Morristown, Lamoille County

Type: Block
Height: 5 feet
Trail Length: 0.5 mile
Water Source: Kenfield Brook
Altitude Gain/Loss: −100 feet

Difficulty: Moderate side of difficult
Hiking Time: 20 minutes
DeLorme Map: Page 46, D-6
Rating: ★★★

DESCRIPTION There are a few different drops within Terrill Gorge. Unfortunately, only the lower falls are accessible. The falls lying upstream require miles of bushwhacking—not exactly leisurely family hiking. From pictures, the upper falls look nice, but they are basically typical cascades. For purposes of this guide, we are only describing the lower falls, leaving the upper falls to be uncovered by the avid hiker.

   A 0.5-mile walk from the parking area leads to the popular, but not overly crowded, swimming hole at the lower falls. The waterfall itself is rather small, and if it were not for the beautiful pool, we would have lowered our overall rating. It is only 5 feet tall, but the 10-foot width does add character and makes the waterfall slightly more impressive. Water flows over a flat-angled rock that could possibly be the remnants of an old dam, although we are not sure. The pool is of a yellow-green tint and becomes as deep as 20 feet in select spots. Its shape is nearly a perfect oval, being about 35 feet wide by 25 feet long. You may see careless people leaping off the rock wall to the left of the falls and be tempted to do the same. We are against this idea, because reaching the ledge they jump off is extraordinarily difficult.

TRAIL INFORMATION From the small pull-off, immediately enter the woods and head down the trail toward the brook. After 0.25 mile on the trail, you will reach the river, which must be crossed; this usually requires the removal of your shoes and socks. Beyond, climb up the riverbank and take a left as soon as you reach a field. Follow the path a few hundred feet back into the woods. Continue along the trail 0.2 mile farther into the woods. Just as you begin to start climbing a steep hill, the falls and pool will be visible on your left. One steep and slippery trail leads down to the pool. Most visitors are better off enjoying the falls from the opposite cliffs, rather than scrambling down this trail. Many more cascades are rumored to lie upstream, but this allegedly requires almost 1.5 miles of tough bushwhacking along the brook.

DIRECTIONS From the junction of VT 108 and VT 100 in Stowe, take VT 100 north for 1.7 miles to a left onto Stage Coach Road. Follow this road for 6.4 miles to a three-car-sized pullout on your left just before a large field, which is marked by a NO TRESPASSING sign along its edges. *To get to Stowe,* take I-89 north from Montpelier to exit 10. Follow VT 100 north.

OTHER WATERFALLS NEARBY Sterling Brook Gorge, Moss Glen Falls (Stowe), Dog's Head Falls, Bingham Falls, Brewster River Gorge.

156

TEXAS FALLS

Hancock, Green Mountain National Forest, Addison County

Type: Punchbowls
Height: 35-foot total drop
Trail Length: Less than 0.1 mile
Water Source: Texas Brook
Altitude Gain/Loss: None

Difficulty: Easy
Hiking Time: Not applicable
DeLorme Map: Page 33, D-14
Rating: ★★★½

DESCRIPTION Texas Falls has long been a favorite Green Mountain National Forest attraction. If it looks familiar, it should: Postcards, hiking guides, and portraits of Vermont have included Texas Falls. So although you may not have had the chance to visit this classic waterfall, its structure may seem all too familiar to you.

Managed by the U.S. Forest Service, Texas Falls, once a favorite swimming hole, is now off-limits due to several injuries. Wooden fencing surrounds the flume and falls, and the only views are from a boardwalk, which you are asked not to stray from. The best view is from a bridge that crosses over the stream. From here you will see two small plunges with a deep green-blue pool between. They are of equal beauty as they flow through a narrow ravine. Because of the beauty and the compactness of the gorge walls, both sets of plunges look more like a flume rushing downstream. Large logs have fallen and now dip into the pools below, causing the waterfall itself to lose some of its appeal.

If you drive up the road a small distance, you will find picnic tables to sit at and have a nice lunch while enjoying the sounds of nature around you. As mentioned, this waterfall is indeed a classic and very well known, well worth a stop and a quick picture to remember your visit.

TRAIL INFORMATION The trail begins across the street from the parking lot. The path to the falls is enclosed entirely by wooden rails, and you are asked not to deviate from the path. The waterfall is only a few yards from the road, making viewing rather easy. Another trail continues at the falls. This is the Texas Falls Nature Trail, a 1.0-mile loop that begins at the falls and travels around the surrounding woods only to return to the waterfall.

DIRECTIONS From Middlebury, take US 7 south to VT 125 east. Travel on VT 125 east past Middlebury Gap and take a left onto the road marked by a GREEN MOUNTAIN FOREST RECREATION AREA sign. This sign is visible from both sides of the road. The parking area is 0.5 mile down the road on your left. This access road is 3.1 miles west of the VT 100 and VT 125 junction in Hancock.

OTHER WATERFALLS NEARBY Middlebury Gorge, Moss Glen Falls (Granville), Falls of Lana, Abbey Pond Cascades.

Texas Falls

157

TROUT RIVER FALLS

Montgomery, Franklin County

Type: Punchbowls and cascades
Height: 10-foot total drop
Trail Length: 0.3 mile
Water Source: Trout River and Hunnah Clark Brook
Altitude Gain/Loss: –50 feet

Difficulty: Easy
Hiking Time: 10 minutes
DeLorme Map: Page 52, E-6
Rating: ★★★½

DESCRIPTION Two brooks converge into a popular swimming hole at Trout River Falls, or Three Holes, as the locals tend to call it. Both falls are drops of about 10 feet into a lime-colored pool. The swirling currents cause this pool to be famous for catching trout. While we were there we saw a family catch more than half-a-dozen trout. The currents may be too strong to swim in for much of the season, but the fish sure seem to like them.

The sounds of the waterfalls surround you as you sit on the rocky beach. The waterfall on the left-hand side consists of many cascades that twist and turn around the rock structures. The waterfall on the right side is a set of punchbowls. The two are equal in beauty, worthy of your admiration while having lunch and watching your children catch sizable trout.

TRAIL INFORMATION The trail begins to the left of the Montgomery Public Safety building. Follow this easy trail 0.3 mile to the base of the falls. As you approach, you will see on your left the Hunnah Clark Brook half of the falls; on your right lie the punchbowls of the Trout River. When we visited, it appeared that there were no cascades upstream on either brook.

DIRECTIONS From the junction of VT 118, VT 58, and VT 242 in Montgomery Center, take VT 242 east for 500 feet and pull into the Montgomery Public Safety building parking lot. Park on your left just before the building. *To get to Montgomery Center,* take VT 105 west from Newport to VT 100 south to VT 58 west.

OTHER WATERFALLS NEARBY West Hill Brook Falls, Big Falls, Willoughby River Falls.

Trout River Falls

158

TWIN FALLS

Westminster, Windham County

Type: Plunge and block
Height: 16-foot total drop
Trail Length: Roadside
Water Source: Saxtons River
Altitude Gain/Loss: –30 feet

Difficulty: Moderate
Hiking Time: Not applicable
DeLorme Map: Page 27, J-10
Rating: ★★★★

DESCRIPTION For a roadside waterfall, Twin Falls sure are difficult to see from the road. The falls are only 50 feet off the road, but with heavy tree coverage, giant boulders, and steep riverbanks blocking your view, you really must scramble down to river level to see Twin Falls.

Twin Falls, as the name suggests, consist of two waterfalls—an upper plunge and, directly below, after the waters of the Saxtons River congregate and swirl in a deep circular pool, the lower section, a block-type waterfall. Below all of this is a large pool—a local swimming-hole favorite—that has a slow-moving current, keeping the water rather chilly but not as cold as at many other waterfall swimming holes you will discover in this guide.

It is apparent that this waterfall is a party spot. There was some trash found on scene, and a little bit of vandalism. If the state would acquire the property and turn this place into a small park, the beauty of Twin Falls could quite easily be restored.

As it is now, there are still plenty of clean places to sit and admire the waterfall, and plenty of places to explore along the gorge. Despite the surroundings, the waterfall itself remains photogenic; do not forget the camera for this one.

TRAIL INFORMATION The falls are located a few feet from the road, although accessing them is far from easy. Scrambling on steep, loose terrain is required to reach the base of the falls. To reach the falls from above, you must mosey along a narrow rock ledge after entering the woods from back down the street. For reaching both the upper and lower falls, there are several obvious paths where people have led the way.

DIRECTIONS Take I-91 north from Brattleboro to exit 5. Follow signs to US 5 north. Take US 5 north for 2.6 miles to a left onto VT 121 west. Follow VT 121 west for 1.0 mile to a left onto Gage Street. Follow this street for 0.4 mile to a pull-off on your right. The parking area is on your right just as you begin to see the river through the woods.

OTHER WATERFALLS NEARBY Cascade Falls, Hamilton Falls.

159

WEST HILL BROOK FALLS

Montgomery, Franklin County

Type: Cascades and slides
Height: 15-foot total drop
Trail Length: 0.1 mile
Water Source: West Hill Brook
Altitude Gain/Loss: None

Difficulty: Easy
Hiking Time: Not applicable
DeLorme Map: Page 52, E-5
Rating: ★★½

Twin Falls

DESCRIPTION The Creamery Bridge, or West Hill Bridge, is a covered bridge of the lattice design spanning West Hill Brook in the town of Montgomery. It is one of six covered bridges located in Montgomery alone. Officially closed to automobile use in September 1999, the bridge is now accessible only by foot. While there are more than 100 covered bridges in the state, seldom was a bridge constructed above a waterfall.

West Hill Brook Falls is a 15-foot drop below the out-of-service bridge. Beginning as a stretch of slides and cascades falling at an angle of about 45 degrees, the falls take on the appearance of a thick blanket before dropping the final few feet as a steep cascade.

Many guidebooks are currently available on the covered bridges of Vermont and the rest of New England. A few new passions for us emerged as we visited more and more waterfalls; a love for covered bridges was one of them. If you found that you enjoyed the waterfall–covered bridge combination, too, check out Covered Bridge Falls of Vermont and Swiftwater Falls of New Hampshire, two very similar places.

TRAIL INFORMATION From the parking area, continue farther down Creamery Bridge Road on foot. In a few hundred feet you will reach the covered bridge and the falls, which begin underneath. Views are limited from the bridge, and there do not seem to be any paths leading around the falls to get a closer look.

DIRECTIONS From the junction of VT 118, VT 58, and VT 242 in Montgomery Center, take VT 118 north for 2.8 miles to a left onto West Hill Road. Another road nearby, Hill West Road, should not be confused with West Hill Road. Follow West Hill Road for 2.6 miles to a left onto Creamery Bridge Road. Take this road for 0.7 mile; the parking area will be on your left, just before the dirt road becomes narrow and descends a hill. *To get to Montgomery Center,* take VT 105 west from Newport to VT 100 south to VT 58 west.

OTHER WATERFALLS NEARBY Trout River Falls, Big Falls, Willoughby River Falls.

160

WILLOUGHBY RIVER FALLS

Barton, Orleans County

Type: Cascades
Height: 8-foot total drop
Trail Length: 0.1 mile
Water Source: Willoughby River
Altitude Gain/Loss: None

Difficulty: Easy
Hiking Time: Not applicable
DeLorme Map: Page 54, G-2
Rating: ★★½

DESCRIPTION Willoughby River Falls flows through a shallow ravine at the edge of the town of Barton. About 100 feet long and 6 feet wide, the falls are more like a giant set of rapids during high-water times.

There are strong currents year-round, and a mild smell of pollution, recognizable as you get closer to the waterfall. These factors prevent people from swimming in this area. The traffic crossing the bridge below the falls causes some distracting noise as well, taking away from any natural experience you hope to find here.

Even though this waterfall sounds as if you may not want to visit, it is worth a brief stop. When the sunlight hits the whitewater, the cascades will glimmer in a photograph. The dark, jagged rocks provide a nice contrast to the low-angled cascades. In spring rainbow trout migrate up the Willoughby River and skip up the falls. Perhaps you will be lucky enough to see them.

TRAIL INFORMATION From the parking lot, walk back down the road and take a left down a dirt road just before crossing back over the one-lane bridge. The falls are 100 feet up the dirt road on your right, visible after you descend a set of stairs toward the river.

DIRECTIONS Take I-91 north from St. Johnsbury to exit 26. Turn onto the combined US 5 south/VT 58 east. Continue on VT 58 east for 0.7 mile beyond the spot where US 5 breaks off. Take a left onto Village Road, which heads toward the village of Brownington. Stay on this road for 0.2 mile, then take a right into the Vermont Fish and Game Access Area parking lot.

OTHER WATERFALLS NEARBY Big Falls, Trout River Falls, West Hill Brook Falls.

161

WOODBURY FALLS
Woodbury, Washington County

Type: Horsetail

Height: 35 feet

Trail Length: Less than 0.1 mile

Water Source: Stream from Mud Pond

Altitude Gain/Loss: None

Difficulty: Easy

Hiking Time: Not applicable

DeLorme Map: Page 47, G-11

Rating: ★★★

DESCRIPTION When you see such beautiful waterfalls as this one, you must ask yourself why they are marked PRIVATE PROPERTY. There are supposedly three different sets of falls here; unfortunately, only one is visible from the road. This waterfall starts off as a narrow staircase of cascades, which then proceeds to fan out, only to condense again into a slim cascade before entering a culvert under the road. The area is incredibly shaded due to all the tree coverage, preventing any light from streaking through. The waterfall only receives a small amount of sunlight during the early morning, when the sun is shining at an angle coming from the road; even then the light is minimal and mostly on the lower part of the waterfall. Still, this waterfall is of great beauty, making it a shame not having the ability to see its other drops. The morning hours provide the best possible chance for a snapshot, so try to stop by then to capture this great roadside waterfall.

TRAIL INFORMATION Years ago the area was not posted, and explorers could wander beyond the roadside view of the waterfall to reach hundreds of feet of additional cascades above. Today Woodbury Falls is private property, and unfortunately the only view is from roadside.

DIRECTIONS From Barre, take VT 14 north through the village of East Calais. Continue for 3.0 miles north of the WOODBURY TOWN LINE sign; the falls will be visible on your left. Parking is available in a small area 0.1 mile farther up the road on your right. We suggest parking there—the road's shoulder is dangerous near the falls.

OTHER WATERFALLS NEARBY Marshfield Falls, Terrill Gorge.

Appendixes

TOP 40 WATERFALLS IN NEW ENGLAND

Although we would love to say that all waterfalls are equally beautiful, and that no waterfall deserves any more attention than another, the fact is we have some personal favorites. Here are our picks of the top 40 waterfalls in New England. Each one has earned an overall rating of either four-and-a-half or five stars.

Angel Falls (ME)

Arethusa Falls (NH)

Bartlett Falls (VT)

Bash Bish Falls (MA)

Beaver Brook Cascades (NH)

Beaver Brook Falls (NH)

Bingham Falls (VT)

Campbell Falls (MA)

Chapman Falls (CT)

Dean's Ravine Falls (CT)

Devil's Pothole (VT)

Diana's Baths (NH)

Dunn Falls (ME)

Falls of Lana (VT)

Falls on the Basin-Cascades Trail (NH)

Falls on the Falling Waters Trail (NH)

Falls on the Flume-Pool Loop (NH)

Glen Ellis Falls (NH)

Gulf Hagas (ME)

Hamilton Falls (VT)

Hay Brook Falls (ME)

Houston Brook Falls (ME)

Kent Falls (CT)

Lye Brook Falls (VT)

Moss Glen Falls—Granville (VT)

Moss Glen Falls—Stowe (VT)

Moxie Falls (ME)

Nancy Cascades (NH)

Old City Falls (VT)

Ripley Falls (NH)

Sabbaday Falls (NH)

Screw Auger Falls—Grafton (ME)

Silver Cascade (NH)

Smalls Falls (ME)

Step Falls (ME)

Tannery Falls (MA)

Trap Falls (MA)

Twin Cascades (MA)

Wahconah Falls (MA)

Waterville Cascades (NH)

TOP 20 WATERFALL SWIMMING HOLES

Bartlett Falls (VT)

Buttermilk Falls (VT)

Devil's Pothole (VT)

Diana's Baths (NH)

Falls at Frenchmen's Hole (ME)

Falls of Lana (VT)

Franconia Falls (NH)

Huntington Gorge (VT)

Jackson Falls (NH)

Lower Falls (NH)

Gulf Hagas (ME)

Moxie Falls (ME)

Old City Falls (VT)

Pikes Falls (VT)

Rattlesnake Flume and Pool (ME)

Smalls Falls (ME)

Steep Falls (ME)

Step Falls (ME)

Swiftwater Falls (Bath, NH)

Terrill Gorge (VT)

THE BEST WATERFALL DAY-TRIPS

In our opinion, nothing reenergizes the soul like the splendor of spending a full day with nature. Make the most of your day trip by putting nearby waterfalls together. Here are our suggestions for multiple-waterfall day trips, in no particular order.

↪

Bash Bish Falls, Race Brook Falls, Campbell Falls (MA),
Buttermilk Falls (Norfolk, CT)

↪

Deer Hill Falls, March Cataract Falls, Money Brook Falls,
Hudson Brook Chasm, Tannery Falls, Twin Falls (MA)

↪

Great Falls of the Housatonic, Dean's Ravine Falls,
Pine Swamp Brook Falls, Kent Falls (CT)

↪

Brewster River Gorge, Bingham Falls, Moss Glen Falls (Stowe),
Sterling Brook Gorge, Terrill Gorge (VT)

↪

Flume Cascade, Silver Cascade, Kedron Flume,
Ripley Falls, Arethusa Falls (NH)

↪

Diana's Baths, Winniweta Falls, Thompson Falls,
Glen Ellis Falls, Crystal Cascade (NH)

↪

Screw Auger Falls (Grafton), Step Falls, Dunn Falls, The Cataracts (ME)

↪

Westfield Falls, Little Wadsworth Falls, Big Wadsworth Falls,
Bear Hill Falls, Seven Falls (CT)

↪

Falls of Lana, Middlebury Gorge, Abbey Pond Cascades,
Bartlett Falls, Bristol Memorial Park Gorge (VT)

⤳

Trap Falls, Doane's Falls, Spirit Falls, Royalston Falls (MA)

⤳

Falls on the Flume-Pool Loop, Falls on the Basin-Cascades Trail,
Georgiana Falls (NH)

⤳

Roaring Brook Falls, Gunn Brook Falls, Slatestone Brook Falls,
Chapel Brook Falls, Pauchaug Brook Falls (MA)

⤳

Pond Brook Falls, Beaver Brook Falls, Dixville Flume,
Huntington Cascades (NH)

⤳

Beaver Brook Cascades, Agassiz Basin, Swiftwater Falls, Paradise Falls
(NH)

THE BEST LONG-DISTANCE WATERFALL DAY-HIKES

(In no particular order)

Falls on the Falling Waters Trail and Mount Lafayette, NH *(page 155)*

Total Hiking Distance: **8.8 miles**

Altitude Gain: **3,750 feet**

Difficulty: **Difficult**

~

Katahdin Stream Falls and Baxter Peak, ME *(page 290)*

Total Hiking Distance: **10.4 miles**

Altitude Gain: **4,200 feet**

Difficulty: **Difficult**

~

Zealand and Thoreau Falls Trail, NH *(page 200)*

Total Hiking Distance: **10.0 miles**

Altitude Gain: **500 feet**

Difficulty: **Moderate**

~

Crystal Cascade and Mount Washington, NH *(page 147)*

Total Hiking Distance: **8.2 miles**

Altitude Gain: **4,200 feet**

Difficulty: **Difficult**

~

Gulf Hagas, ME *(page 54)*

Total Hiking Distance: **8.6 miles**

Altitude Gain: **600 feet**

Difficulty: **Moderate side of difficult**

~

Race Brook Falls, Mount Race, and Mount Everett, MA
(page 109)

Total Hiking Distance: **7.0 miles**
Altitude Gain: **2,300 feet**
Difficulty: **Moderate side of difficult**

∽

Beaver Brook Cascades and Mount Moosilauke, NH
(page 138)

Total Hiking Distance: **8.0 miles**
Altitude Gain: **3,100 feet**
Difficulty: **Difficult**

∽

Falls on the Basin-Cascades Trail and Lonesome Lake, NH *(page 152)*

Total Hiking Distance: **6.0 miles**
Altitude Gain: **1,000 feet**
Difficulty: **Moderate**

∽

Franconia Falls and No. 13 Falls, NH *(page 166)*

Total Hiking Distance: **17.0 miles**
Altitude Gain: **600 feet**
Difficulty: **Moderate**

SCENIC WATERFALLS OF BAXTER STATE PARK IN MAINE

Katahdin Stream Falls

Trail Length: **1.2 miles**
Water Source: **Katahdin Stream**
Delorme Baxter Map: **J-5**

Notes: Katahdin Stream Falls is the culmination of three drops totaling 60 feet in height. The waterfall maintains a strong year-round flow. Perhaps the best known of Baxter's waterfalls, this natural feature can be seen from the Hunt Trail, which is one of the more popular routes to the summit of Mount Katahdin. Be aware that Baxter Peak, Katahdin's tallest point, requires a strenuous round-trip hike totaling 10.4 miles and an elevation gain of 4,200 feet. The trailhead for the falls and the Hunt Trail is at the Katahdin Stream Campground. This optional round-trip hike is often touted as one of the best the Northeast has to offer.

Grand Falls

Trail Length: **2.8 miles**
Water Source: **Wassataquoik Stream**
Delorme Baxter Map: **F-7**

Notes: The Grand Falls Trail leaves from Russell Pond, a backcountry campsite reached only by a long access trail. Although we have yet to visit Grand Falls, we have heard that it is quite magnificent and makes for a pleasant half-day trip.

Green Falls

Trail Length: **3.2 miles**
Water Source: **Unknown**
Delorme Baxter Map: **F-5**

Notes: Green Falls is a remote waterfall just south of Wassataquoik

Lake. Just like nearby Grand Falls, Green Falls is accessed via a trail (the Wassataquoik Lake Trail) that starts at Russell Pond. There is a sketch of Green Falls in DeLorme's "Map and Guide to Baxter State Park"—an essential map if you are visiting the area—that will give you a good idea of how beautiful the falls is. The falls are supposedly named for the emerald-green moss that thrives around their path.

Little Abol Falls

Trail Length: **1.0 miles**
Water Source: **Tributary of Abol Stream**
Delorme Baxter Map: **J&K-5**

Notes: The Little Abol Falls Trail begins at the Abol Campground and leads to a mountain stream with 15 feet of cascades over pink-brown Katahdin granite. Little Abol Falls provides a nice place for a picnic, and is an easy stroll from the campground.

South Branch Falls

Trail Length: **0.7 mile**
Water Source: **South Branch Ponds Brook**
Delorme Baxter Map: **D-6**

Notes: This set of cascades is accessed by the South Branch Falls Trail. The trail leaves the side of the road that leads to the South Branch Pond Campground. The trail is generally rated moderate, but we are unsure of any specific hiking dangers or challenges.

Niagara Falls

Trail Length: **1.25 miles**
Water Source: **Nesowadnehunk Stream**
Delorme Baxter Map: **K-4**

Notes: Two falls, Little Niagara Falls and Big Niagara Falls, are located just south of the Daicey Pond Campground on Nesowadnehunk

Stream. To access these waterfalls, travel south on the Appalachian Trail from the campground. Little Niagara Falls is reached after hiking for about 1.0 mile, with Big Niagara Falls 0.3 mile beyond that.

Howe Brook Falls

Trail Length: **3.0 miles**
Water Source: **Howe Brook**
Delorme Baxter Map: **D-7**

Notes: Take the Pogy Notch Trail for 1.0 mile south of the South Branch Pond Campground to a left onto the Howe Brook Trail. Follow the Howe Brook Trail 2.0 miles to a large waterfall. Many other small falls and cascades are seen before reaching the main attraction.

Notes